LET'S GET READY TO ROBATTLE!

CONTENTS

What are Medabots?

Medabots are "pet" robots complete with artificial intelligence and individual personalities. As they train and compete in Robattles, they evolve and gain more powers and strength.

Ikki:
Ikki dreams about one day becoming the Robattle champion of the world! He's still a novice, but his victory against the Screws has earned him quite a reputation.

Metabee:
Strong-willed and independent, Metabee is Ikki's feisty Medabot. He's always looking for a good Robattle to get into.

Henry:
Your friendly neighborhood convenience store clerk with a secret past—Henry is a former Robattle champion!

Erika and Brass:
Ikki's best friend, Erika is a strong-minded girl who writes her own newspaper. Always on the lookout for a good story, Erika will always go the extra mile to get a scoop! Erika's Medabot, Brass, is quite the eager reporter's assistant.

Mr. Referee:
Mr. Referee always manages to appear wherever and whenever a Robattle breaks out. He referees all Robattles abiding by the strictest standards of fair play. Mr. Referee is known for dramatic and exciting entrances.

The Phantom Renegade:
A mysterious masked man. Who is he and what is he up to? Kids seem to look up to him as something of a superhero.

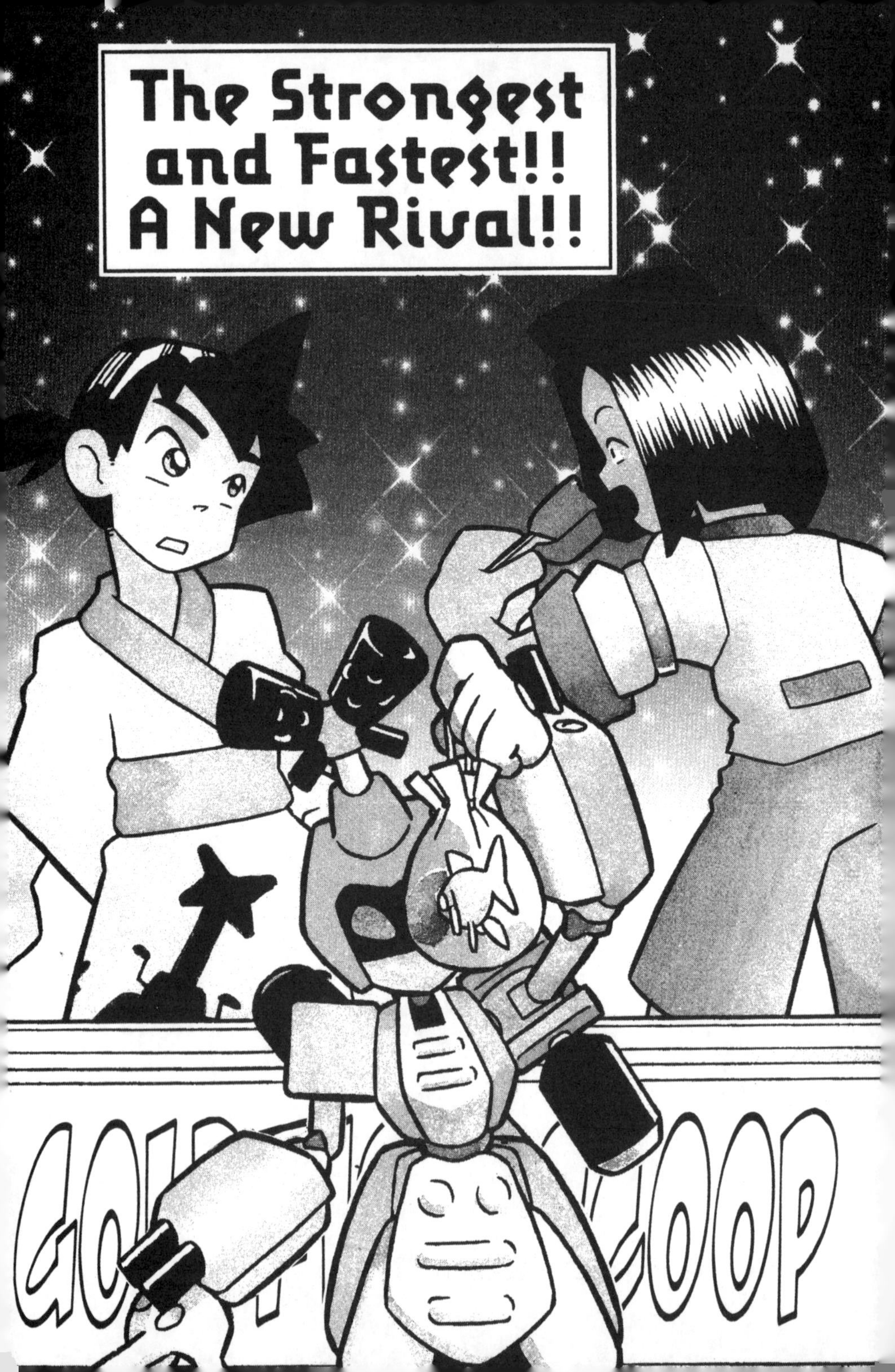
The Strongest
and Fastest!!
A New Rival!!

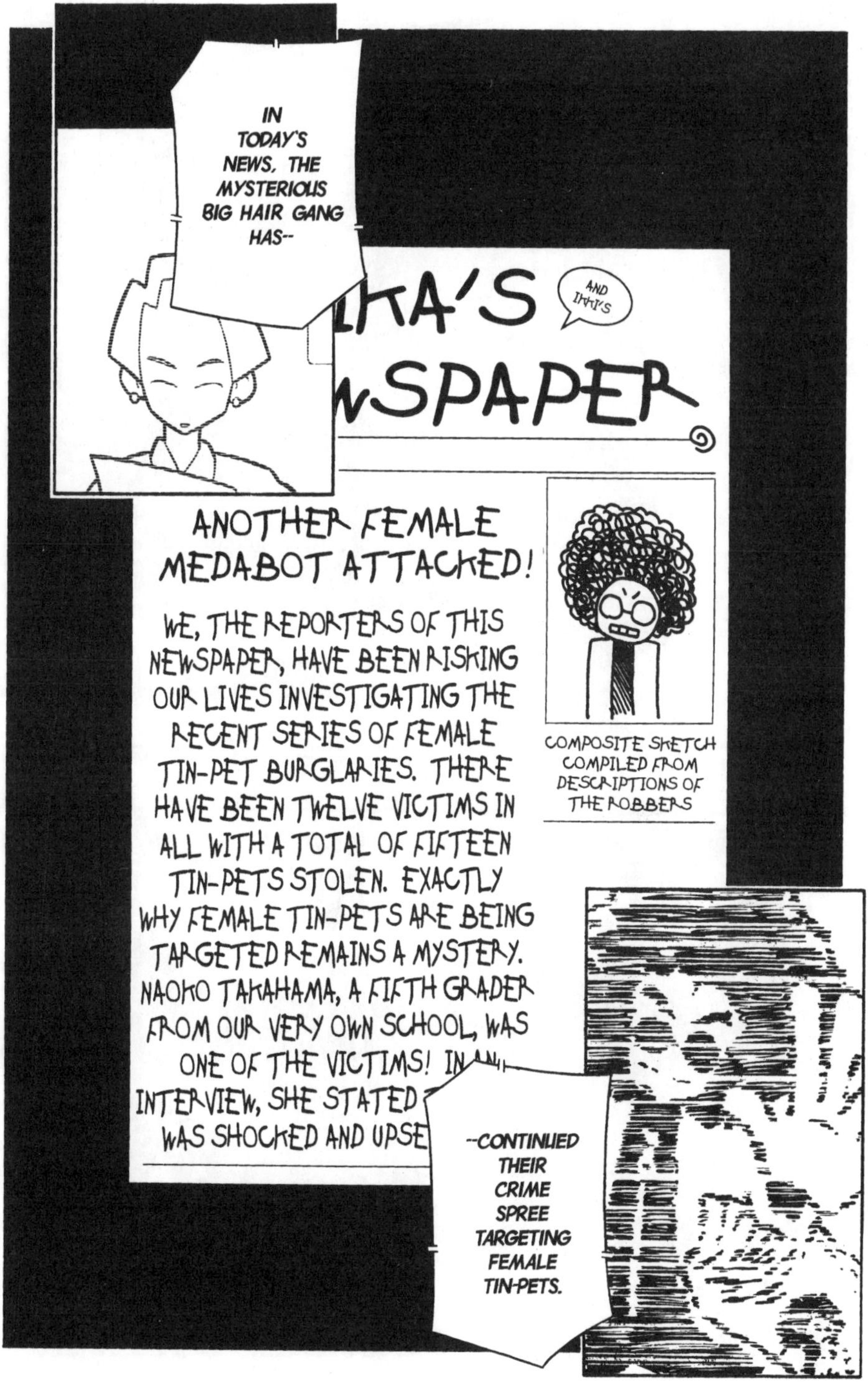

IN TODAY'S NEWS, THE MYSTERIOUS BIG HAIR GANG HAS--
IKA'S
AND IKKI'S
WSPAPER
ANOTHER FEMALE MEDABOT ATTACKED!
WE, THE REPORTERS OF THIS NEWSPAPER, HAVE BEEN RISKING OUR LIVES INVESTIGATING THE RECENT SERIES OF FEMALE TIN-PET BURGLARIES. THERE HAVE BEEN TWELVE VICTIMS IN ALL WITH A TOTAL OF FIFTEEN TIN-PETS STOLEN. EXACTLY WHY FEMALE TIN-PETS ARE BEING TARGETED REMAINS A MYSTERY. NAOKO TAKAHAMA, A FIFTH GRADER FROM OUR VERY OWN SCHOOL, WAS ONE OF THE VICTIMS! IN
INTERVIEW, SHE STATED
WAS SHOCKED AND UPSE
COMPOSITE SKETCH COMPILED FROM DESCRIPTIONS OF THE ROBBERS
--CONTINUED THEIR CRIME SPREE TARGETING FEMALE TIN-PETS.

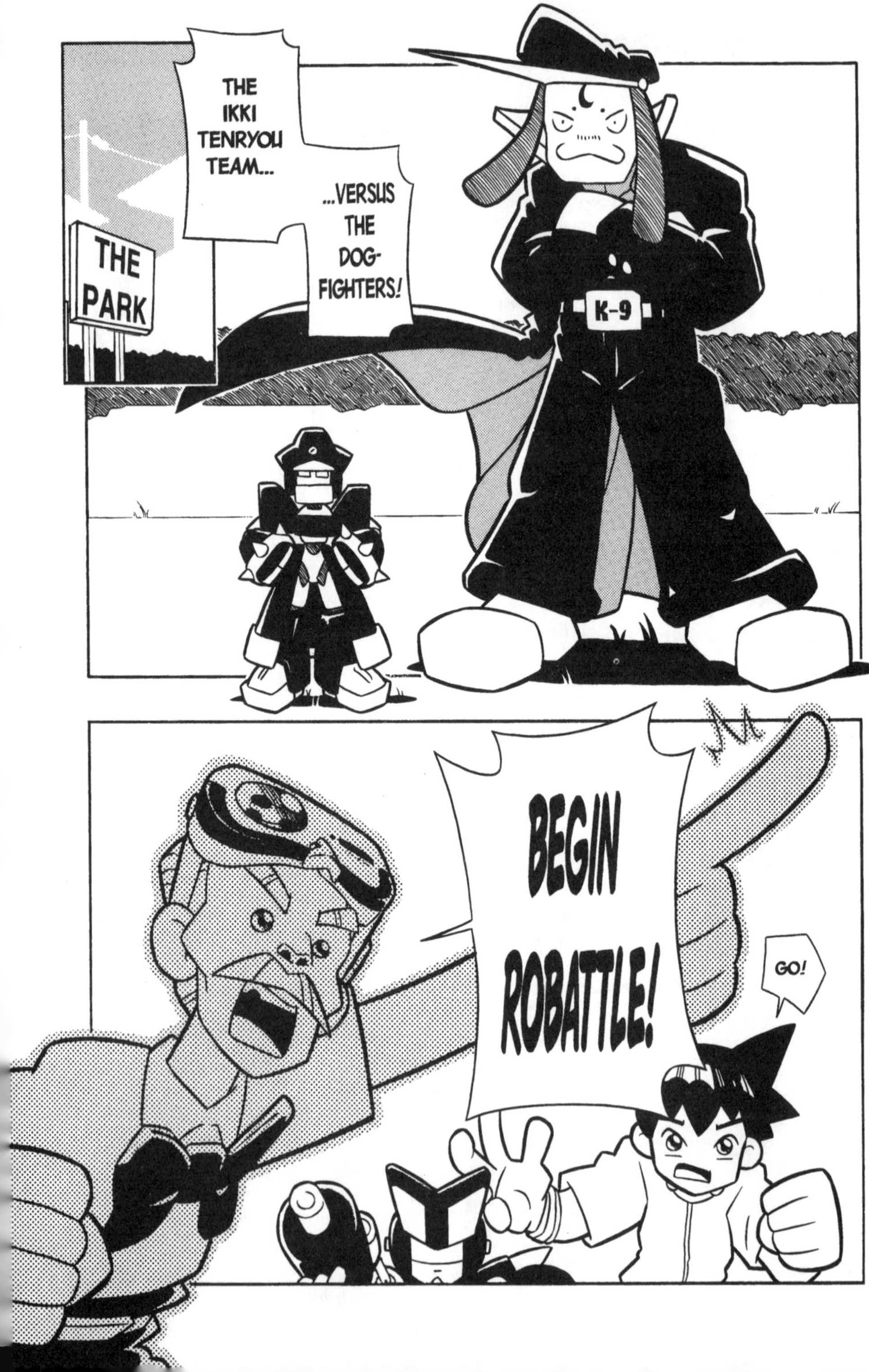
THE IKKI TENRYOU TEAM...
THE PARK
...VERSUS THE DOG-FIGHTERS!
K-9
BEGIN ROBATTLE!
GO!

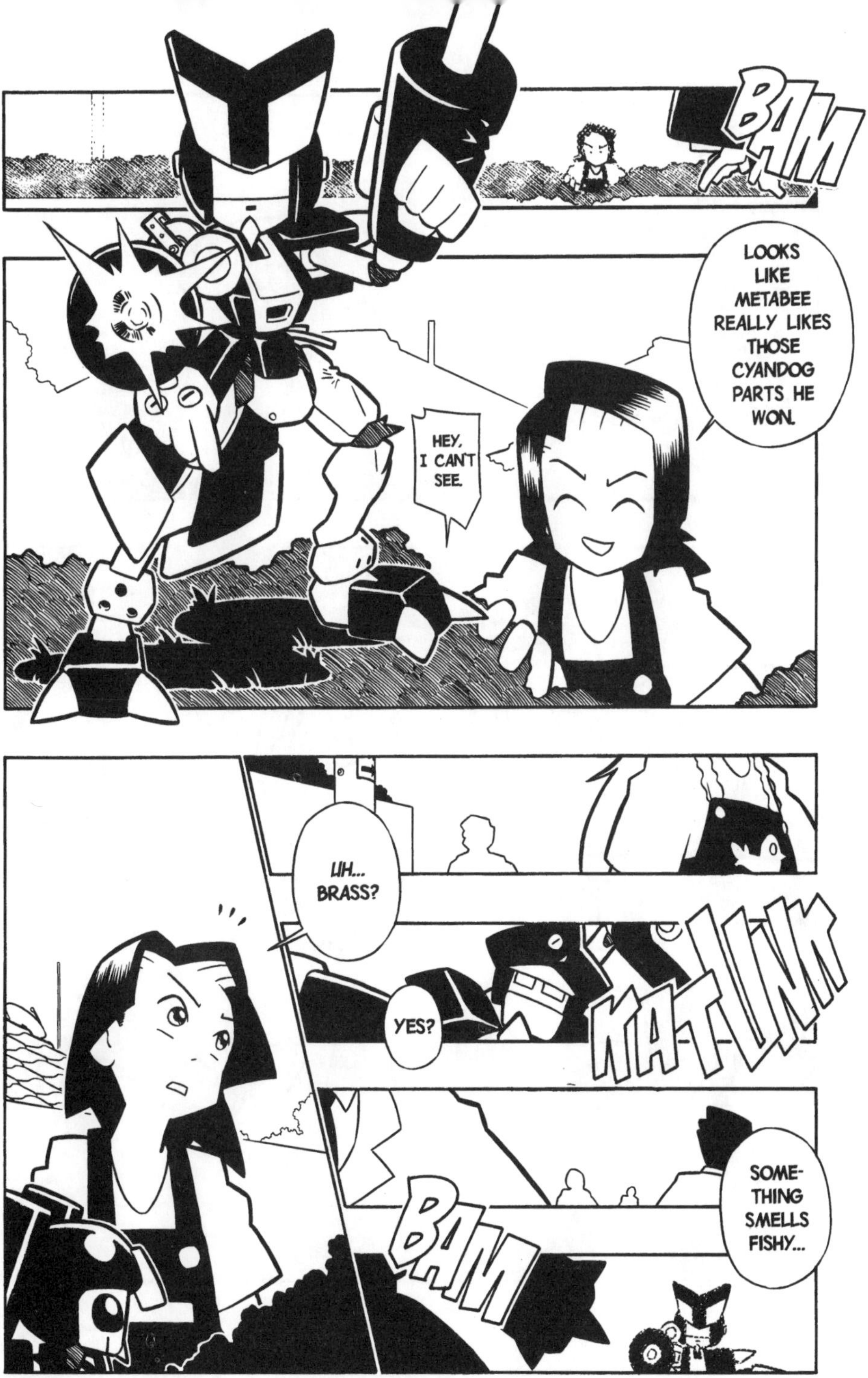

BAM
HEY, I CAN'T SEE.
LOOKS LIKE METABEE REALLY LIKES THOSE CYANDOG PARTS HE WON.
UH... BRASS?
YES?
KA-TUNK
BAM
SOME-THING SMELLS FISHY...

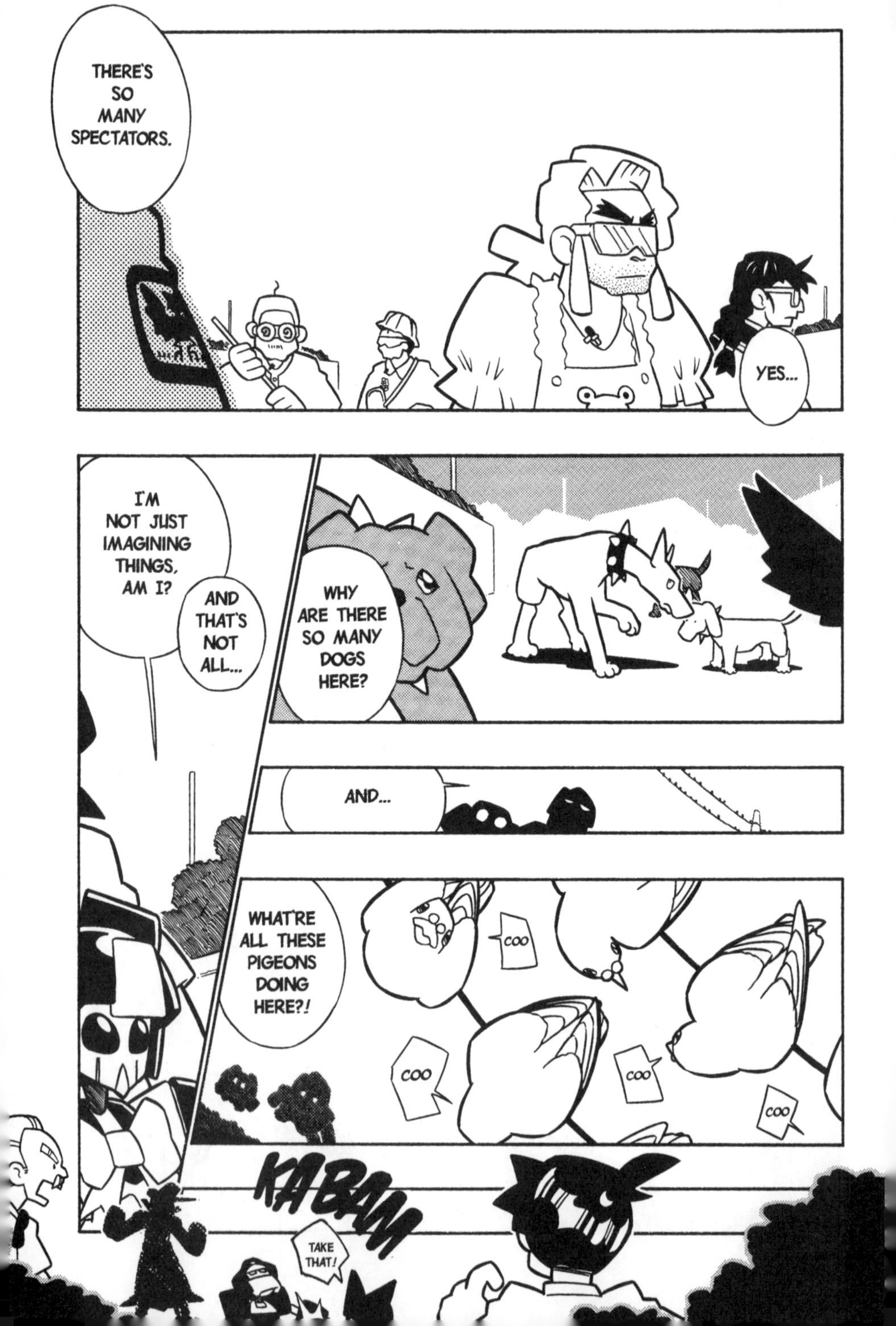
THERE'S SO MANY SPECTATORS.
YES...
I'M NOT JUST IMAGINING THINGS, AM I?
AND THAT'S NOT ALL...
WHY ARE THERE SO MANY DOGS HERE?
AND...
WHAT'RE ALL THESE PIGEONS DOING HERE?!
COO
COO
COO
COO
KA BAM
TAKE THAT!

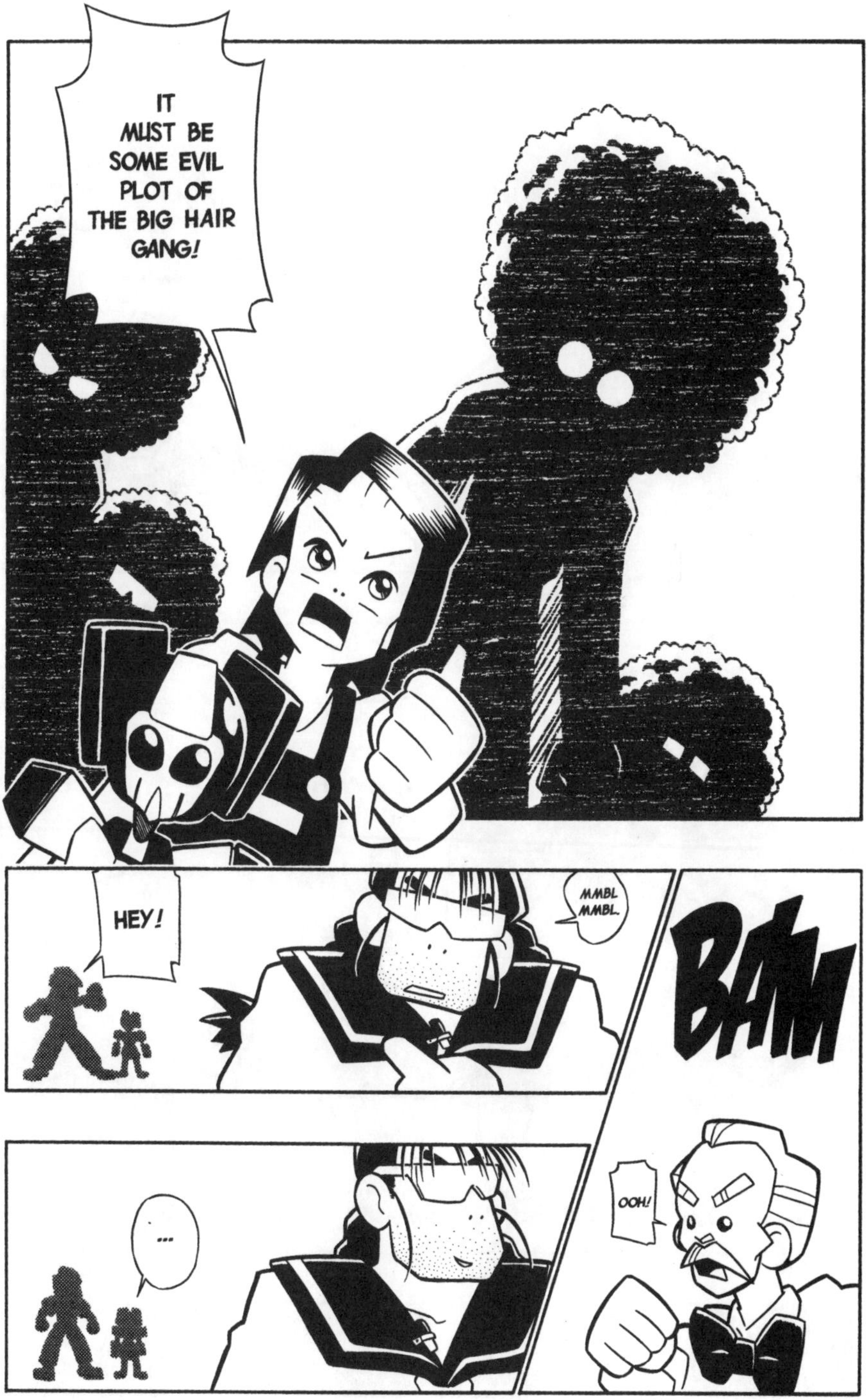
IT MUST BE SOME EVIL PLOT OF THE BIG HAIR GANG!
HEY!
MMBL MMBL.
BAM
...
OOH!

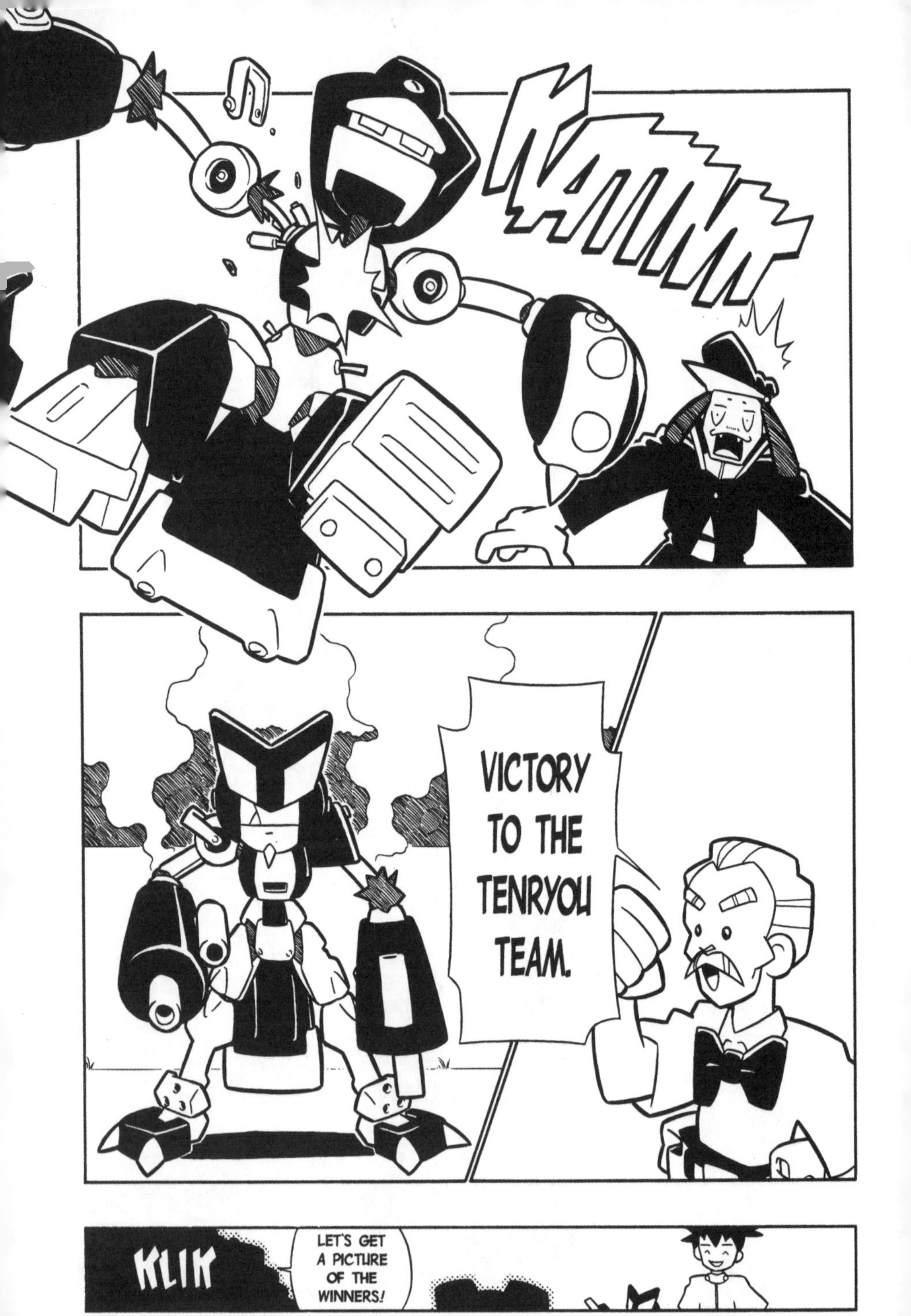
KANNNK
VICTORY TO THE TENRYOU TEAM.
KLIK
LET'S GET A PICTURE OF THE WINNERS!

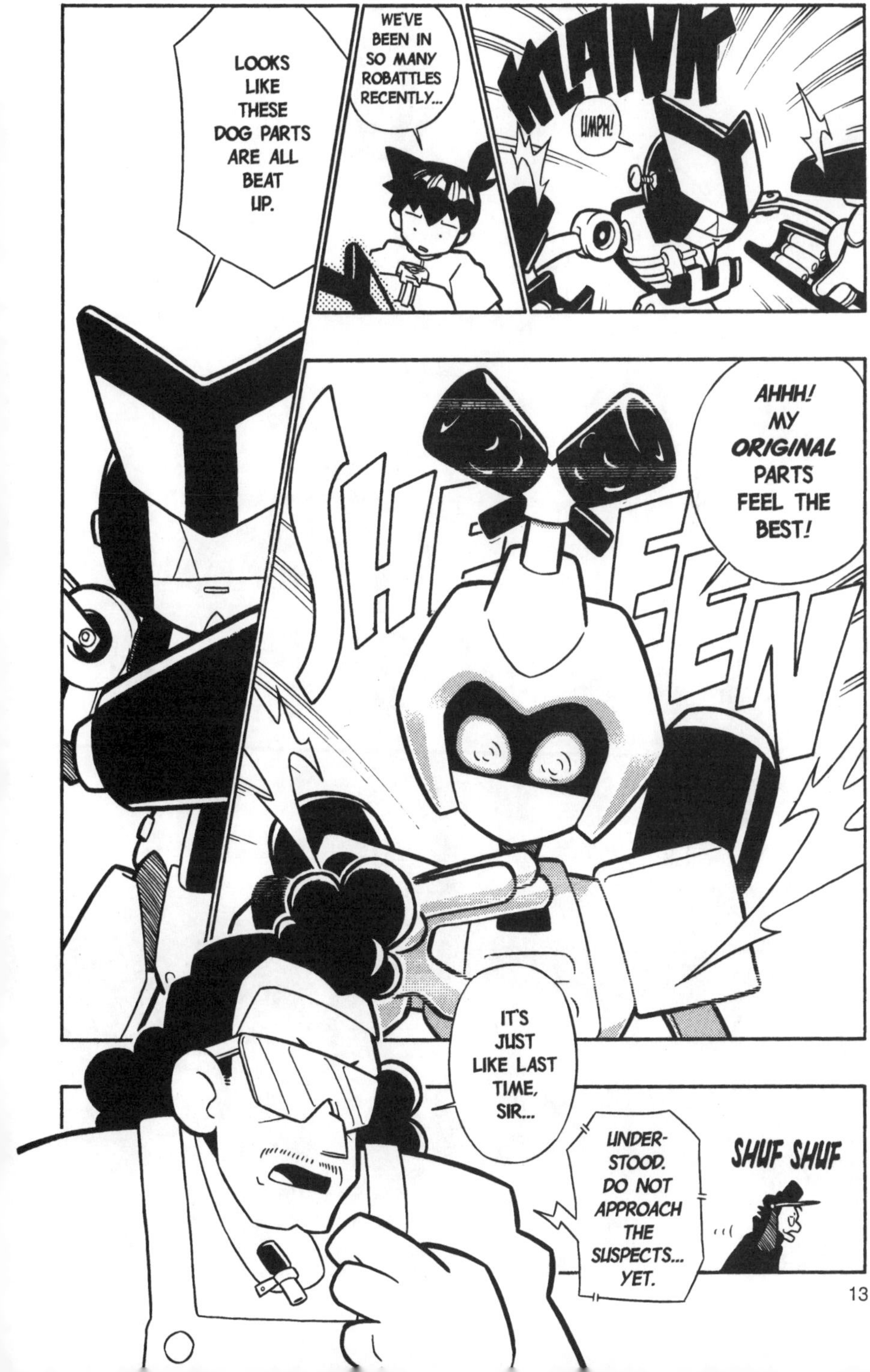
LOOKS LIKE THESE DOG PARTS ARE ALL BEAT UP.
WE'VE BEEN IN SO MANY ROBATTLES RECENTLY...
KLANK
UMPH!
SHEEEN
AHHH! MY ORIGINAL PARTS FEEL THE BEST!
IT'S JUST LIKE LAST TIME, SIR...
UNDER-STOOD. DO NOT APPROACH THE SUSPECTS... YET.
SHUF SHUF

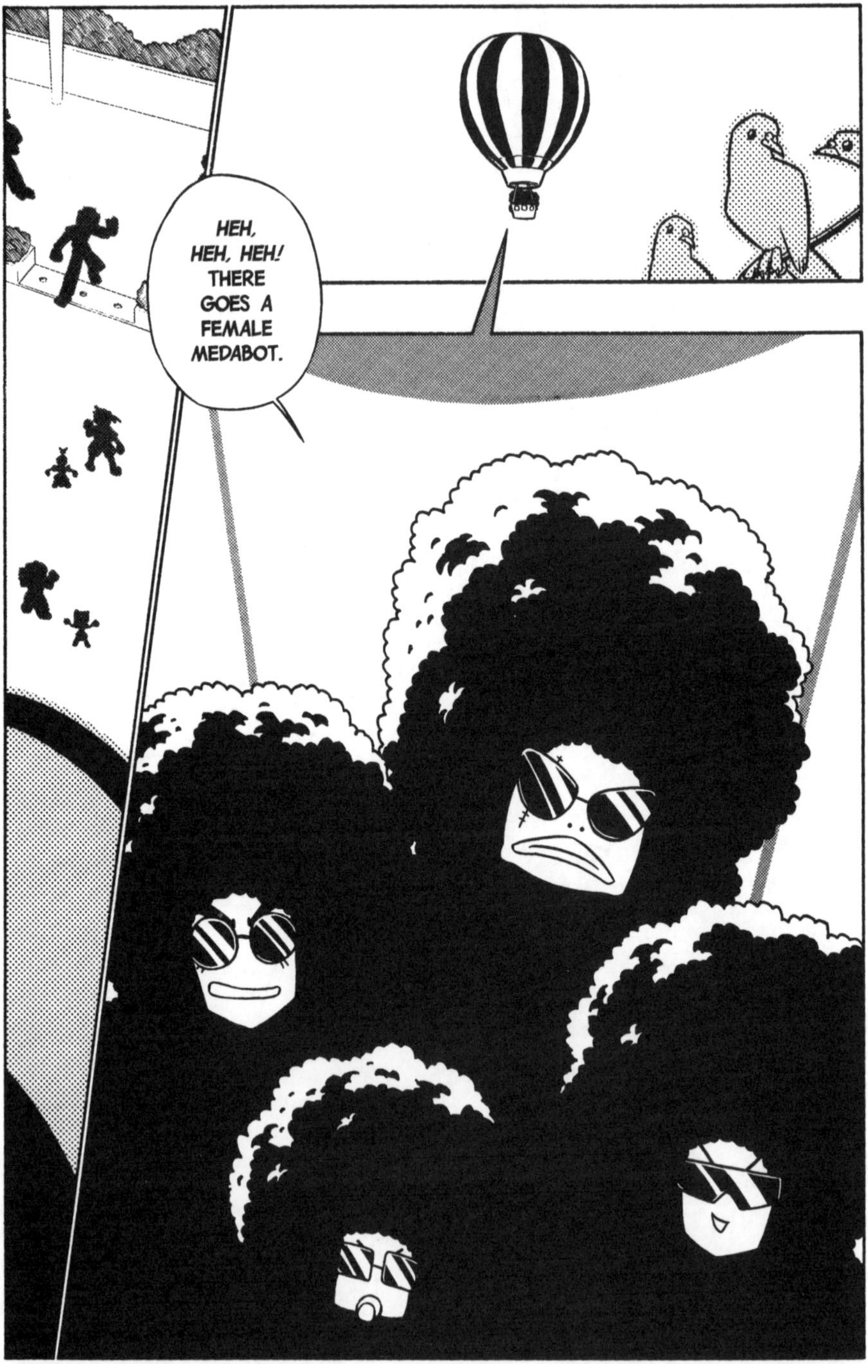
HEH, HEH, HEH! THERE GOES A FEMALE MEDABOT.

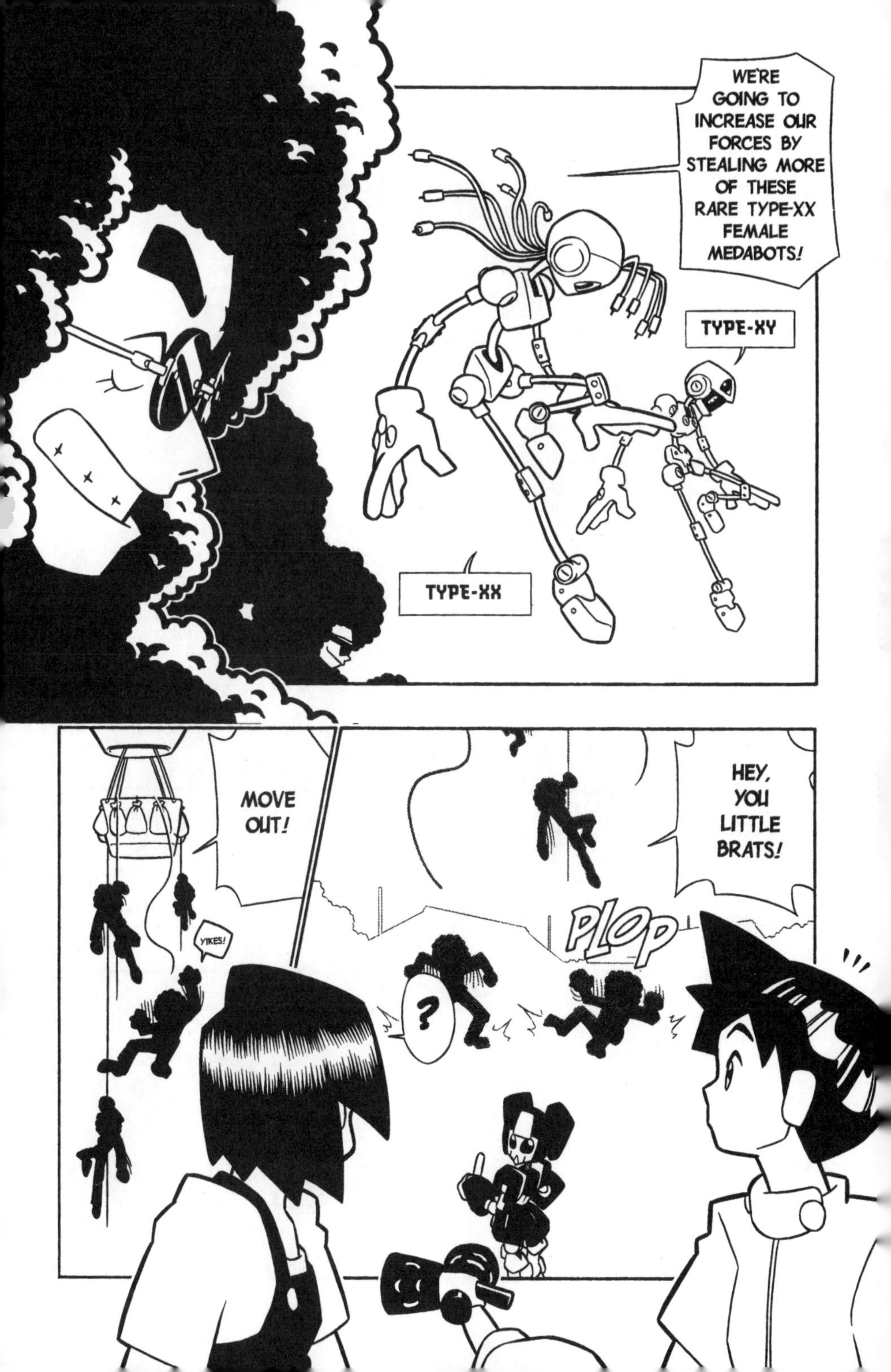
WE'RE GOING TO INCREASE OUR FORCES BY STEALING MORE OF THESE RARE TYPE-XX FEMALE MEDABOTS!
TYPE-XY
TYPE-XX
MOVE OUT!
HEY, YOU LITTLE BRATS!
YIKES!
PLOP
?

WE'RE THE BIG HAIR GANG!

I JUST KNEW SOMETHING WAS WRONG!!

TRANSPORT MEDABOT!

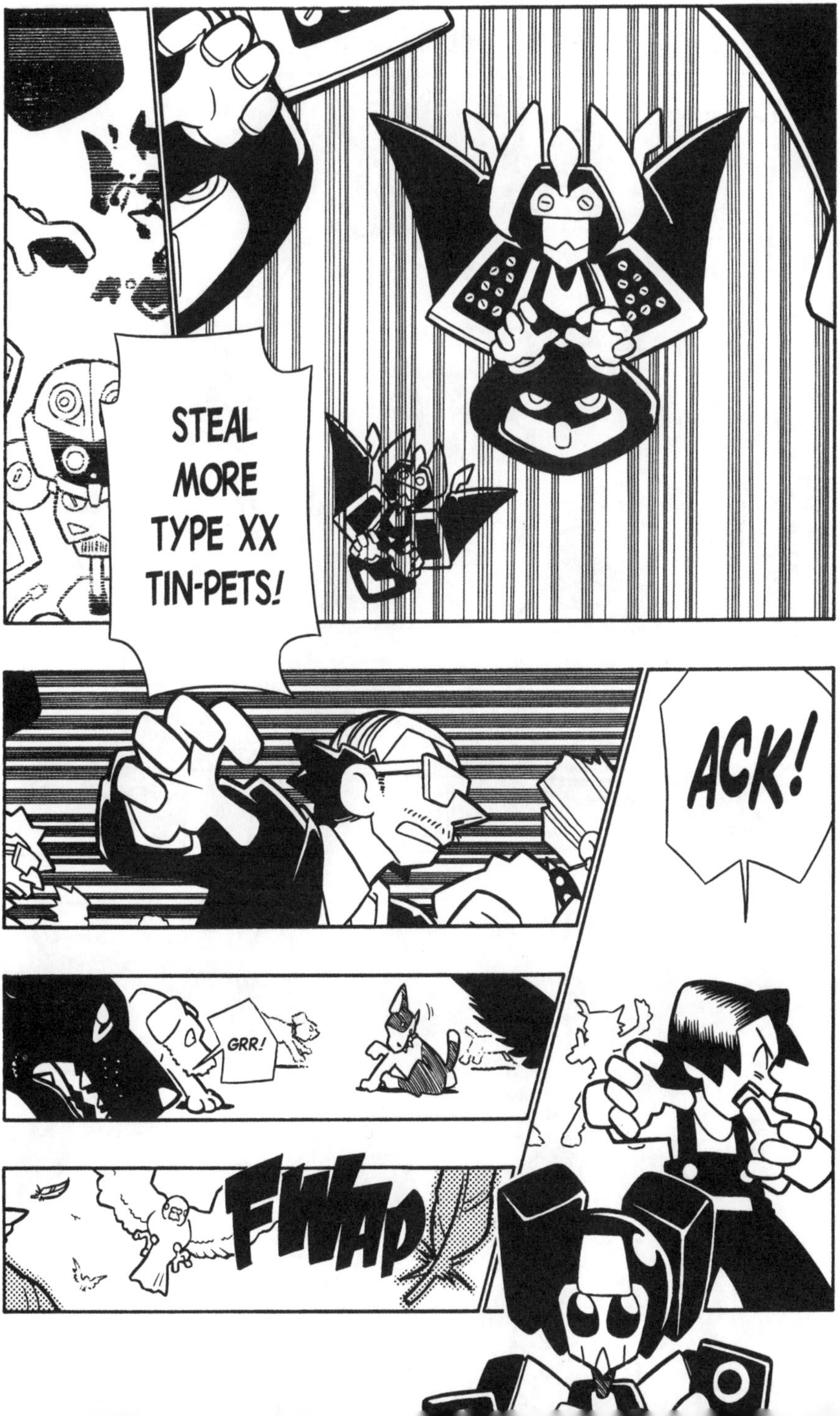
STEAL MORE TYPE XX TIN-PETS!
ACK!
GRR!
FWAP

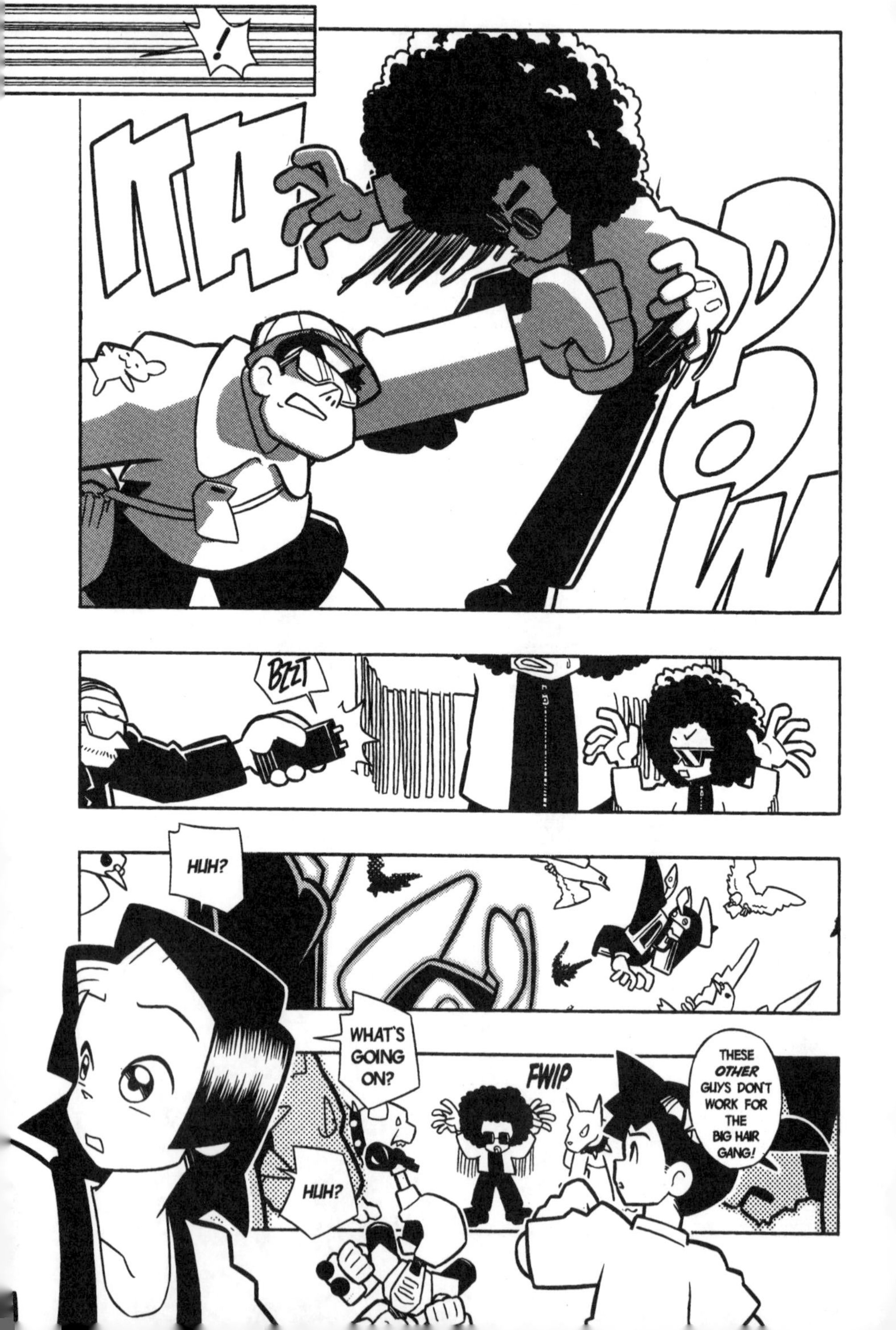
!
BZZT
HUH?
WHAT'S GOING ON?
FWIP
THESE *OTHER* GUYS DON'T WORK FOR THE BIG HAIR GANG!
HUH?

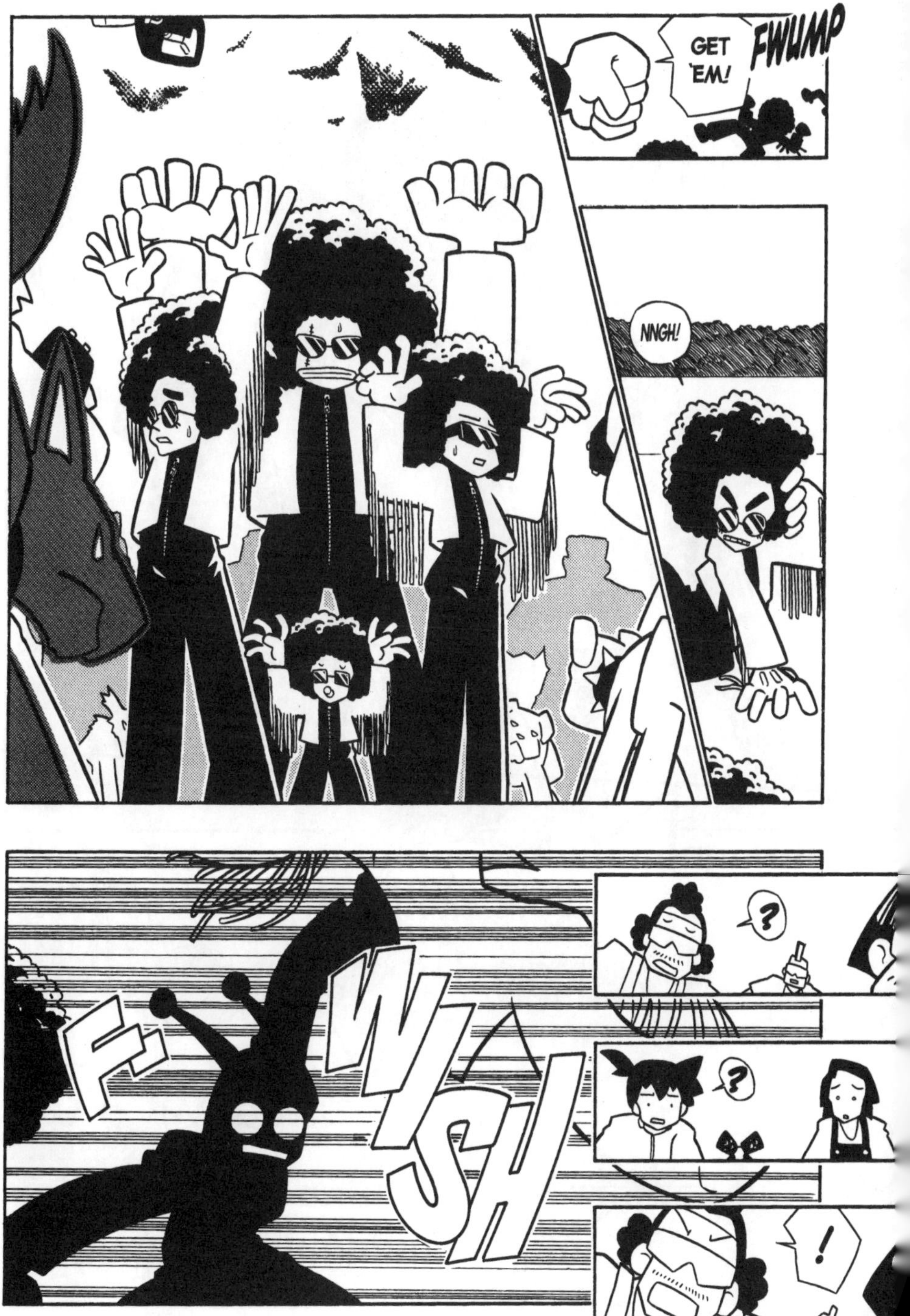
GET 'EM!
FWUMP
NNGH!
FWISH
?
?
!

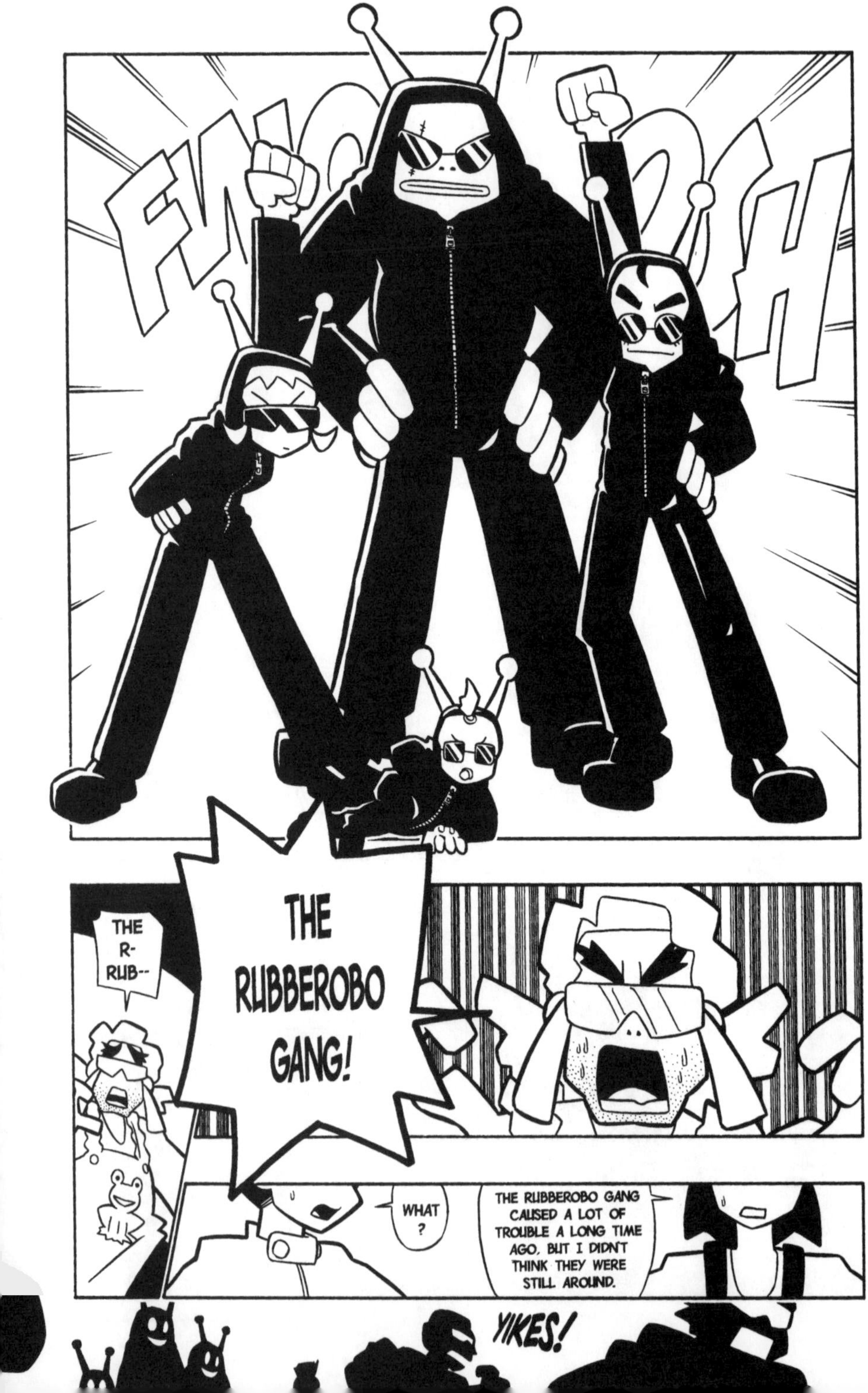
THE R-RUB--
THE RUBBEROBO GANG!
WHAT?
THE RUBBEROBO GANG CAUSED A LOT OF TROUBLE A LONG TIME AGO, BUT I DIDN'T THINK THEY WERE STILL AROUND.
YIKES!

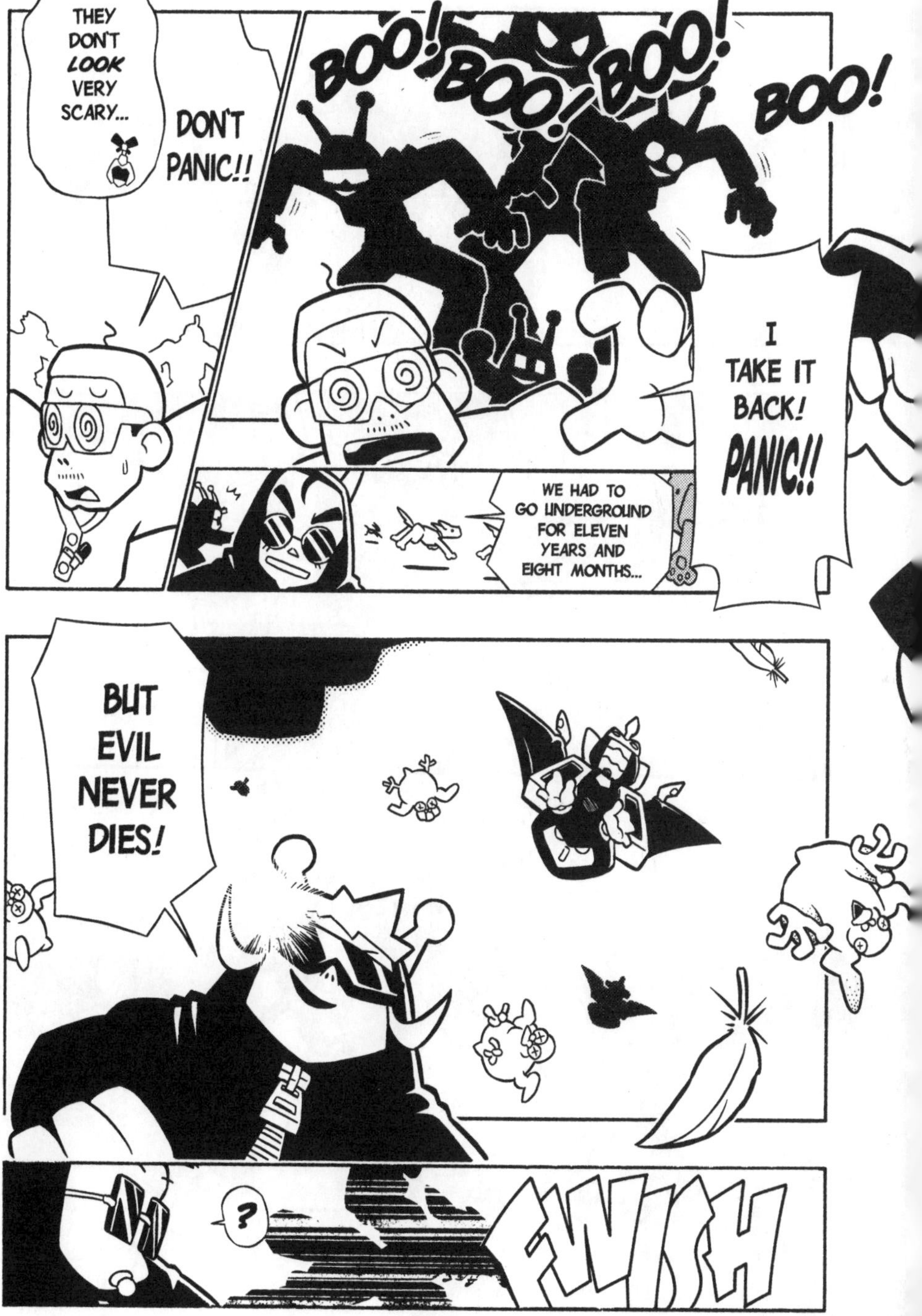
THEY DON'T LOOK VERY SCARY...
DON'T PANIC!!
BOO! BOO! BOO! BOO!
I TAKE IT BACK! PANIC!!
WE HAD TO GO UNDERGROUND FOR ELEVEN YEARS AND EIGHT MONTHS...
BUT EVIL NEVER DIES!
?
FINISH

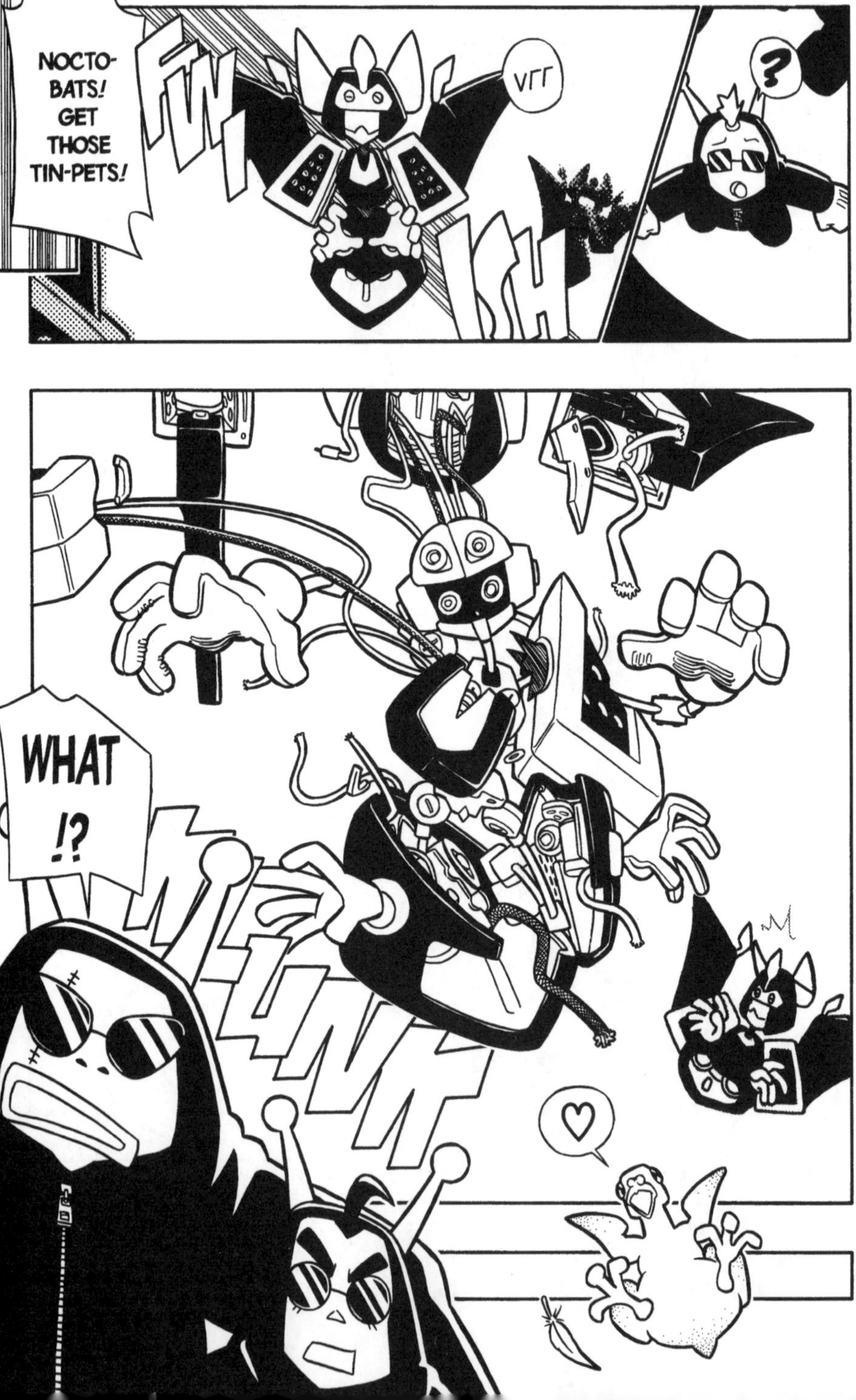
NOCTO-BATS! GET THOSE TIN-PETS!
VRR
?
WHAT !?

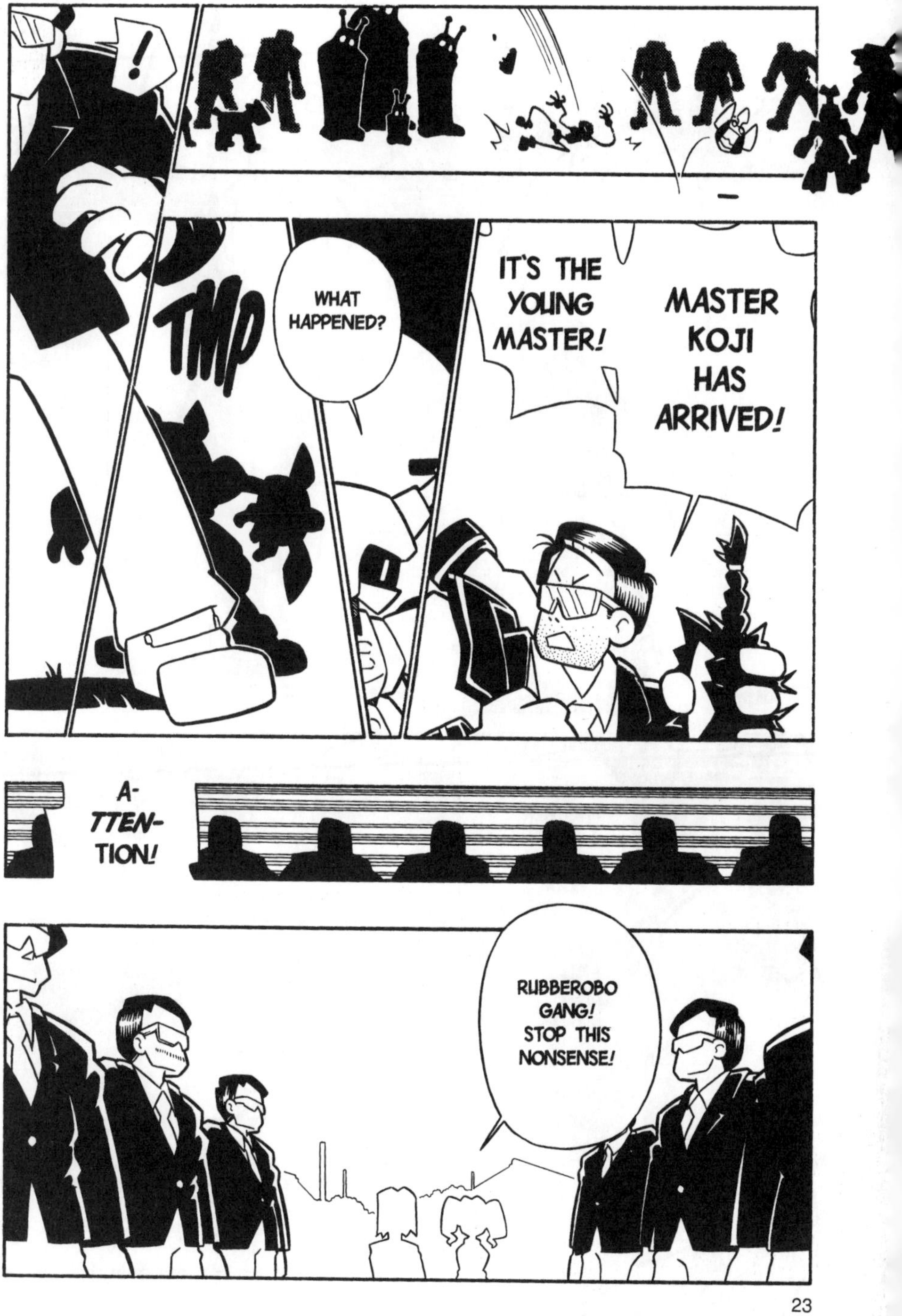
!
TMP
WHAT HAPPENED?
IT'S THE YOUNG MASTER!
MASTER KOJI HAS ARRIVED!
A-TTEN-TION!
RUBBEROBO GANG! STOP THIS NONSENSE!

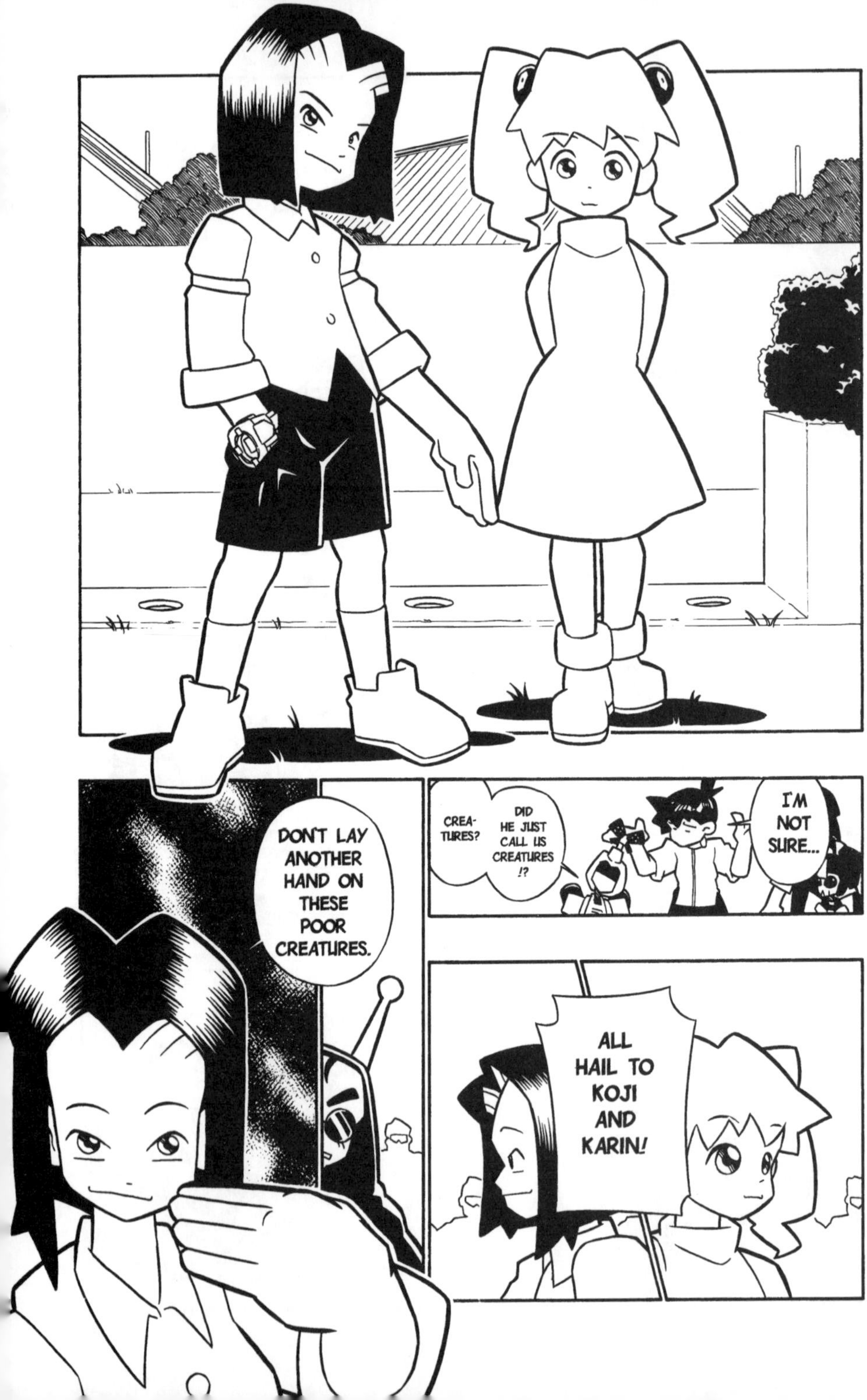
DON'T LAY ANOTHER HAND ON THESE POOR CREATURES.
CREA-TURES?
DID HE JUST CALL US CREATURES !?
I'M NOT SURE...
ALL HAIL TO KOJI AND KARIN!

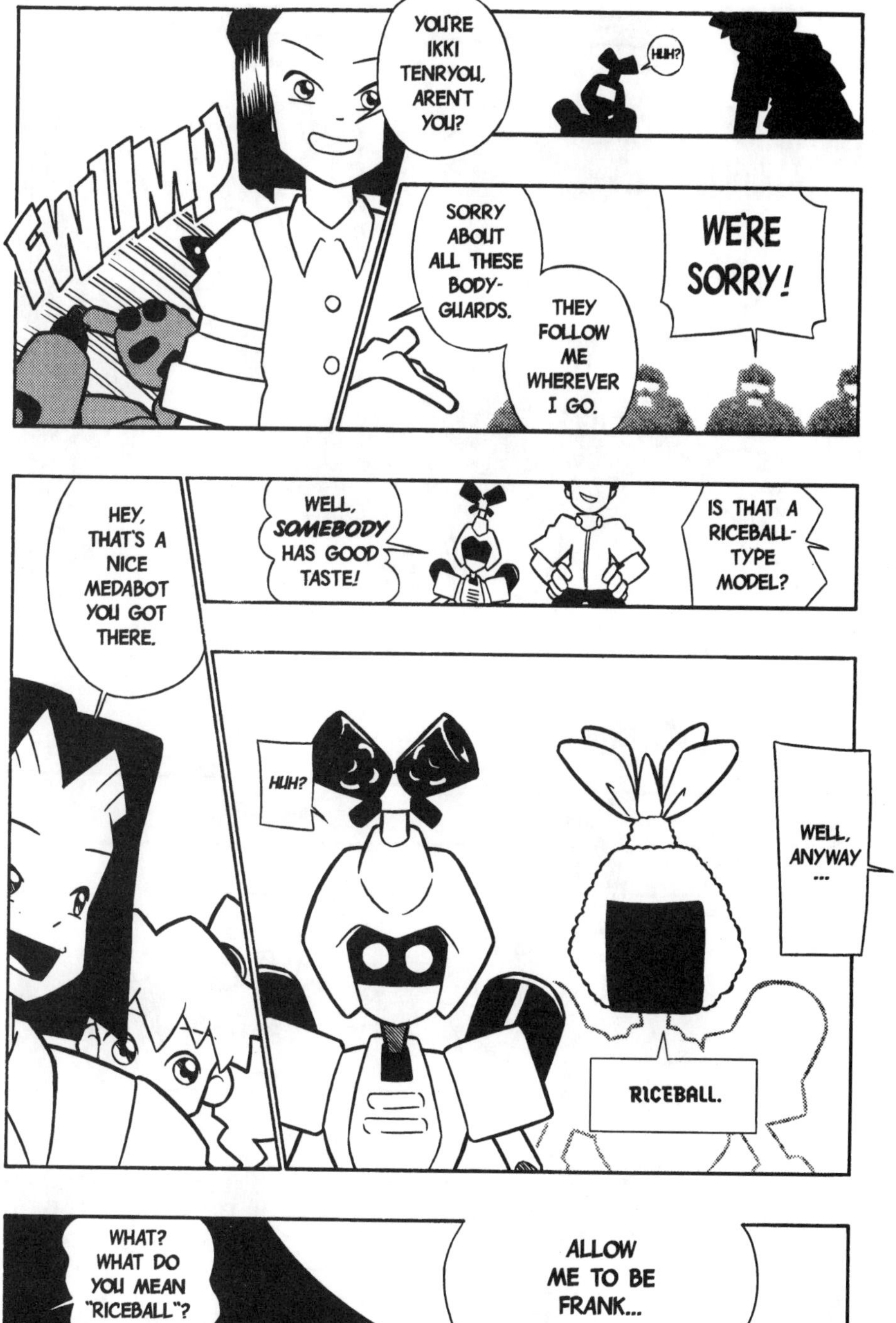
FWUMP
YOU'RE IKKI TENRYOU, AREN'T YOU?
HUH?
SORRY ABOUT ALL THESE BODY-GUARDS.
THEY FOLLOW ME WHEREVER I GO.
WE'RE SORRY!
HEY, THAT'S A NICE MEDABOT YOU GOT THERE.
WELL, SOMEBODY HAS GOOD TASTE!
IS THAT A RICEBALL-TYPE MODEL?
HUH?
RICEBALL.
WELL, ANYWAY ...
WHAT? WHAT DO YOU MEAN "RICEBALL"?
ALLOW ME TO BE FRANK...

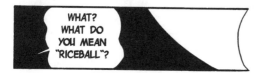

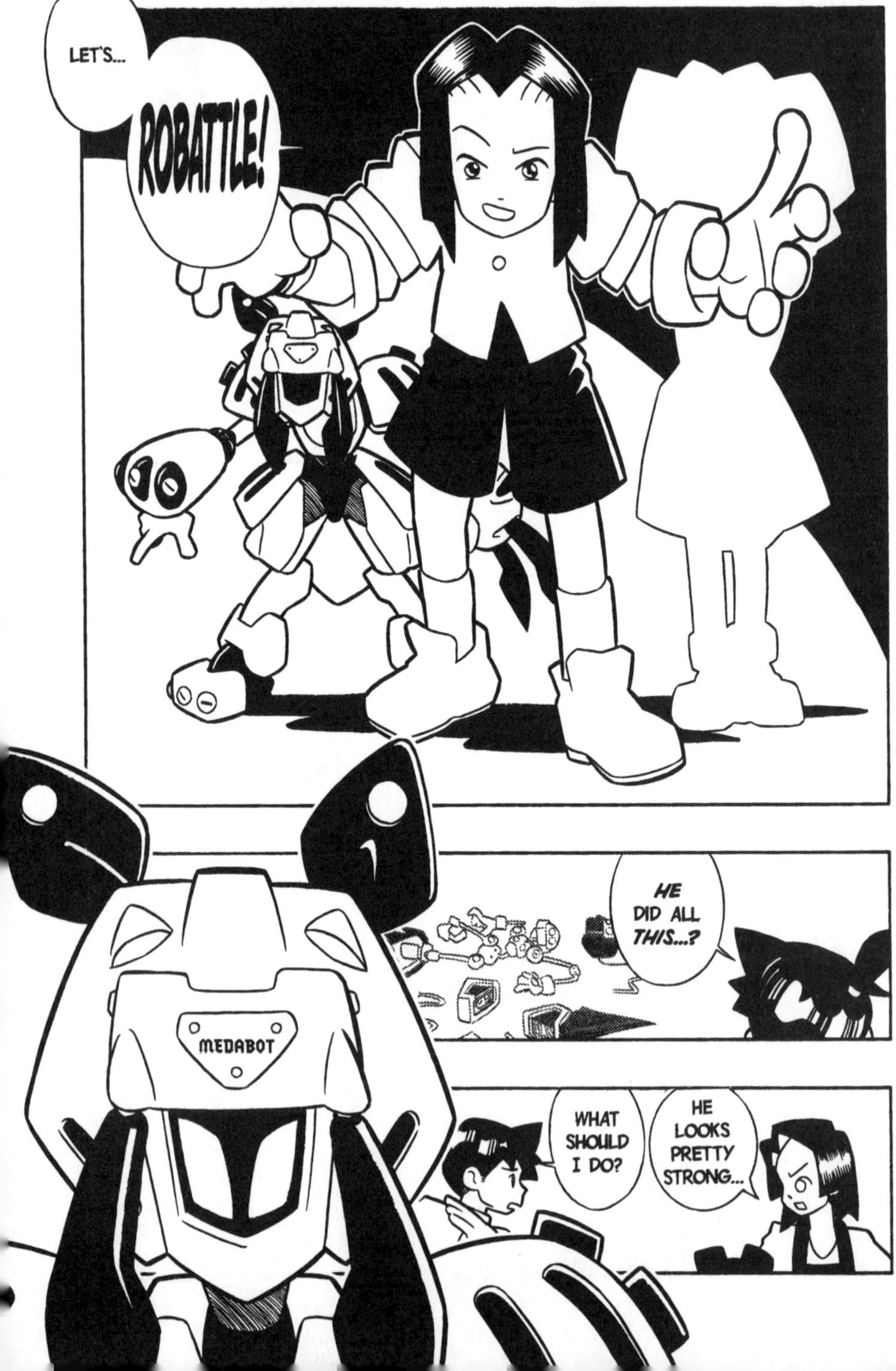
LET'S...
ROBATTLE!
HE DID ALL THIS...?
MEDABOT
WHAT SHOULD I DO?
HE LOOKS PRETTY STRONG...

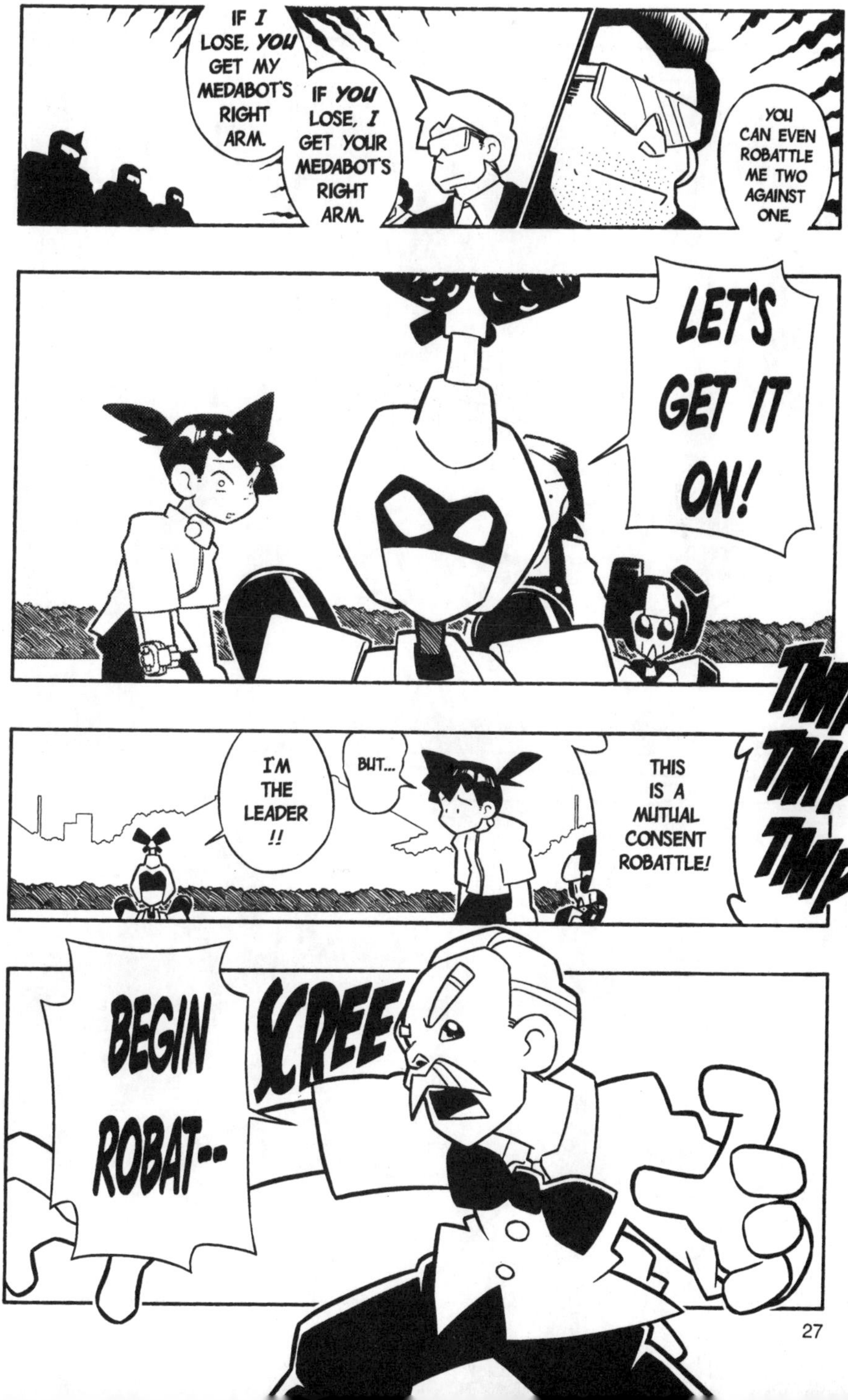
IF I LOSE, YOU GET MY MEDABOT'S RIGHT ARM.
IF YOU LOSE, I GET YOUR MEDABOT'S RIGHT ARM.
YOU CAN EVEN ROBATTLE ME TWO AGAINST ONE.
LET'S GET IT ON!
TMP TMP TMP
I'M THE LEADER !!
BUT...
THIS IS A MUTUAL CONSENT ROBATTLE!
BEGIN ROBAT--
SCREE

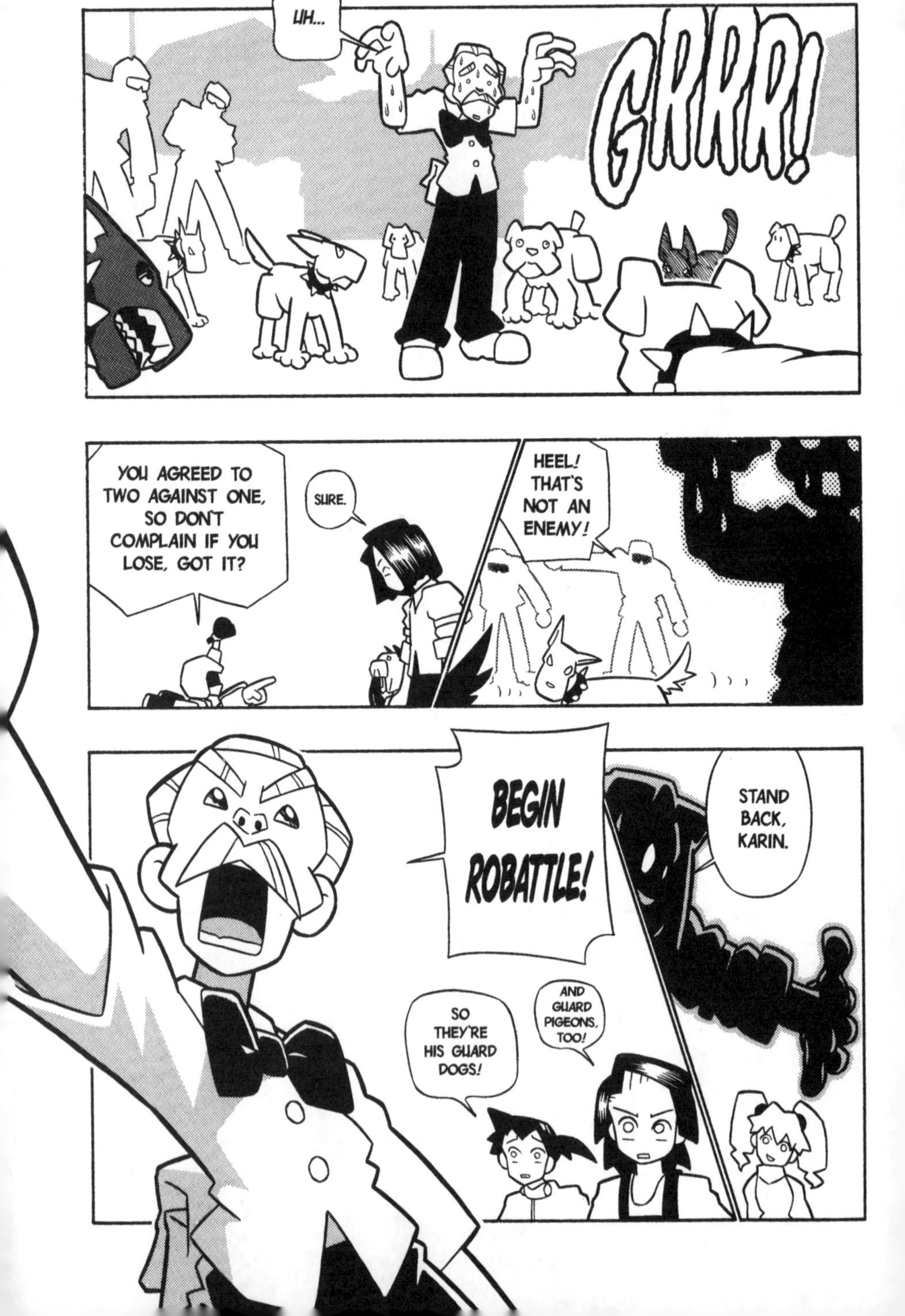
UH...
GRRR!
YOU AGREED TO TWO AGAINST ONE, SO DON'T COMPLAIN IF YOU LOSE, GOT IT?
SURE.
HEEL! THAT'S NOT AN ENEMY!
BEGIN ROBATTLE!
STAND BACK, KARIN.
SO THEY'RE HIS GUARD DOGS!
AND GUARD PIGEONS, TOO!

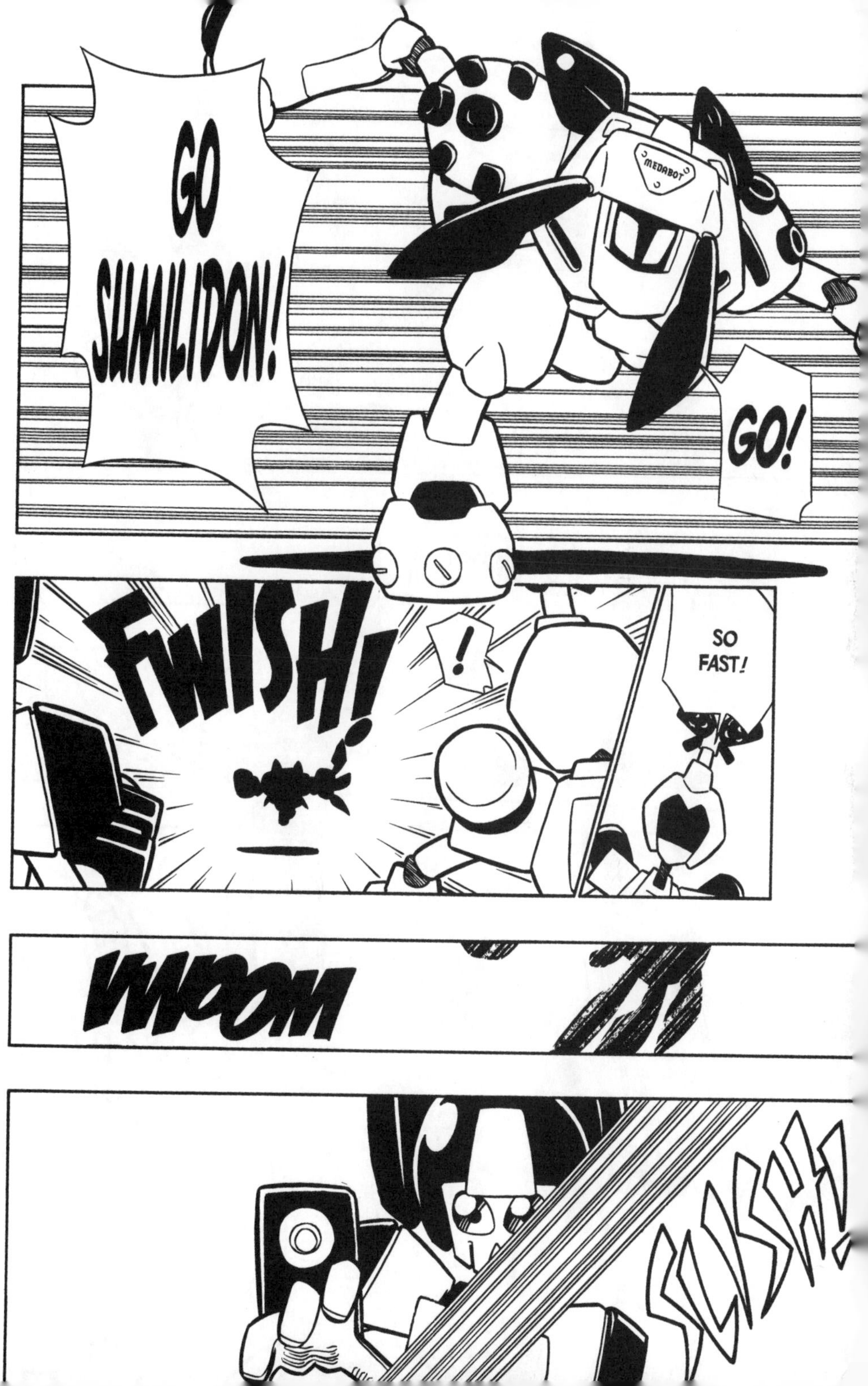
GO SHMILIDON!
GO!
FWISH!
!
SO FAST!
VMOOM
SLISH!

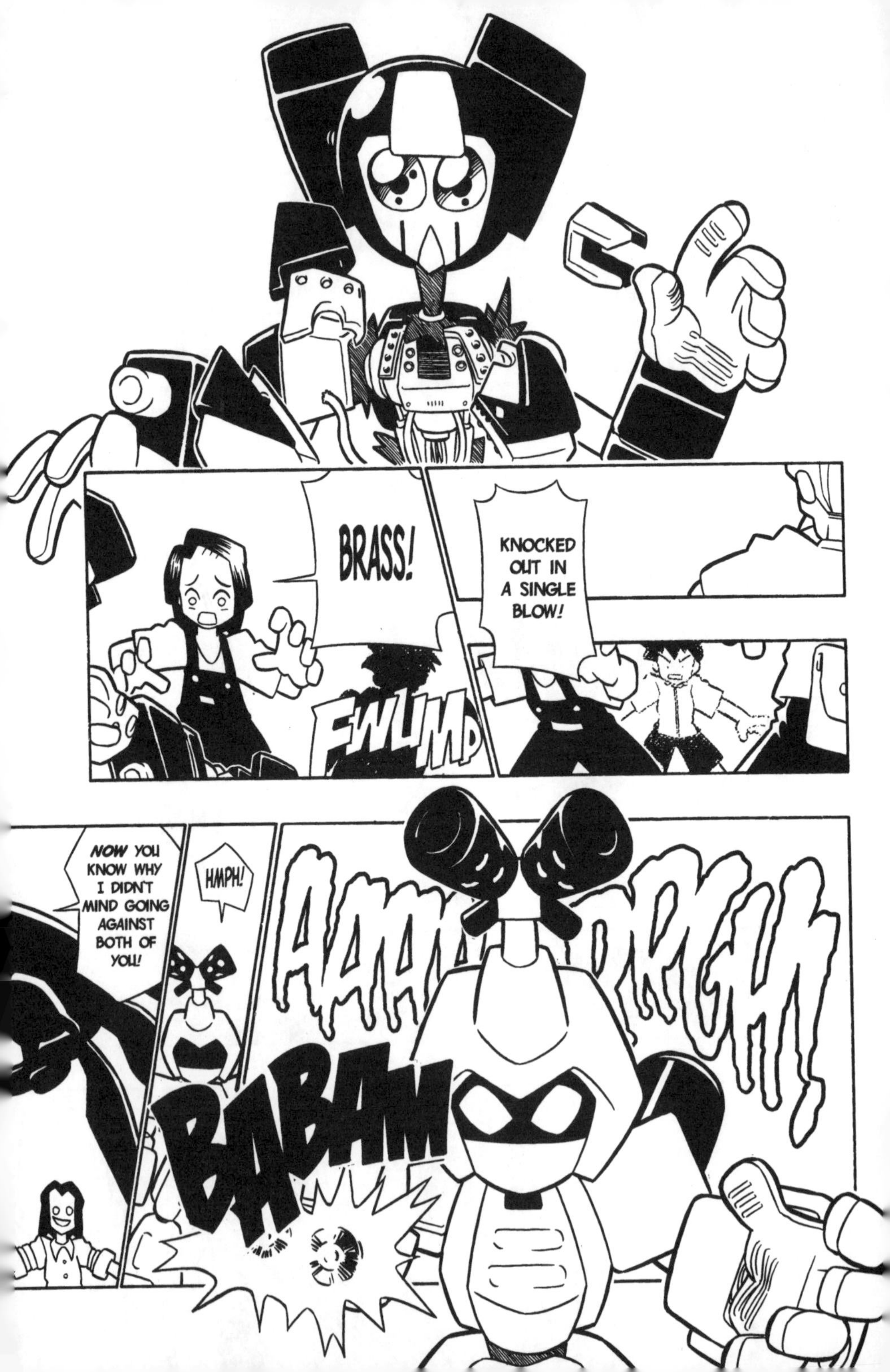
BRASS!
KNOCKED OUT IN A SINGLE BLOW!
FWUMP
NOW YOU KNOW WHY I DIDN'T MIND GOING AGAINST BOTH OF YOU!
HMPH!
BABAM

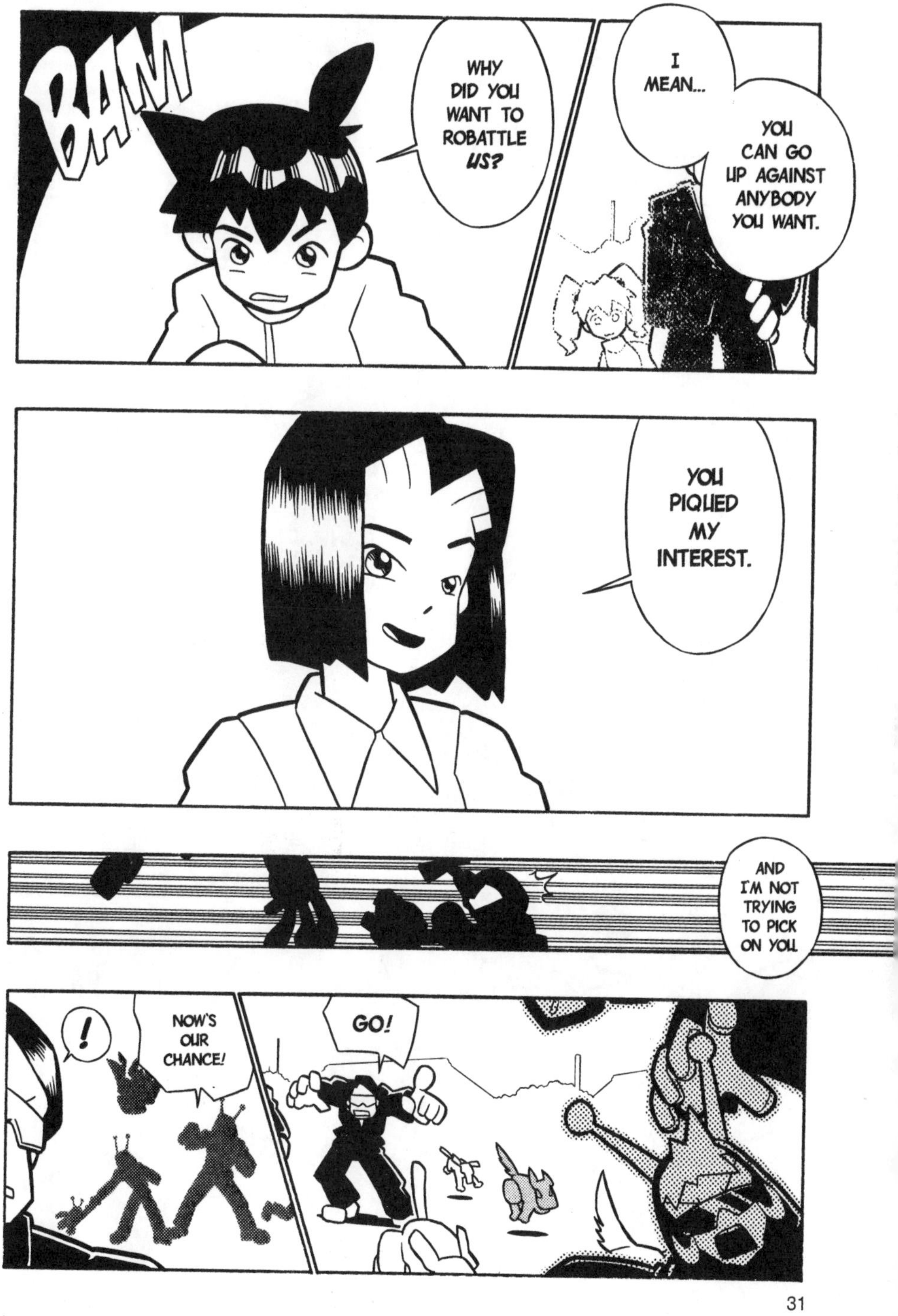
BAM
WHY DID YOU WANT TO ROBATTLE US?
I MEAN...
YOU CAN GO UP AGAINST ANYBODY YOU WANT.
YOU PIQUED MY INTEREST.
AND I'M NOT TRYING TO PICK ON YOU.
!
NOW'S OUR CHANCE!
GO!

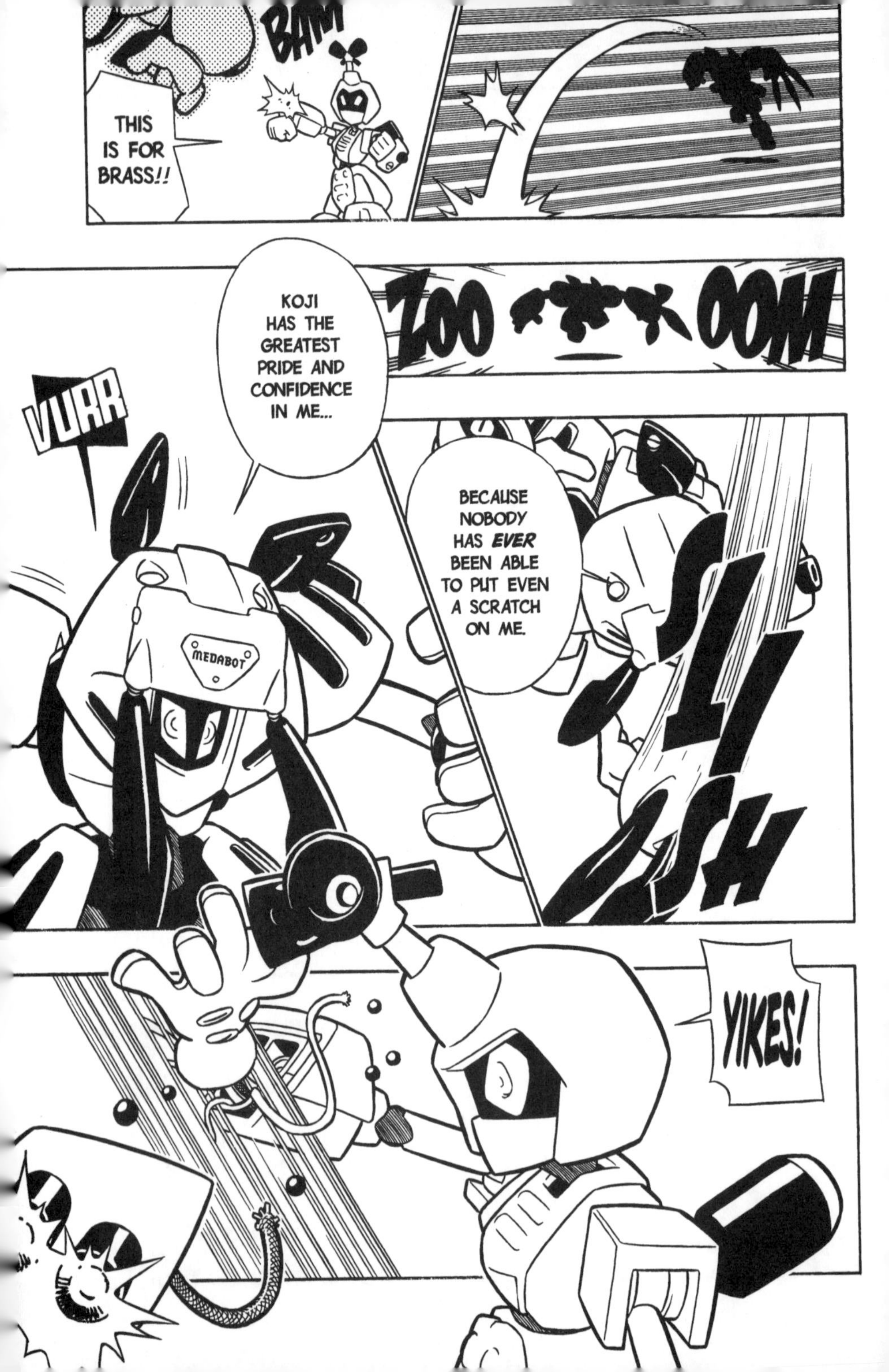
BAM
THIS IS FOR BRASS!!
KOJI HAS THE GREATEST PRIDE AND CONFIDENCE IN ME...
ZOO OOM
VURR
BECAUSE NOBODY HAS *EVER* BEEN ABLE TO PUT EVEN A SCRATCH ON ME.
YIKES!

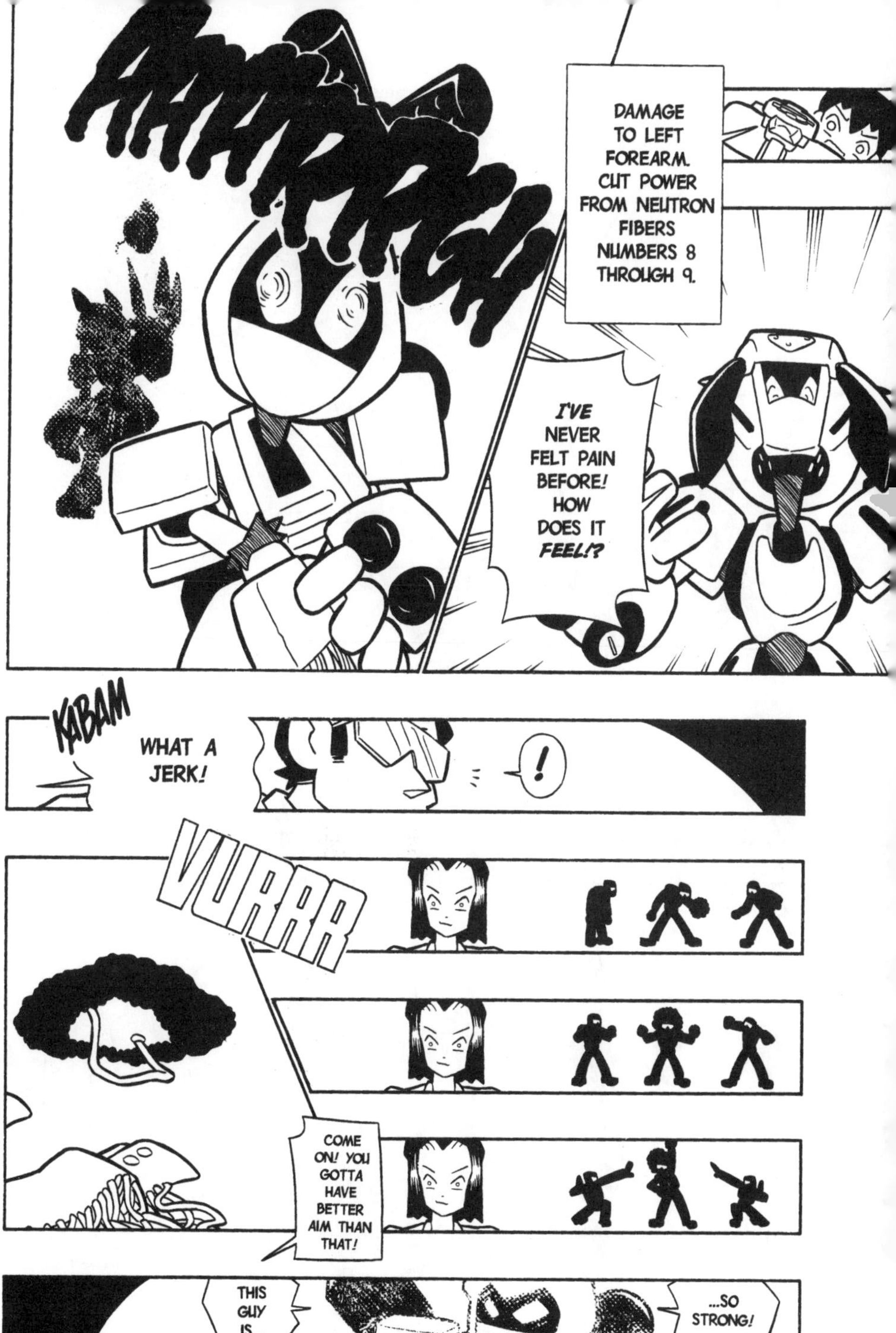
DAMAGE TO LEFT FOREARM. CUT POWER FROM NEUTRON FIBERS NUMBERS 8 THROUGH 9.
I'VE NEVER FELT PAIN BEFORE! HOW DOES IT FEEL!?
KABAM
WHAT A JERK!
!
VURRR
COME ON! YOU GOTTA HAVE BETTER AIM THAN THAT!
THIS GUY IS...
...SO STRONG!

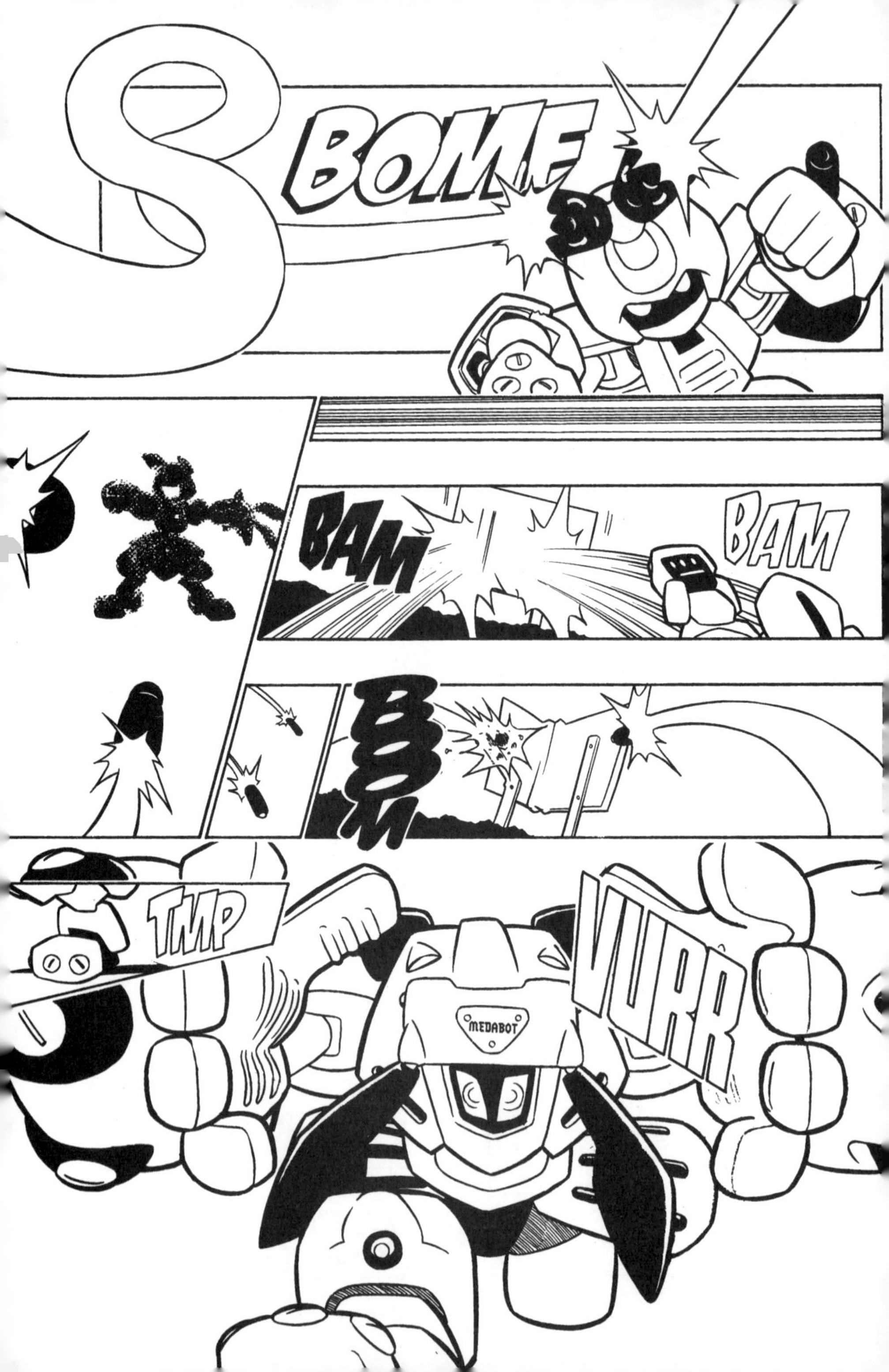
BOMF
BAM
BAM
BOOM
TMP
VURR
MEDABOT

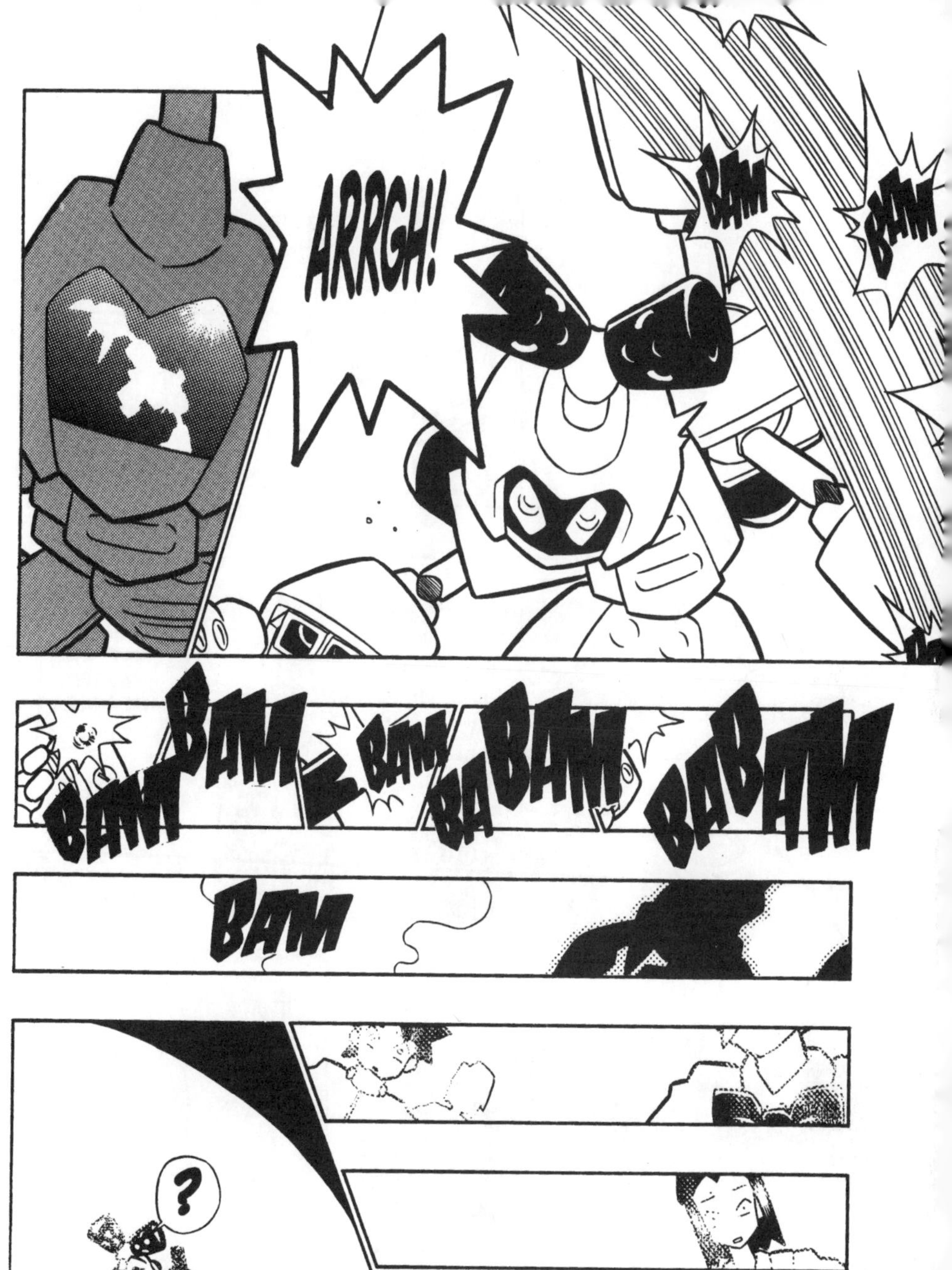
ARRGH!
BAM
BAM
BAM
BAM
BAM
BABAM
BABAM
BAM
?
HEY!

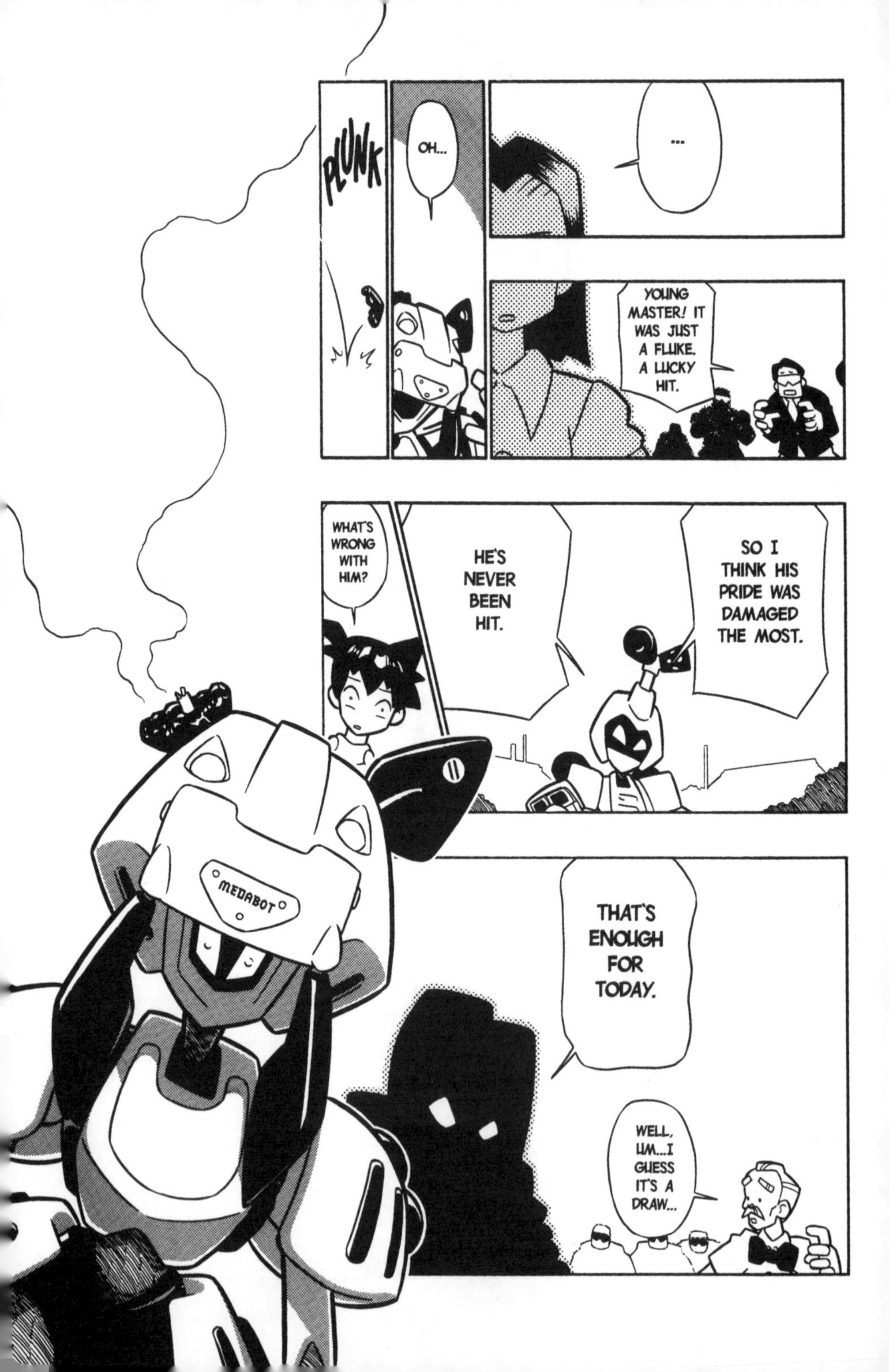

PLUNK
OH...
...
YOUNG MASTER! IT WAS JUST A FLUKE. A LUCKY HIT.
WHAT'S WRONG WITH HIM?
HE'S NEVER BEEN HIT.
SO I THINK HIS PRIDE WAS DAMAGED THE MOST.
MEDABOT
THAT'S ENOUGH FOR TODAY.
WELL, UM...I GUESS IT'S A DRAW...

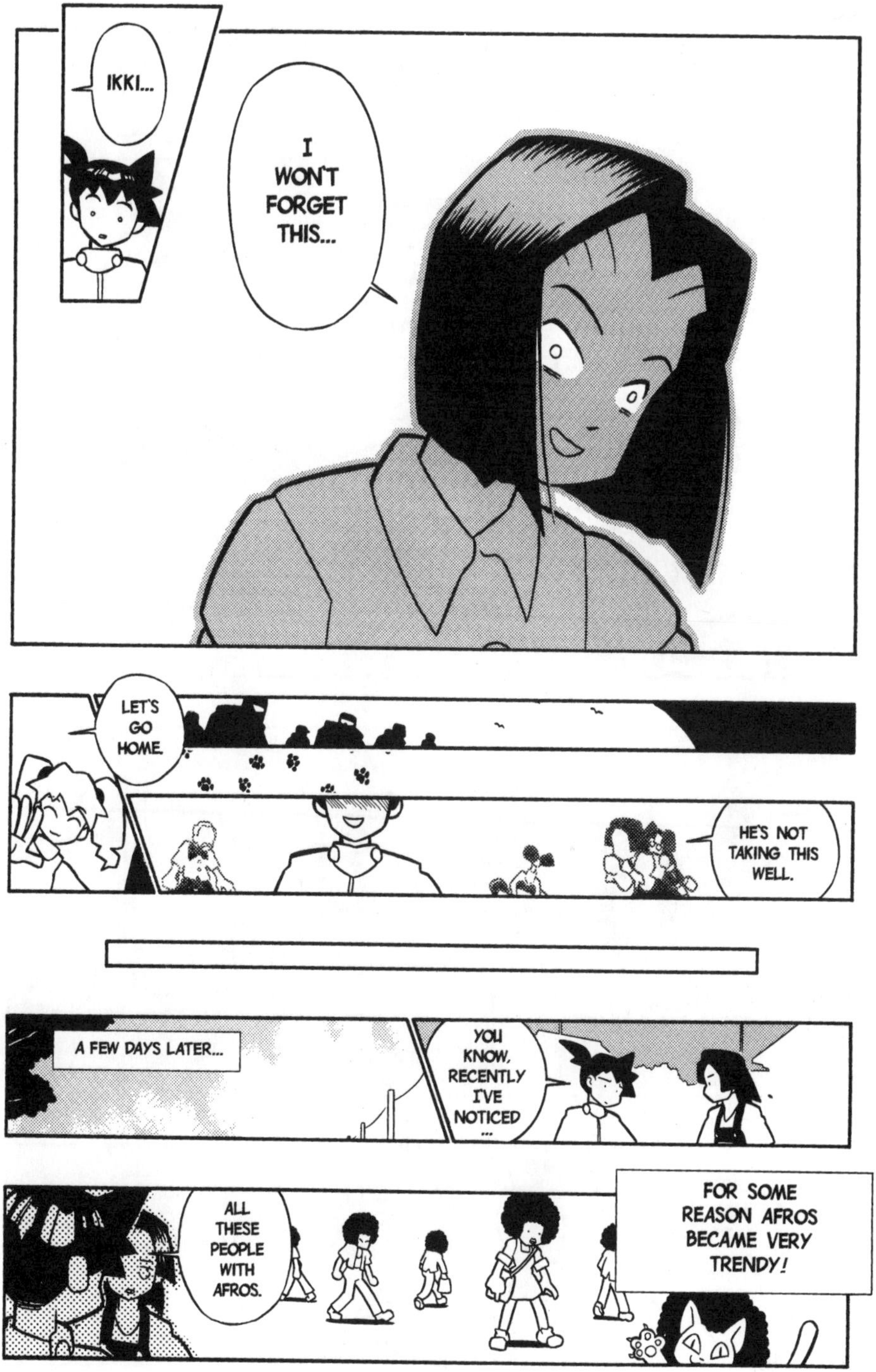
IKKI...
I WON'T FORGET THIS...
LET'S GO HOME.
HE'S NOT TAKING THIS WELL.
A FEW DAYS LATER...
YOU KNOW, RECENTLY I'VE NOTICED ...
ALL THESE PEOPLE WITH AFROS.
FOR SOME REASON AFROS BECAME VERY TRENDY!

A NEW BONUS FEATURE! WHAT'S BEEN ON OUR MINDS!

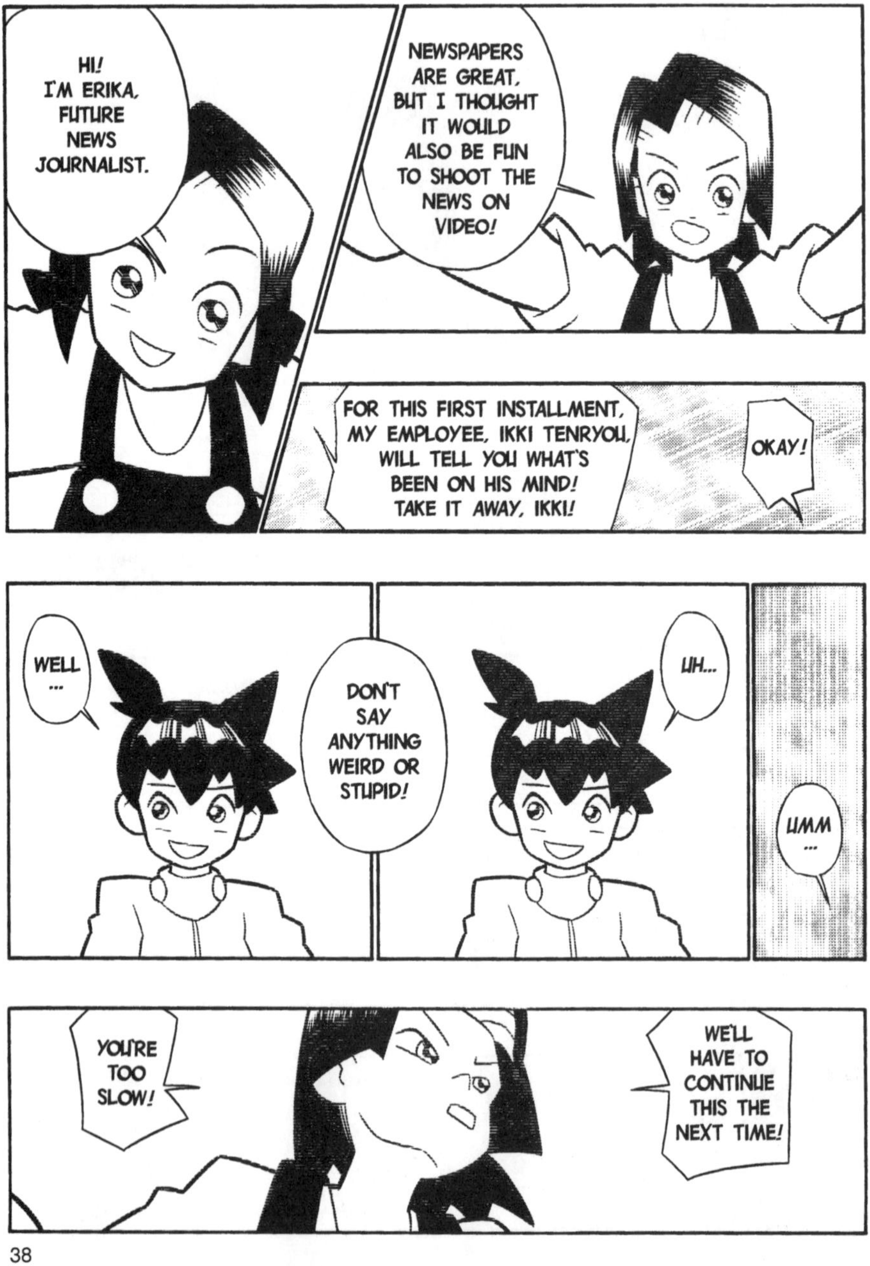
HI! I'M ERIKA, FUTURE NEWS JOURNALIST.
NEWSPAPERS ARE GREAT, BUT I THOUGHT IT WOULD ALSO BE FUN TO SHOOT THE NEWS ON VIDEO!
FOR THIS FIRST INSTALLMENT, MY EMPLOYEE, IKKI TENRYOU, WILL TELL YOU WHAT'S BEEN ON HIS MIND! TAKE IT AWAY, IKKI!
OKAY!
WELL...
DON'T SAY ANYTHING WEIRD OR STUPID!
UH...
UMM...
YOU'RE TOO SLOW!
WE'LL HAVE TO CONTINUE THIS THE NEXT TIME!

The Guardian of the Forest!? The KWG!!

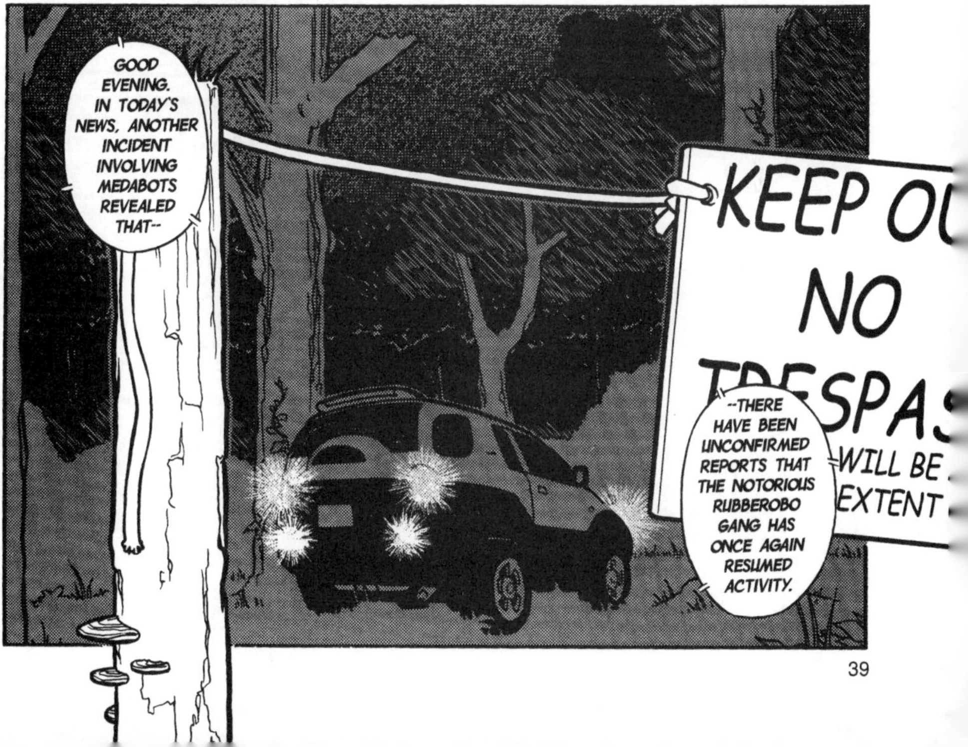
GOOD EVENING. IN TODAY'S NEWS, ANOTHER INCIDENT INVOLVING MEDABOTS REVEALED THAT--
KEEP OU
NO
TRESPAS
WILL BE
EXTENT
--THERE HAVE BEEN UNCONFIRMED REPORTS THAT THE NOTORIOUS RUBBEROBO GANG HAS ONCE AGAIN RESUMED ACTIVITY.

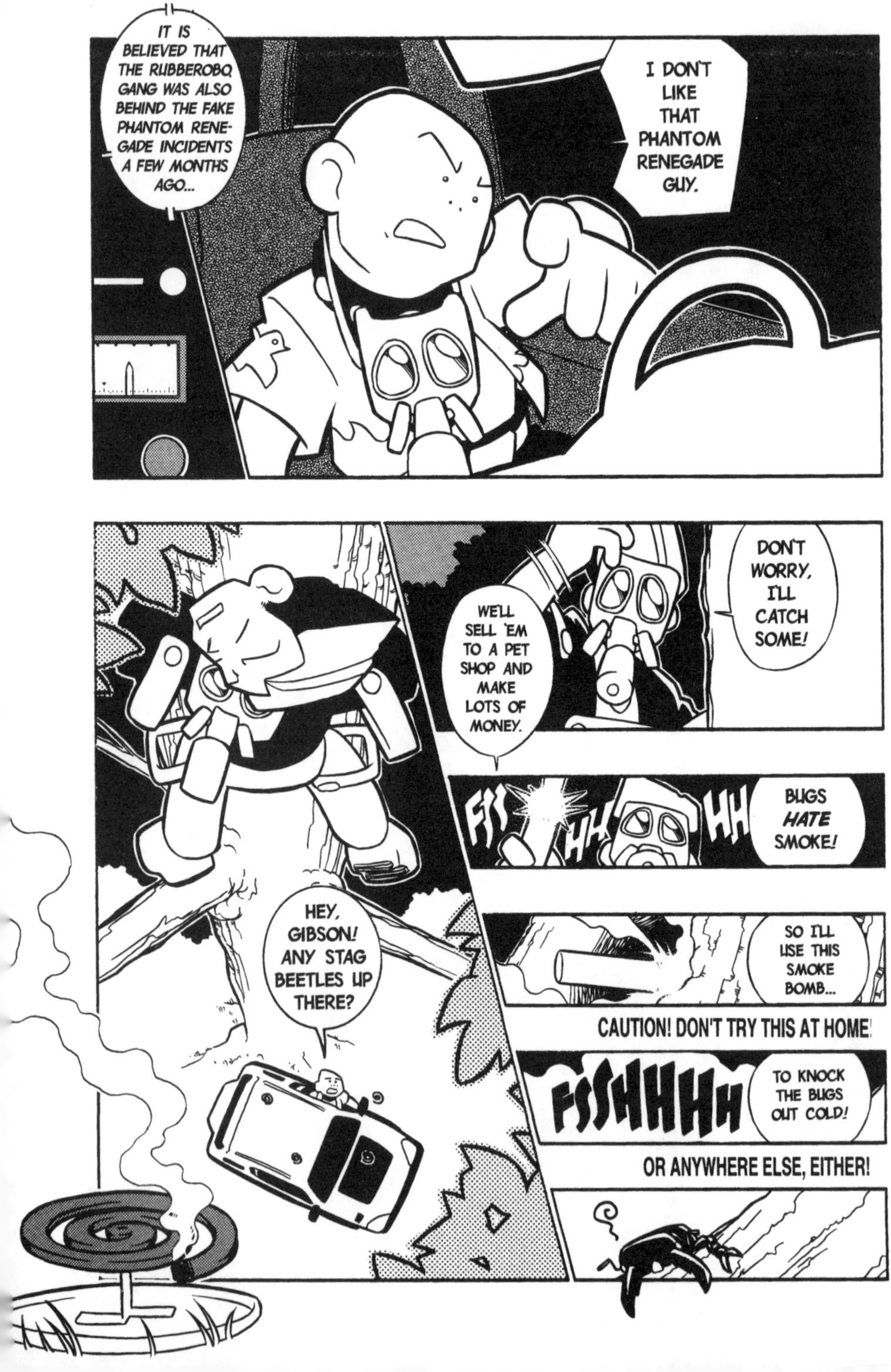
IT IS BELIEVED THAT THE RUBBEROBQ GANG WAS ALSO BEHIND THE FAKE PHANTOM RENEGADE INCIDENTS A FEW MONTHS AGO...
I DON'T LIKE THAT PHANTOM RENEGADE GUY.
HEY, GIBSON! ANY STAG BEETLES UP THERE?
DON'T WORRY, I'LL CATCH SOME!
WE'LL SELL 'EM TO A PET SHOP AND MAKE LOTS OF MONEY.
FSSHHHH
BUGS HATE SMOKE!
SO I'LL USE THIS SMOKE BOMB...
CAUTION! DON'T TRY THIS AT HOME!
FSSHHHHH
TO KNOCK THE BUGS OUT COLD!
OR ANYWHERE ELSE, EITHER!

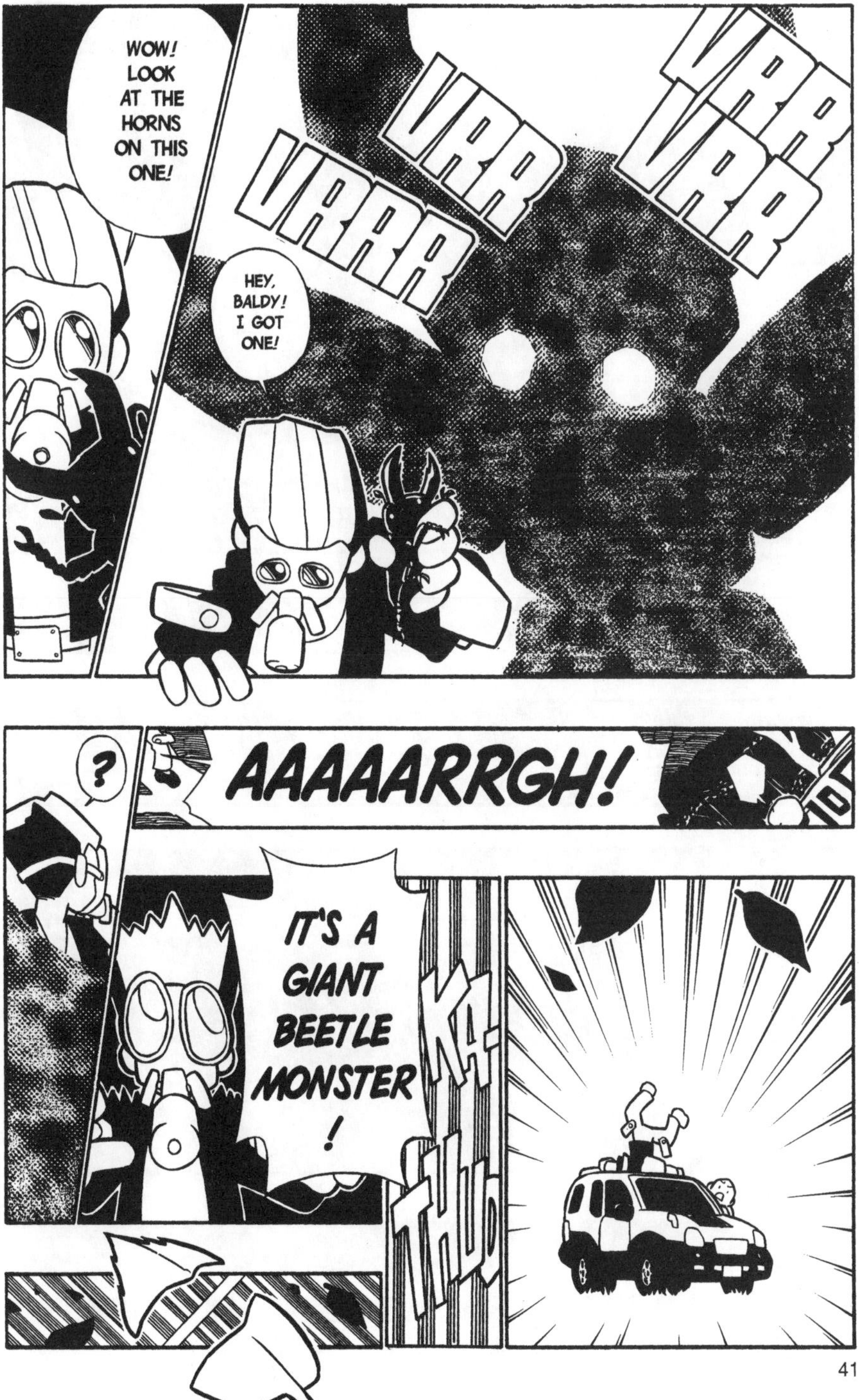
WOW! LOOK AT THE HORNS ON THIS ONE!
URRR
URR
URR
URR
HEY, BALDY! I GOT ONE!
?
AAAAARRGH!
IT'S A GIANT BEETLE MONSTER!
KA-THUD

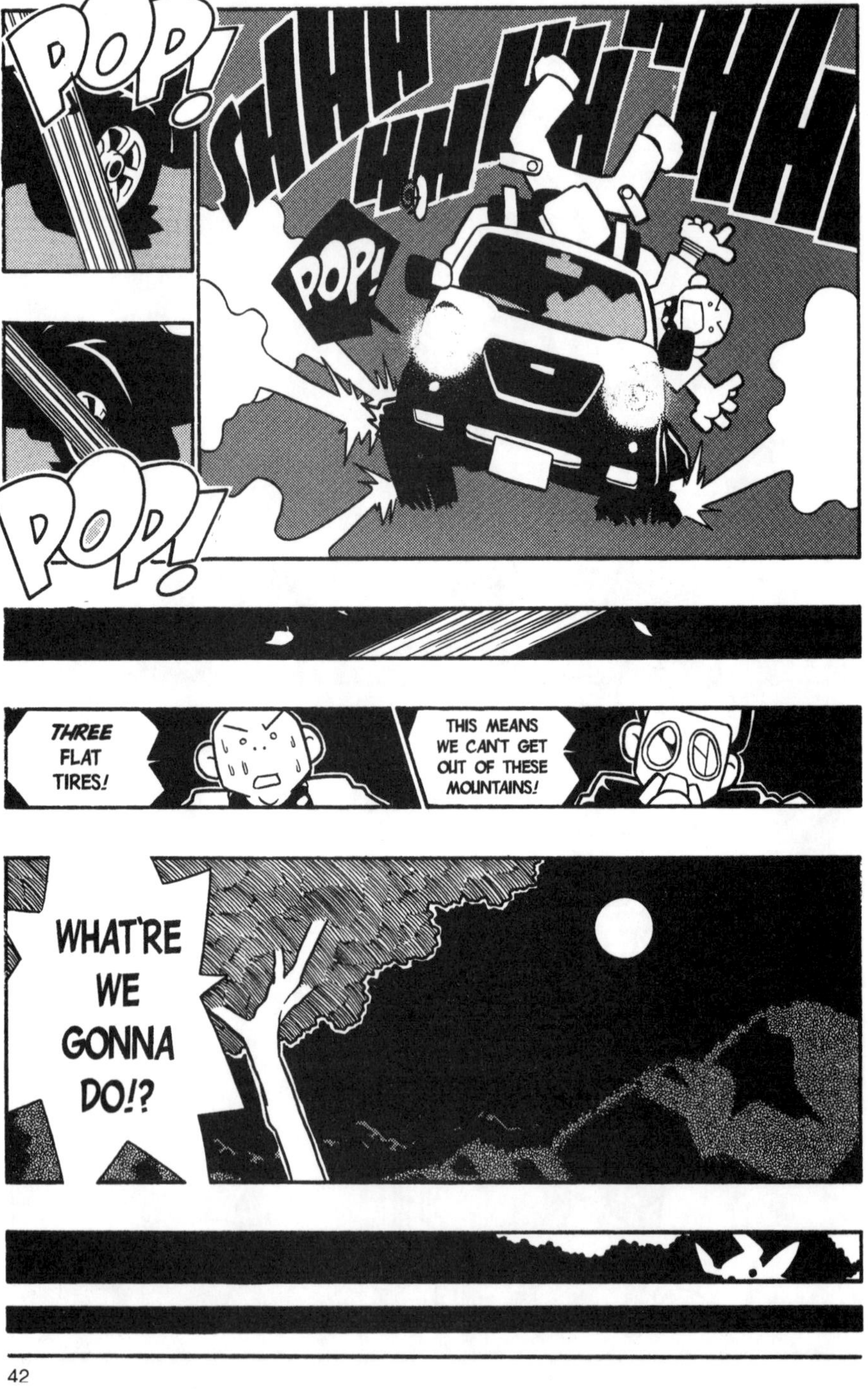
POP!
SHHHHHHHHHHHHH
POP!
POP!
THREE FLAT TIRES!
THIS MEANS WE CAN'T GET OUT OF THESE MOUNTAINS!
WHAT'RE WE GONNA DO!?

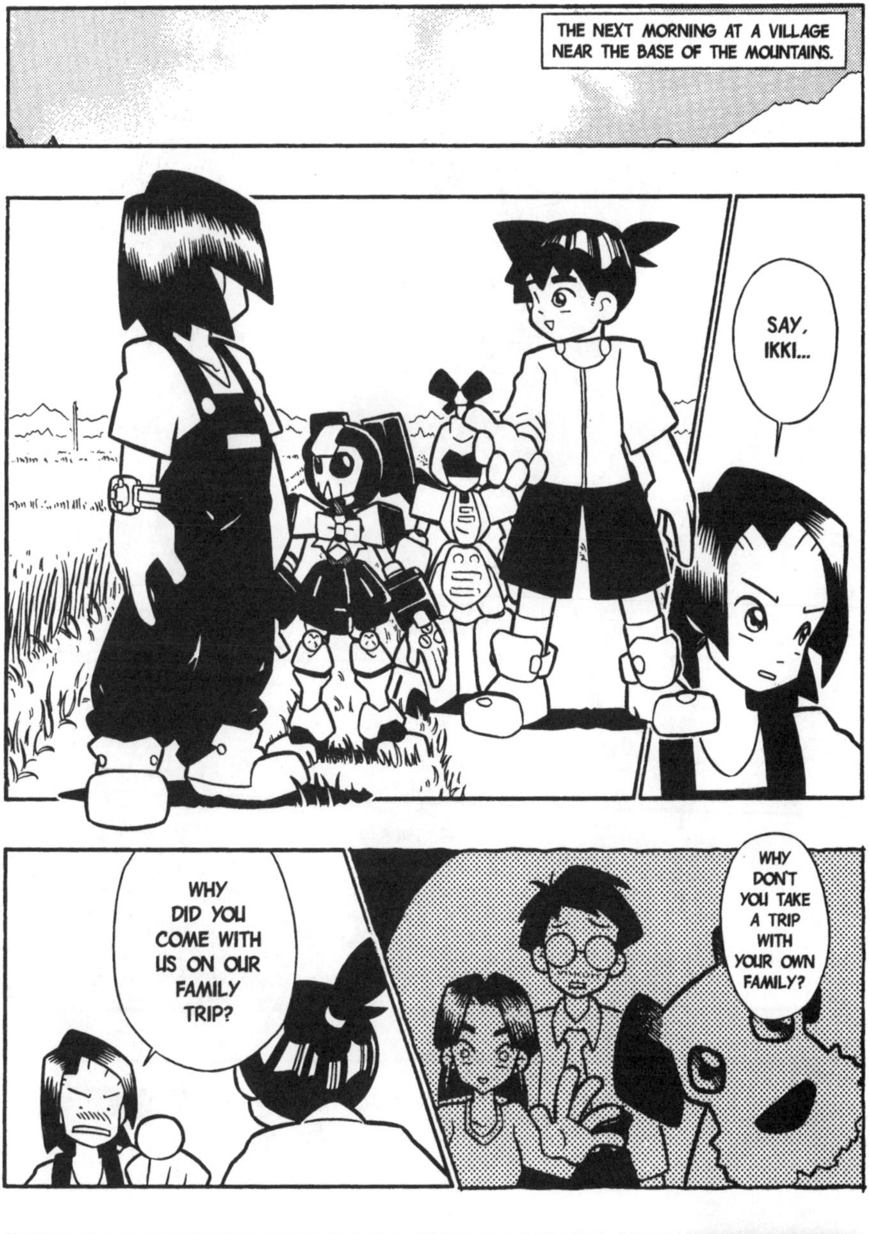
THE NEXT MORNING AT A VILLAGE NEAR THE BASE OF THE MOUNTAINS.
SAY, IKKI...
WHY DID YOU COME WITH US ON OUR FAMILY TRIP?
WHY DON'T YOU TAKE A TRIP WITH YOUR OWN FAMILY?
MY DAD SAYS HE'S TOO BUSY...
WELL, HELLO!

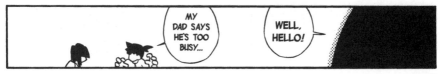

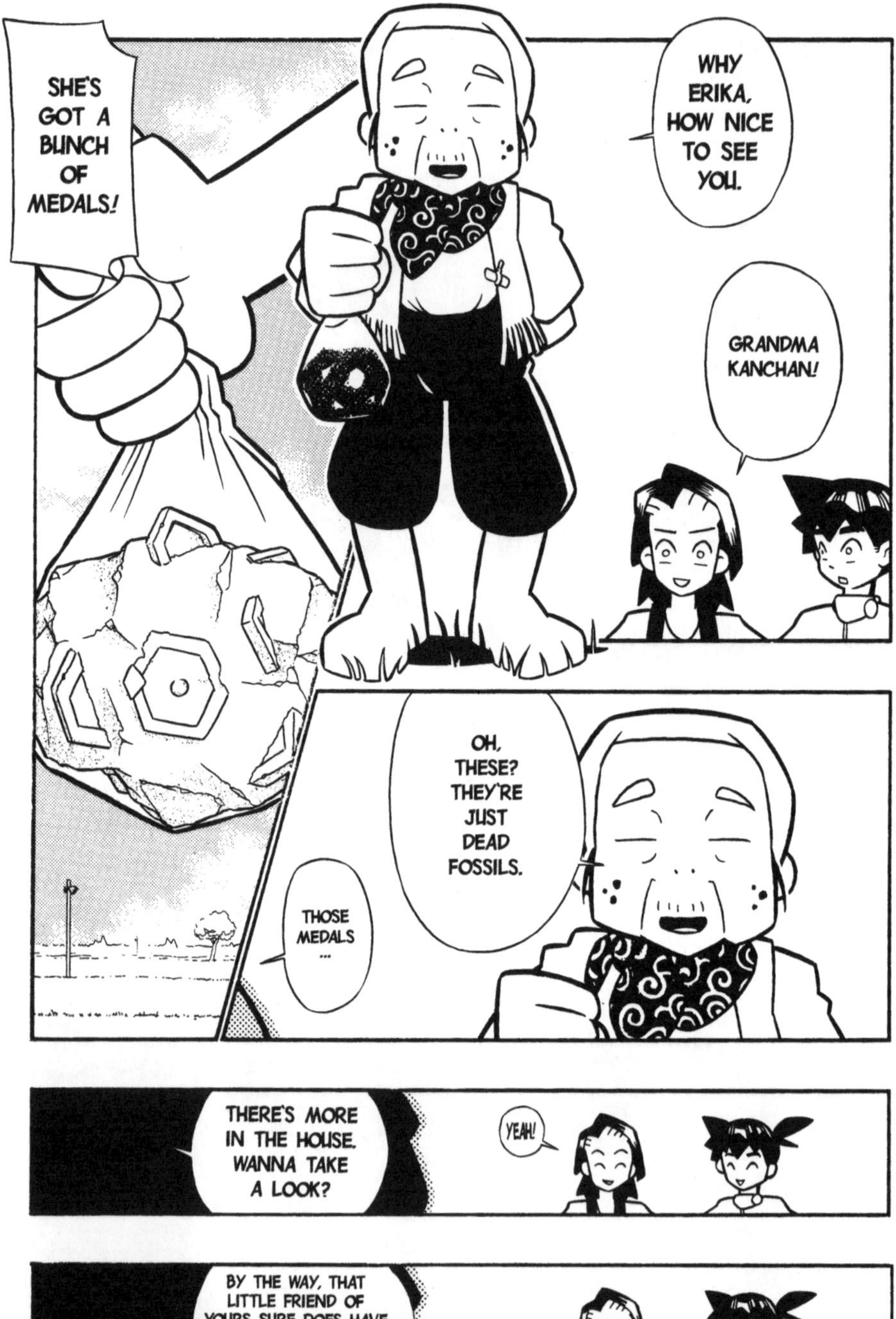

SHE'S GOT A BUNCH OF MEDALS!
WHY ERIKA, HOW NICE TO SEE YOU.
GRANDMA KANCHAN!
THOSE MEDALS ...
OH, THESE? THEY'RE JUST DEAD FOSSILS.
THERE'S MORE IN THE HOUSE. WANNA TAKE A LOOK?
YEAH!
BY THE WAY, THAT LITTLE FRIEND OF YOURS SURE DOES HAVE A STRANGE HAIRCUT. ARE TOPKNOTS POPULAR THESE DAYS?

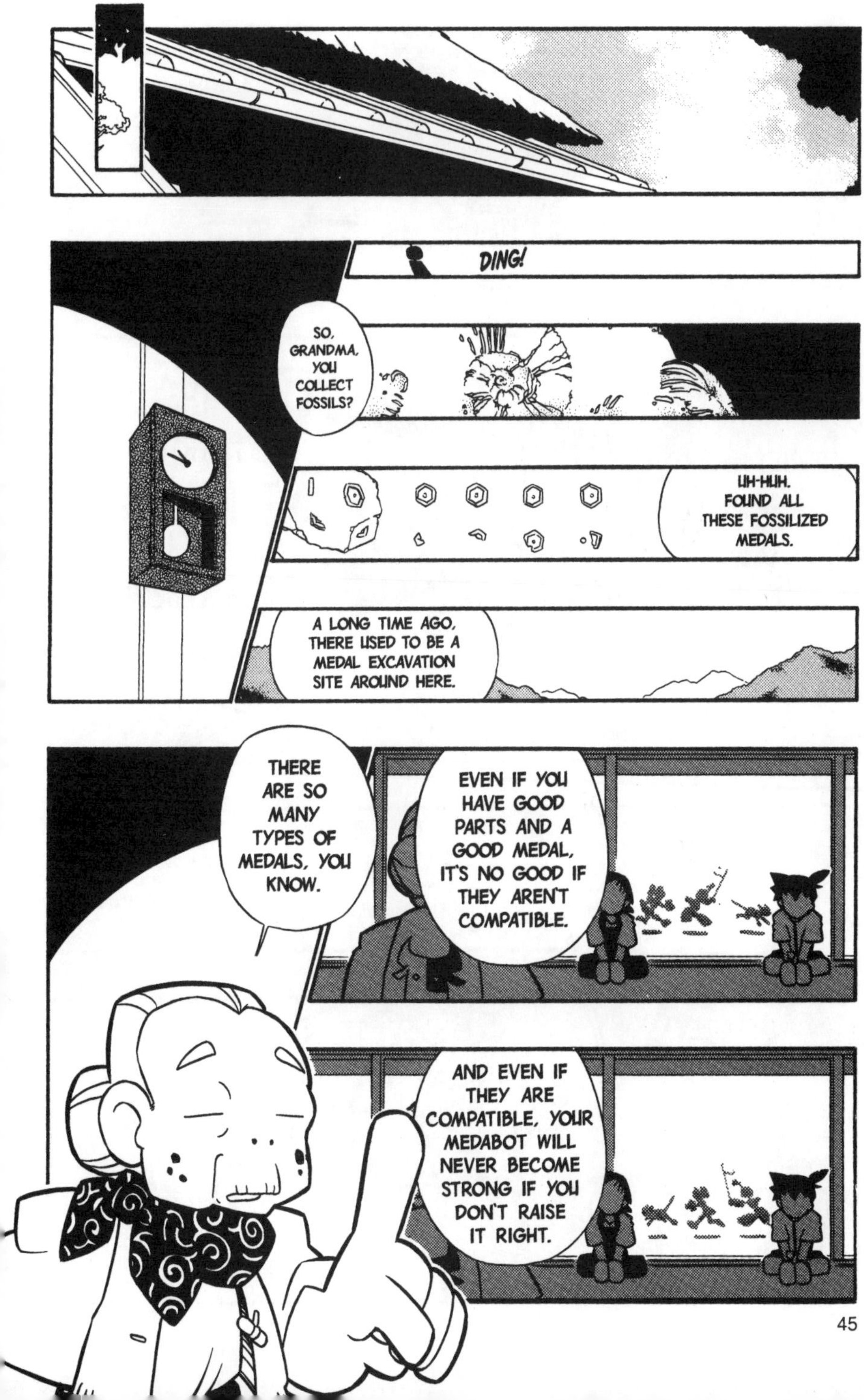
DING!
SO, GRANDMA, YOU COLLECT FOSSILS?
UH-HUH. FOUND ALL THESE FOSSILIZED MEDALS.
A LONG TIME AGO, THERE USED TO BE A MEDAL EXCAVATION SITE AROUND HERE.
THERE ARE SO MANY TYPES OF MEDALS, YOU KNOW.
EVEN IF YOU HAVE GOOD PARTS AND A GOOD MEDAL, IT'S NO GOOD IF THEY AREN'T COMPATIBLE.
AND EVEN IF THEY ARE COMPATIBLE, YOUR MEDABOT WILL NEVER BECOME STRONG IF YOU DON'T RAISE IT RIGHT.

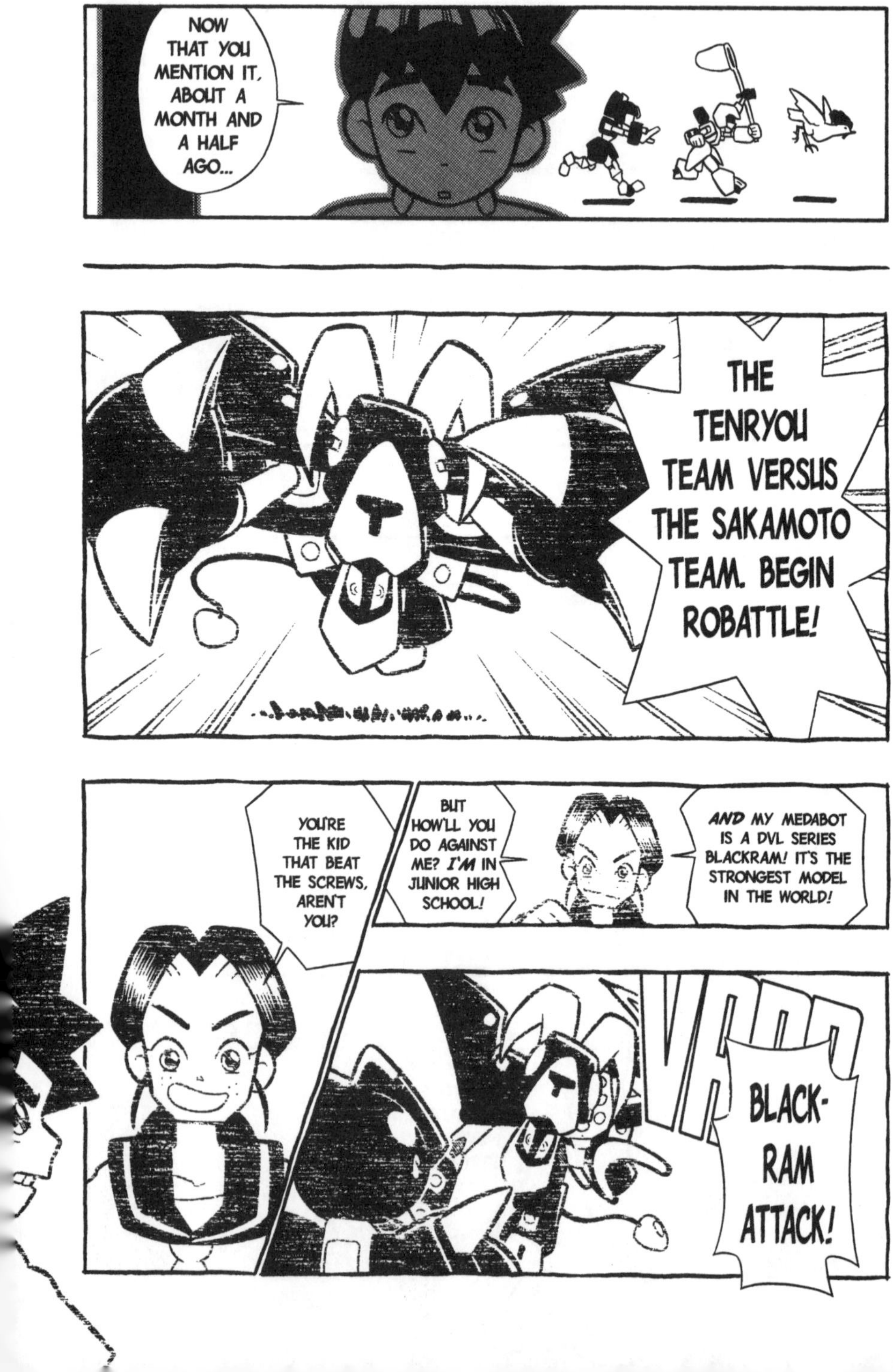
NOW THAT YOU MENTION IT, ABOUT A MONTH AND A HALF AGO...
THE TENRYOU TEAM VERSUS THE SAKAMOTO TEAM. BEGIN ROBATTLE!
YOU'RE THE KID THAT BEAT THE SCREWS, AREN'T YOU?
BUT HOW'LL YOU DO AGAINST ME? *I'M* IN JUNIOR HIGH SCHOOL!
AND MY MEDABOT IS A DVL SERIES BLACKRAM! IT'S THE STRONGEST MODEL IN THE WORLD!
BLACK-RAM ATTACK!

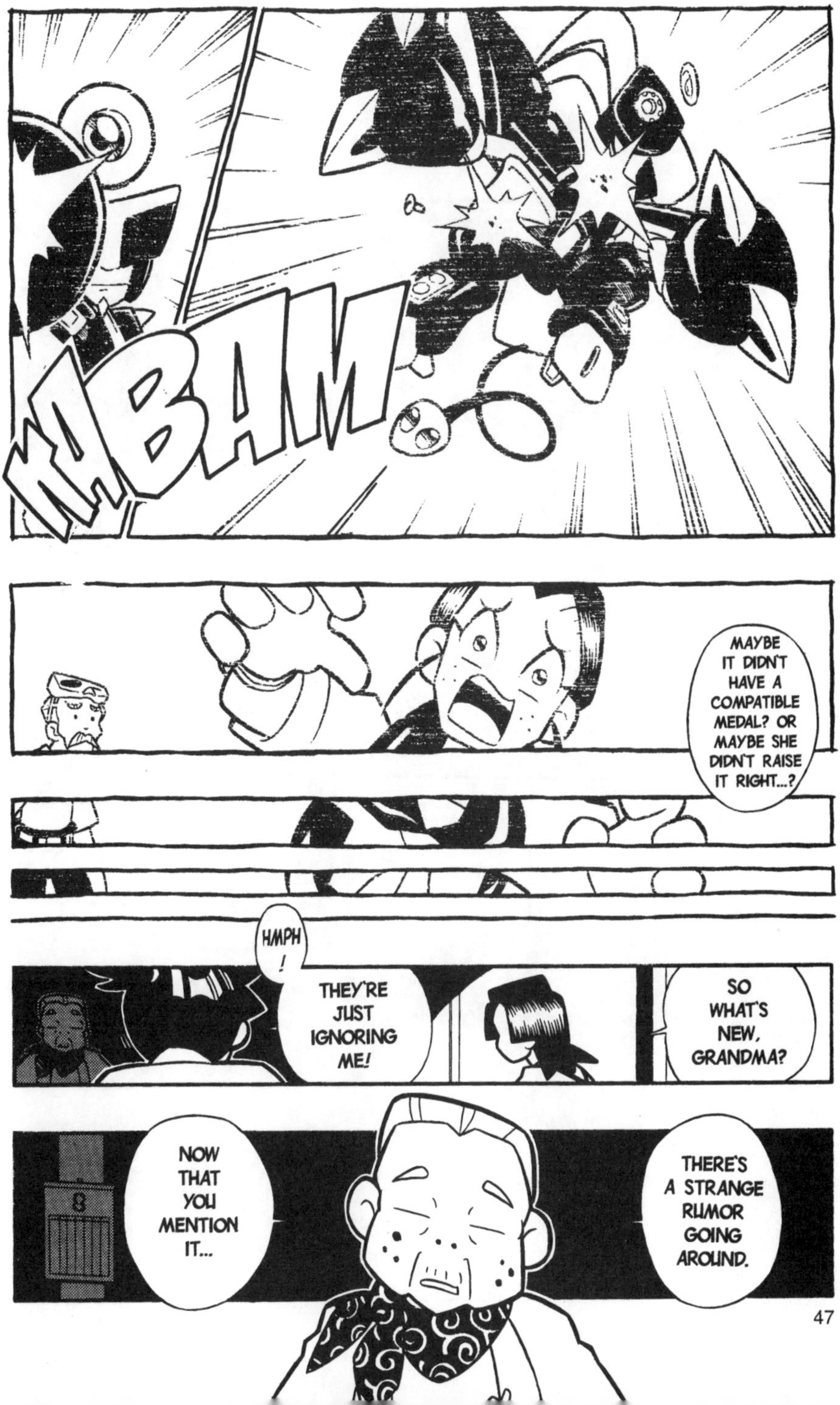
WHAM
BAM
MAYBE IT DIDN'T HAVE A COMPATIBLE MEDAL? OR MAYBE SHE DIDN'T RAISE IT RIGHT...?
HMPH!
THEY'RE JUST IGNORING ME!
SO WHAT'S NEW, GRANDMA?
NOW THAT YOU MENTION IT...
THERE'S A STRANGE RUMOR GOING AROUND.

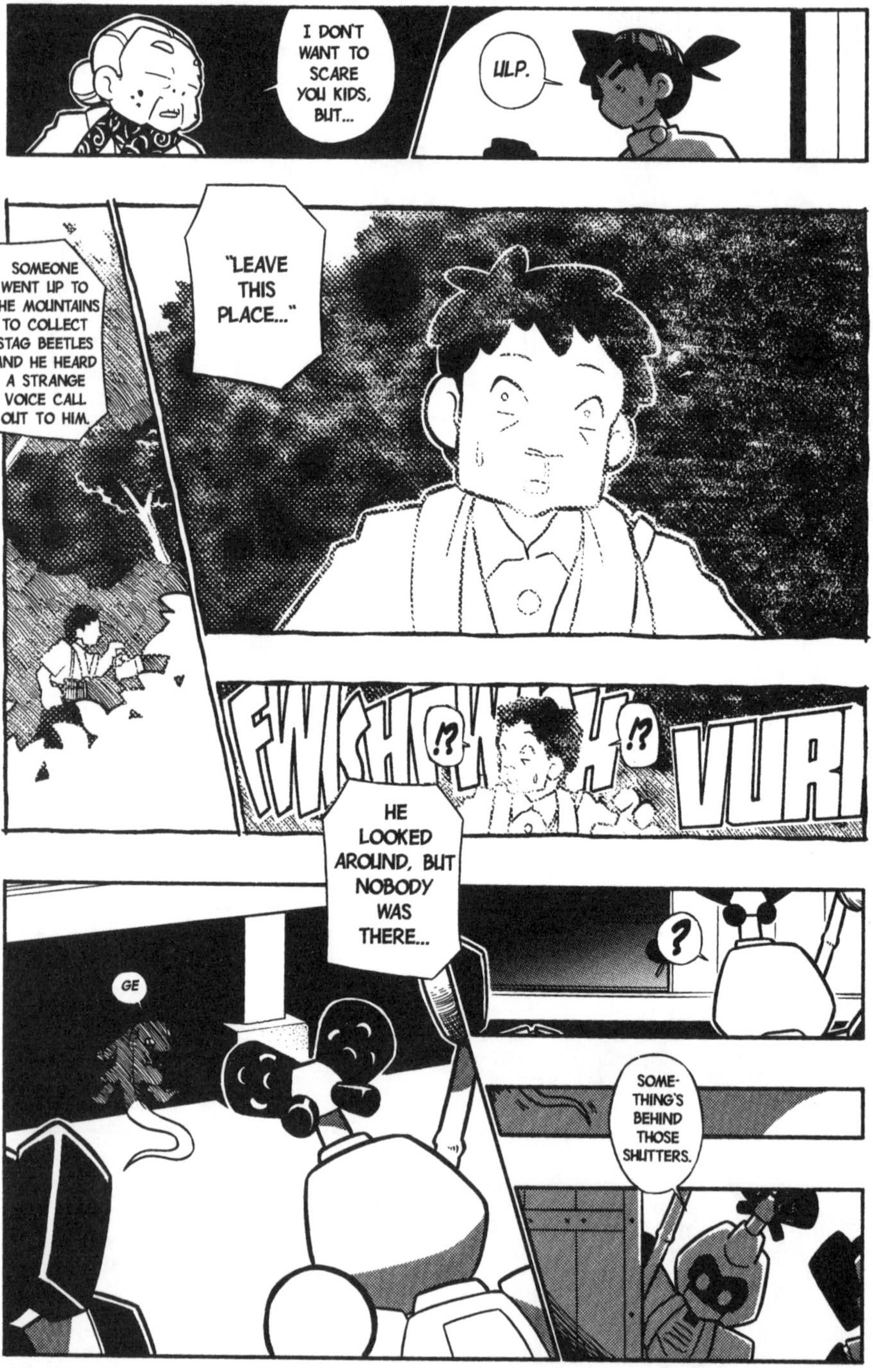

I DON'T WANT TO SCARE YOU KIDS, BUT...
ULP.
SOMEONE WENT UP TO THE MOUNTAINS TO COLLECT STAG BEETLES AND HE HEARD A STRANGE VOICE CALL OUT TO HIM.
"LEAVE THIS PLACE..."
FWISHOWWH
!?
!?
VURI
HE LOOKED AROUND, BUT NOBODY WAS THERE...
?
GE
SOME-THING'S BEHIND THOSE SHUTTERS.

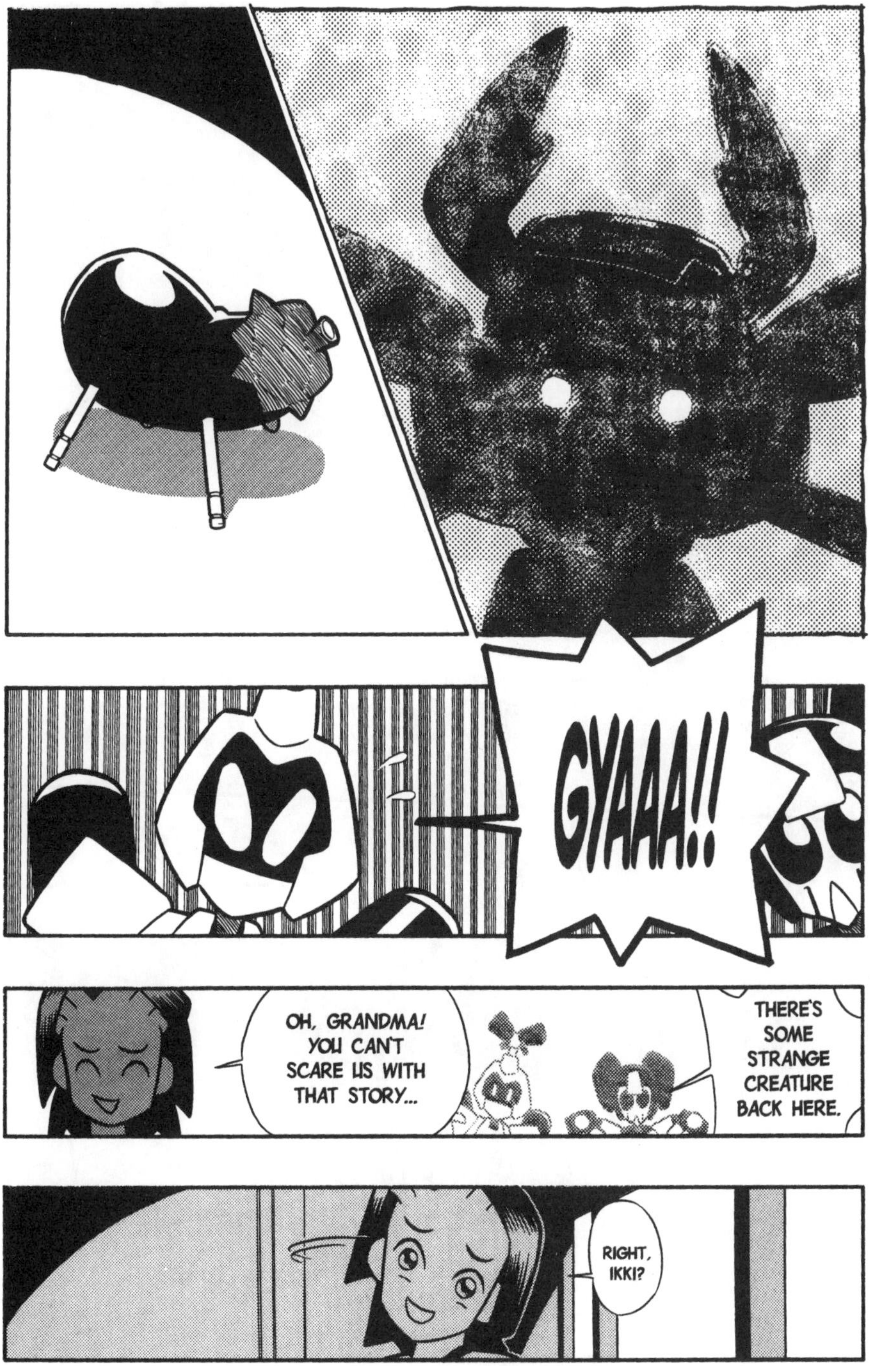
GYAAA!!
OH, GRANDMA! YOU CAN'T SCARE US WITH THAT STORY...
THERE'S SOME STRANGE CREATURE BACK HERE.
RIGHT, IKKI?

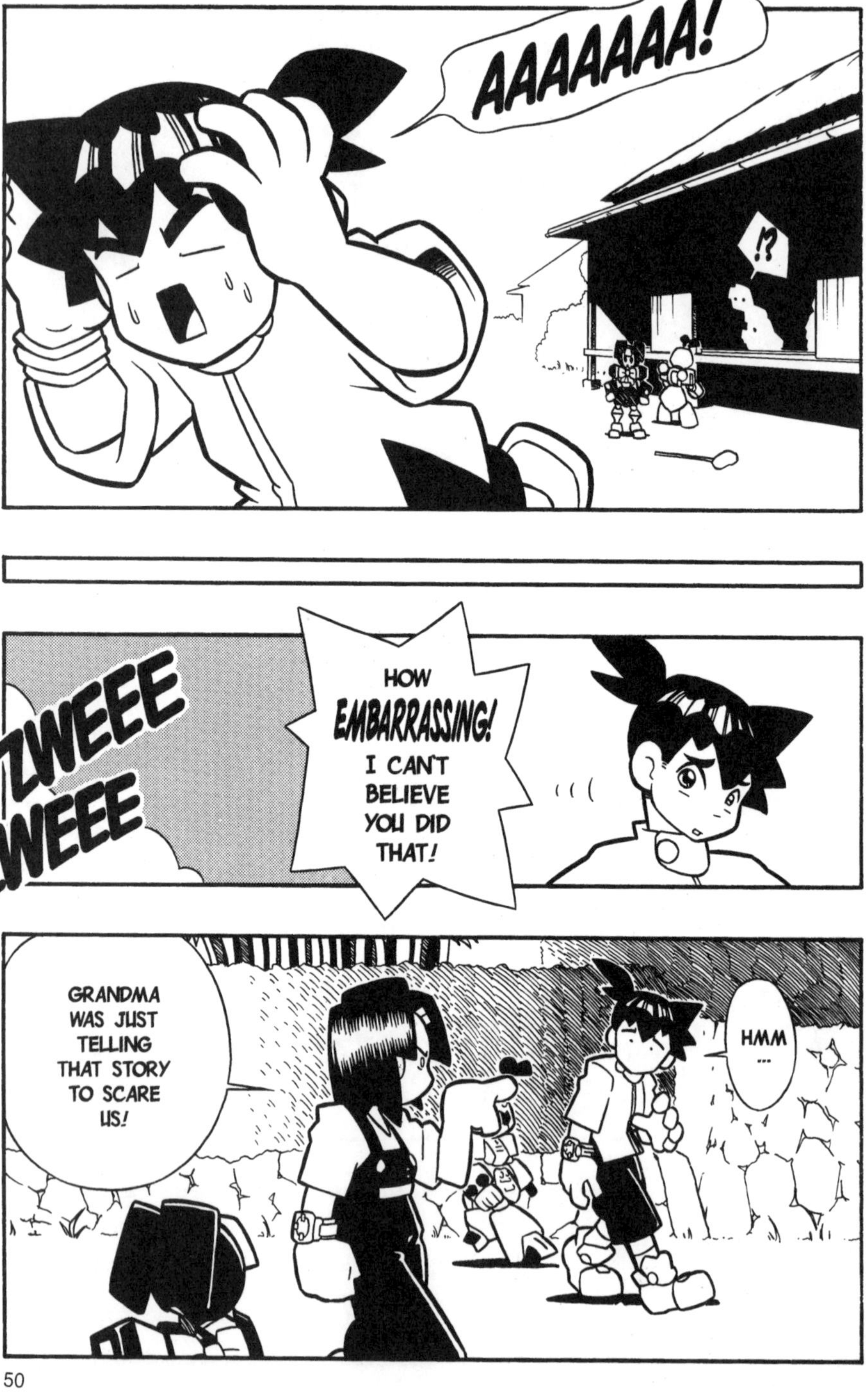
AAAAAAA!
!?
ZWEEE ZWEEE
HOW EMBARRASSING! I CAN'T BELIEVE YOU DID THAT!
GRANDMA WAS JUST TELLING THAT STORY TO SCARE US!
HMM ...

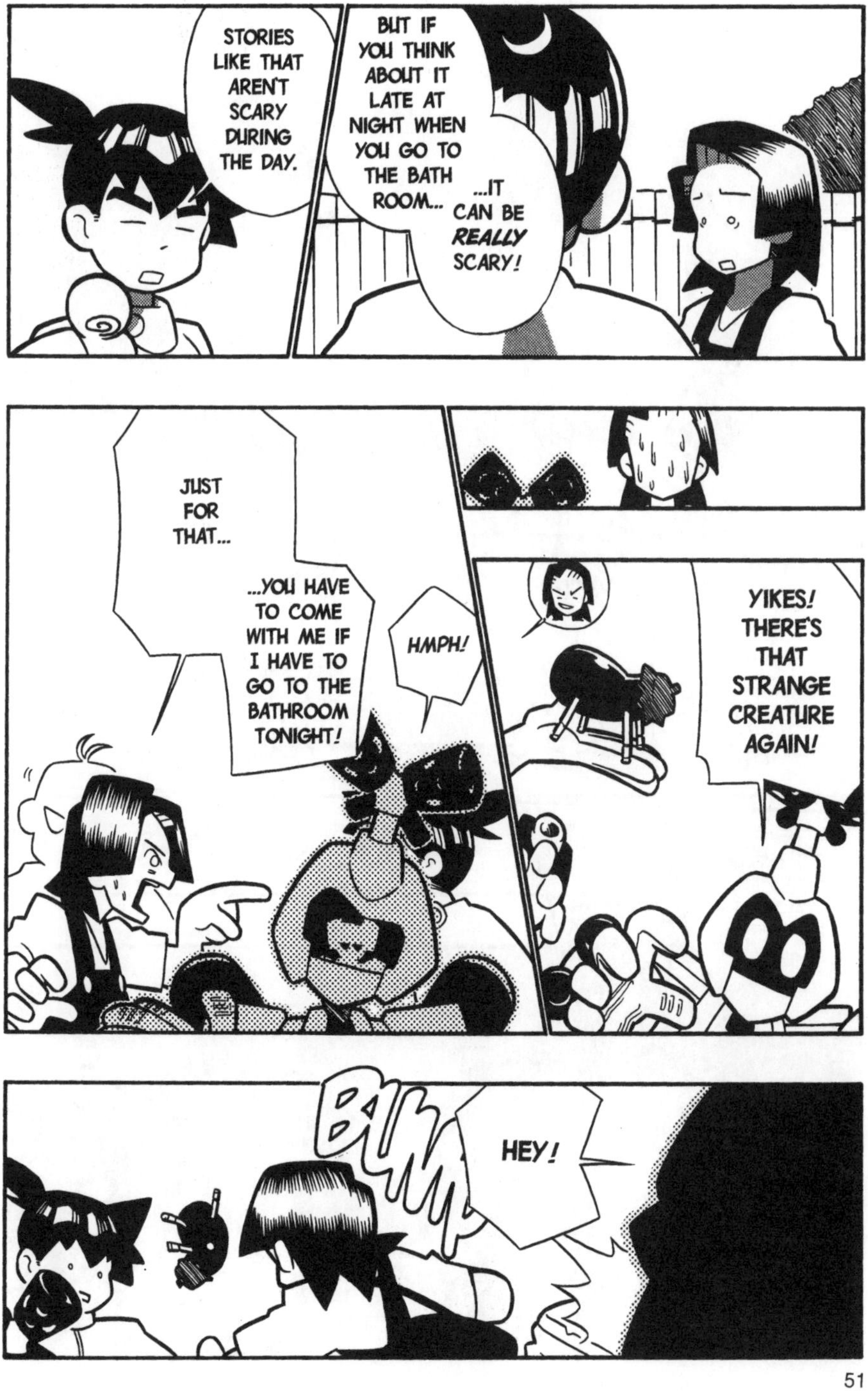
STORIES LIKE THAT AREN'T SCARY DURING THE DAY.
BUT IF YOU THINK ABOUT IT LATE AT NIGHT WHEN YOU GO TO THE BATH ROOM...
...IT CAN BE REALLY SCARY!
JUST FOR THAT...
...YOU HAVE TO COME WITH ME IF I HAVE TO GO TO THE BATHROOM TONIGHT!
HMPH!
YIKES! THERE'S THAT STRANGE CREATURE AGAIN!
BAM
HEY!

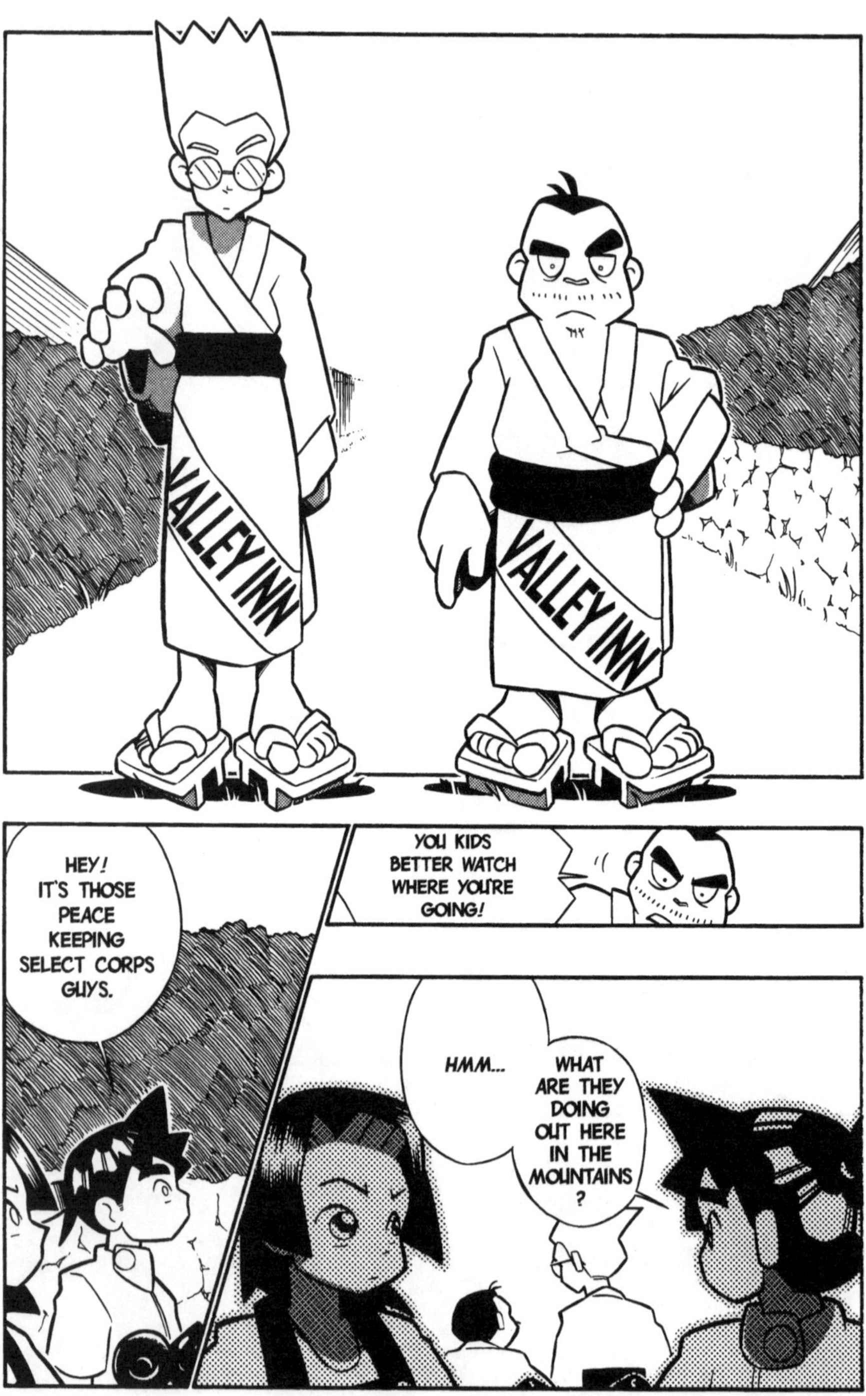
VALLEY INN
VALLEY INN
HEY! IT'S THOSE PEACE KEEPING SELECT CORPS GUYS.
YOU KIDS BETTER WATCH WHERE YOU'RE GOING!
HMM...
WHAT ARE THEY DOING OUT HERE IN THE MOUNTAINS?

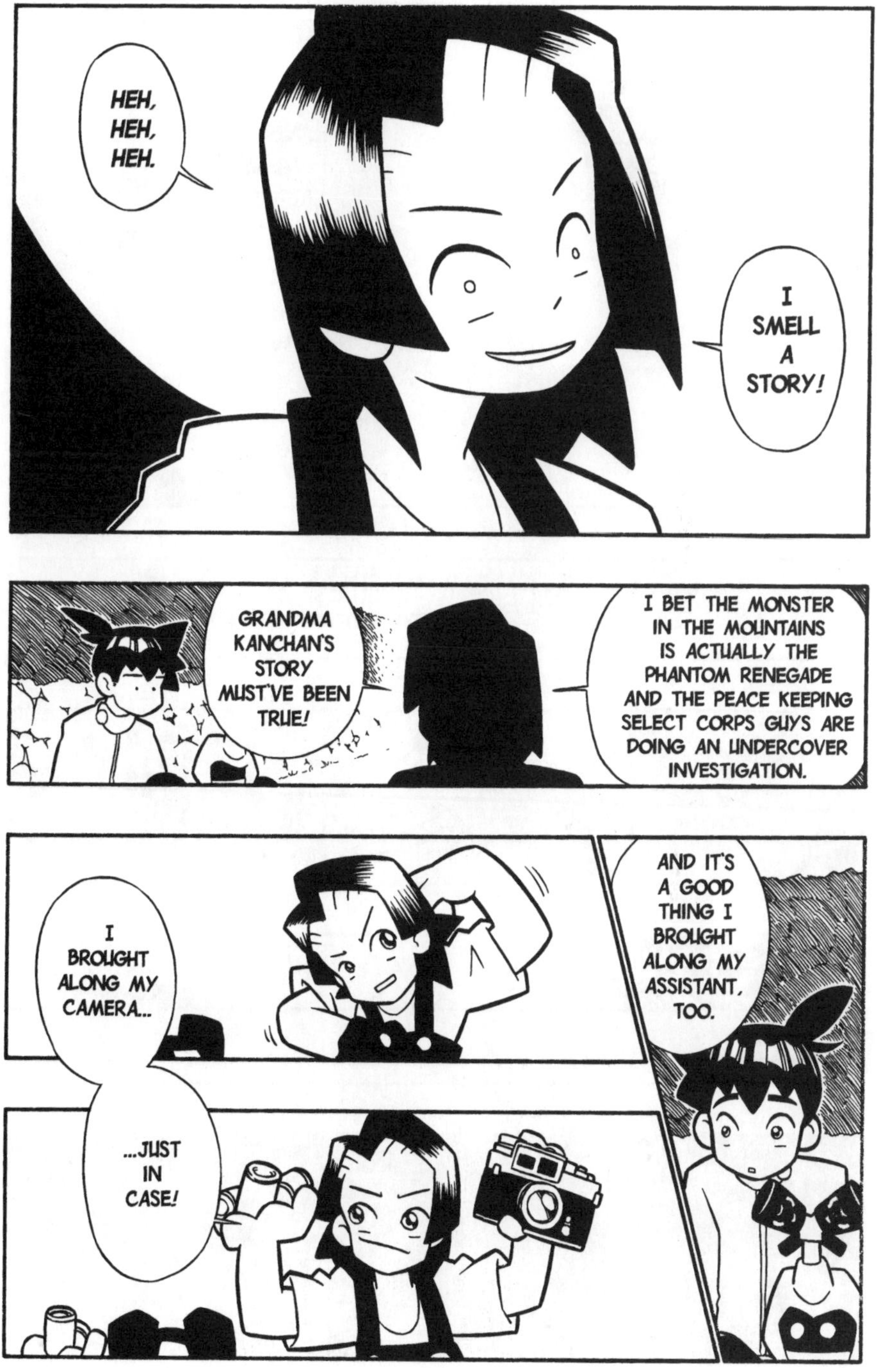
HEH, HEH, HEH.
I SMELL A STORY!
GRANDMA KANCHAN'S STORY MUST'VE BEEN TRUE!
I BET THE MONSTER IN THE MOUNTAINS IS ACTUALLY THE PHANTOM RENEGADE AND THE PEACE KEEPING SELECT CORPS GUYS ARE DOING AN UNDERCOVER INVESTIGATION.
I BROUGHT ALONG MY CAMERA...
...JUST IN CASE!
AND IT'S A GOOD THING I BROUGHT ALONG MY ASSISTANT, TOO.

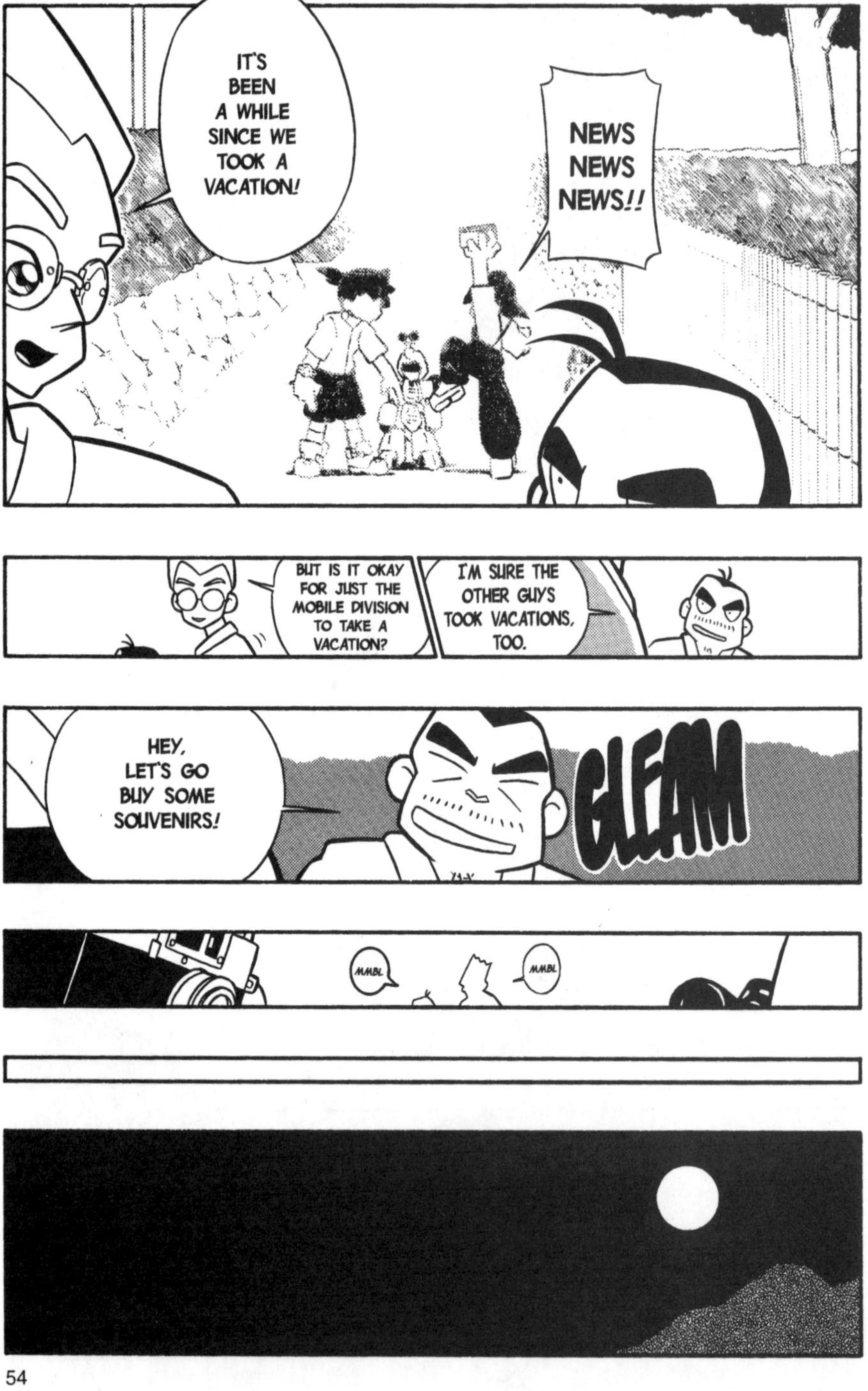
IT'S BEEN A WHILE SINCE WE TOOK A VACATION!
NEWS NEWS NEWS!!
BUT IS IT OKAY FOR JUST THE MOBILE DIVISION TO TAKE A VACATION?
I'M SURE THE OTHER GUYS TOOK VACATIONS, TOO.
HEY, LET'S GO BUY SOME SOUVENIRS!
GLEAM
MMBL
MMBL

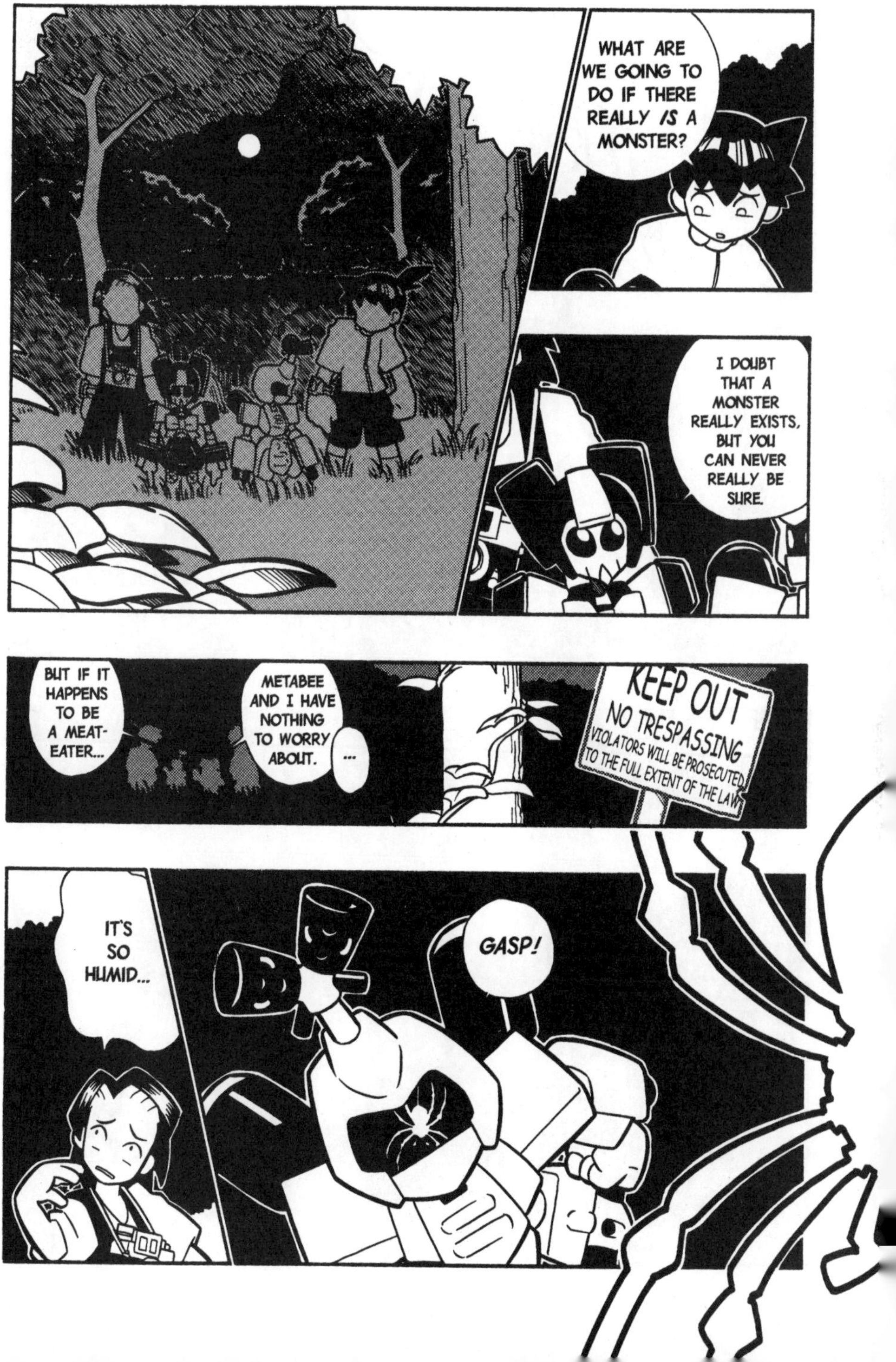
WHAT ARE WE GOING TO DO IF THERE REALLY *IS* A MONSTER?
I DOUBT THAT A MONSTER REALLY EXISTS, BUT YOU CAN NEVER REALLY BE SURE.
BUT IF IT HAPPENS TO BE A MEAT-EATER...
METABEE AND I HAVE NOTHING TO WORRY ABOUT.
...
KEEP OUT
NO TRESPASSING
VIOLATORS WILL BE PROSECUTED TO THE FULL EXTENT OF THE LAW
IT'S SO HUMID...
GASP!

BAM BA
BABA
AAAAA!!
BAM
WHAT ARE YOU DOING?
MMBL
...
MMBL

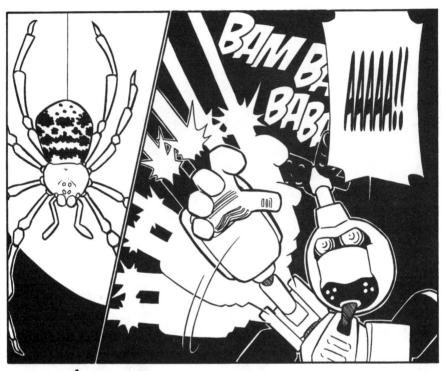

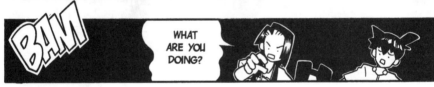

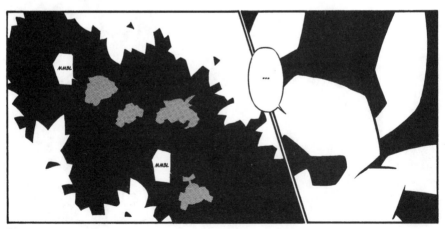

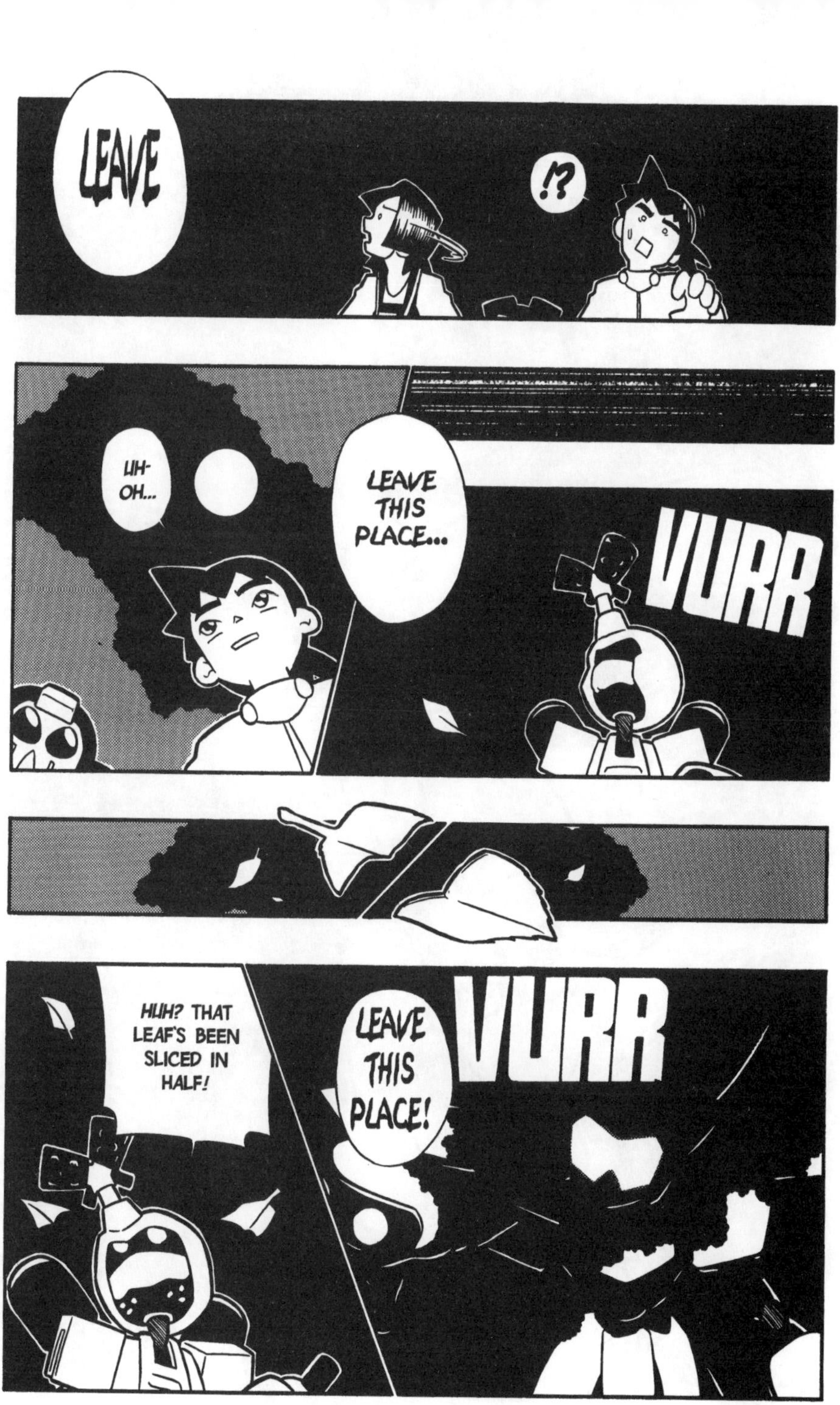
LEAVE
!?
UH-OH...
LEAVE THIS PLACE...
VURR
HUH? THAT LEAF'S BEEN SLICED IN HALF!
LEAVE THIS PLACE!
VURR

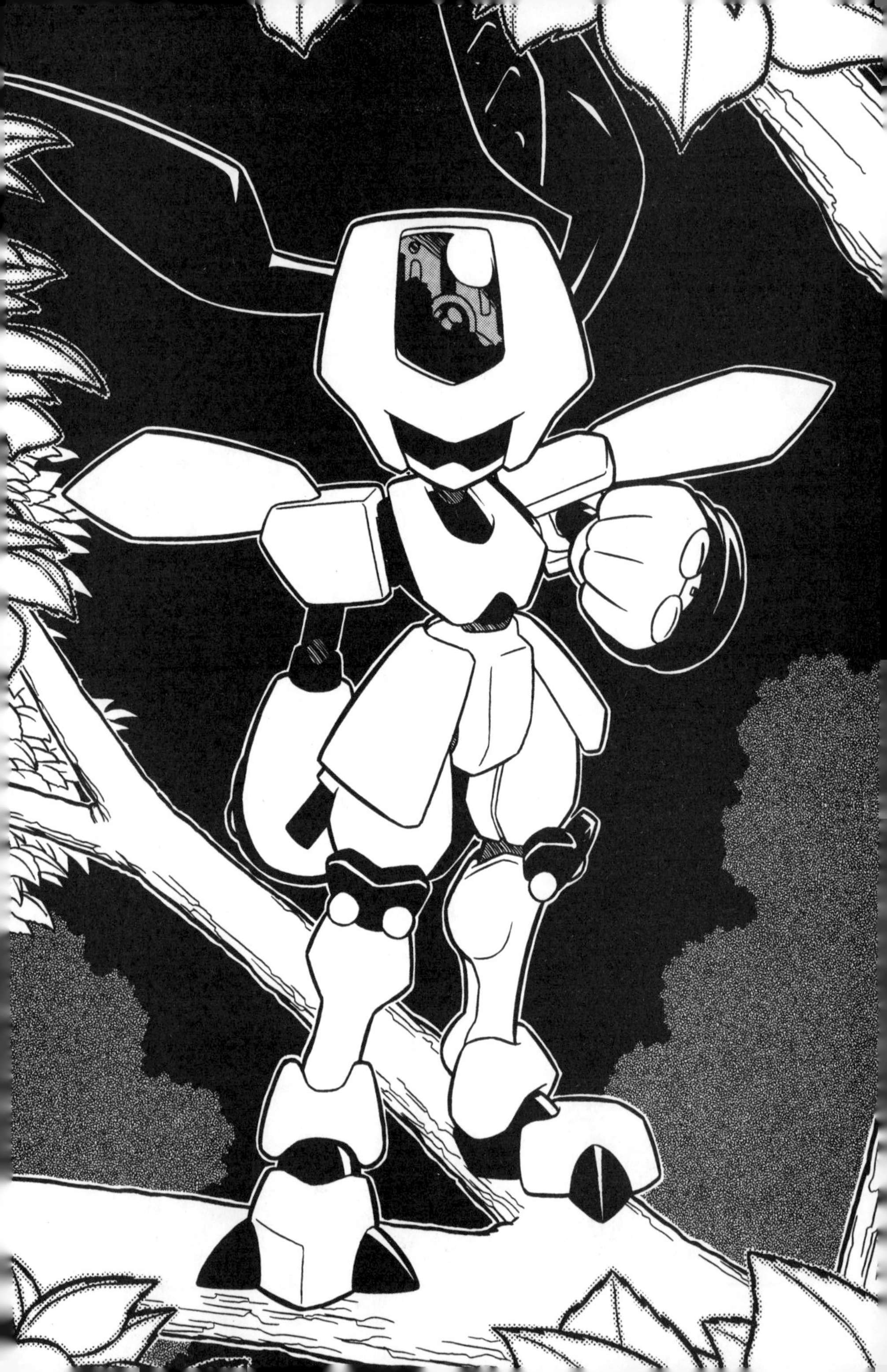

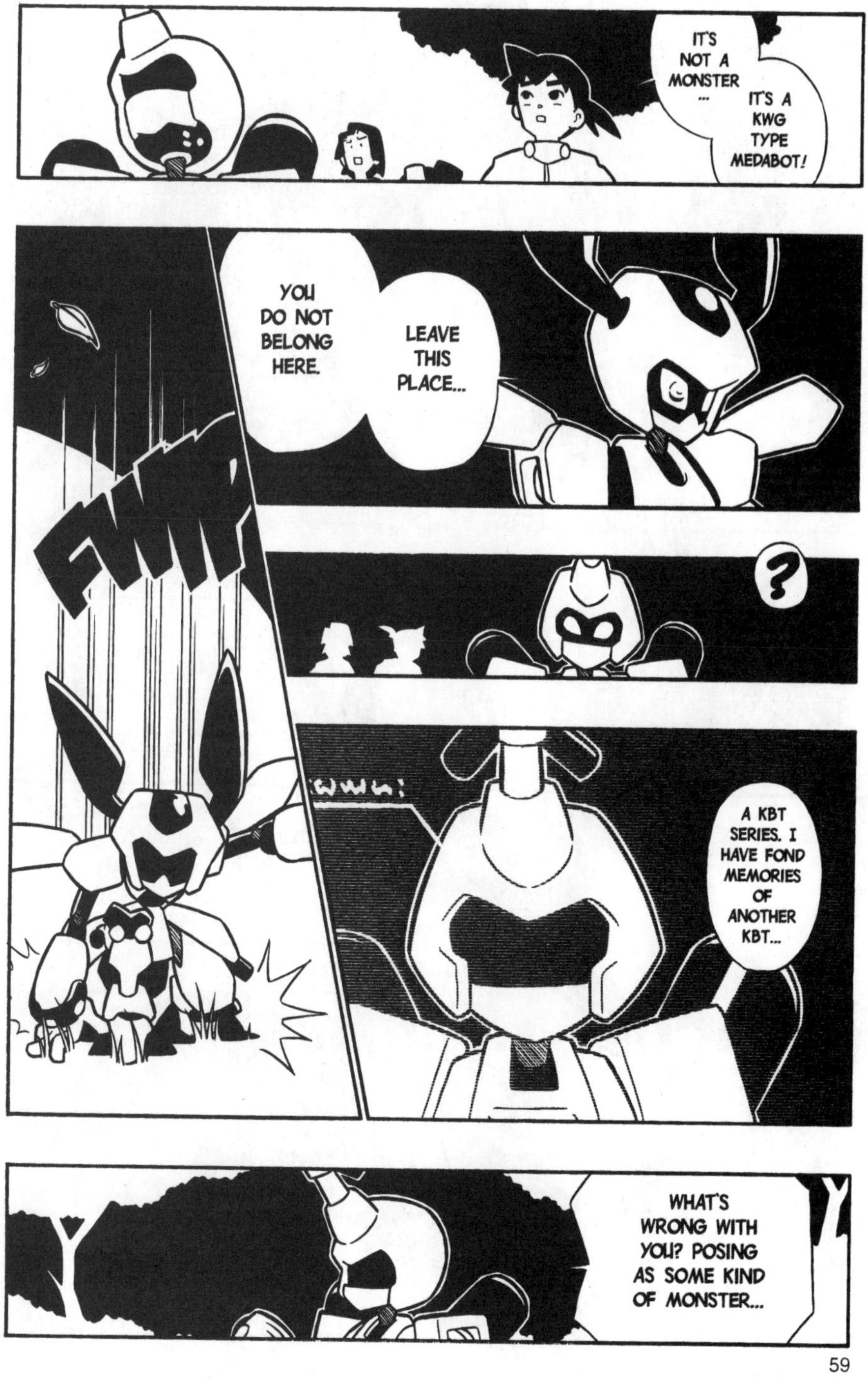
IT'S NOT A MONSTER ...
IT'S A KWG TYPE MEDABOT!
YOU DO NOT BELONG HERE.
LEAVE THIS PLACE...
?
A KBT SERIES. I HAVE FOND MEMORIES OF ANOTHER KBT...
WHAT'S WRONG WITH YOU? POSING AS SOME KIND OF MONSTER...

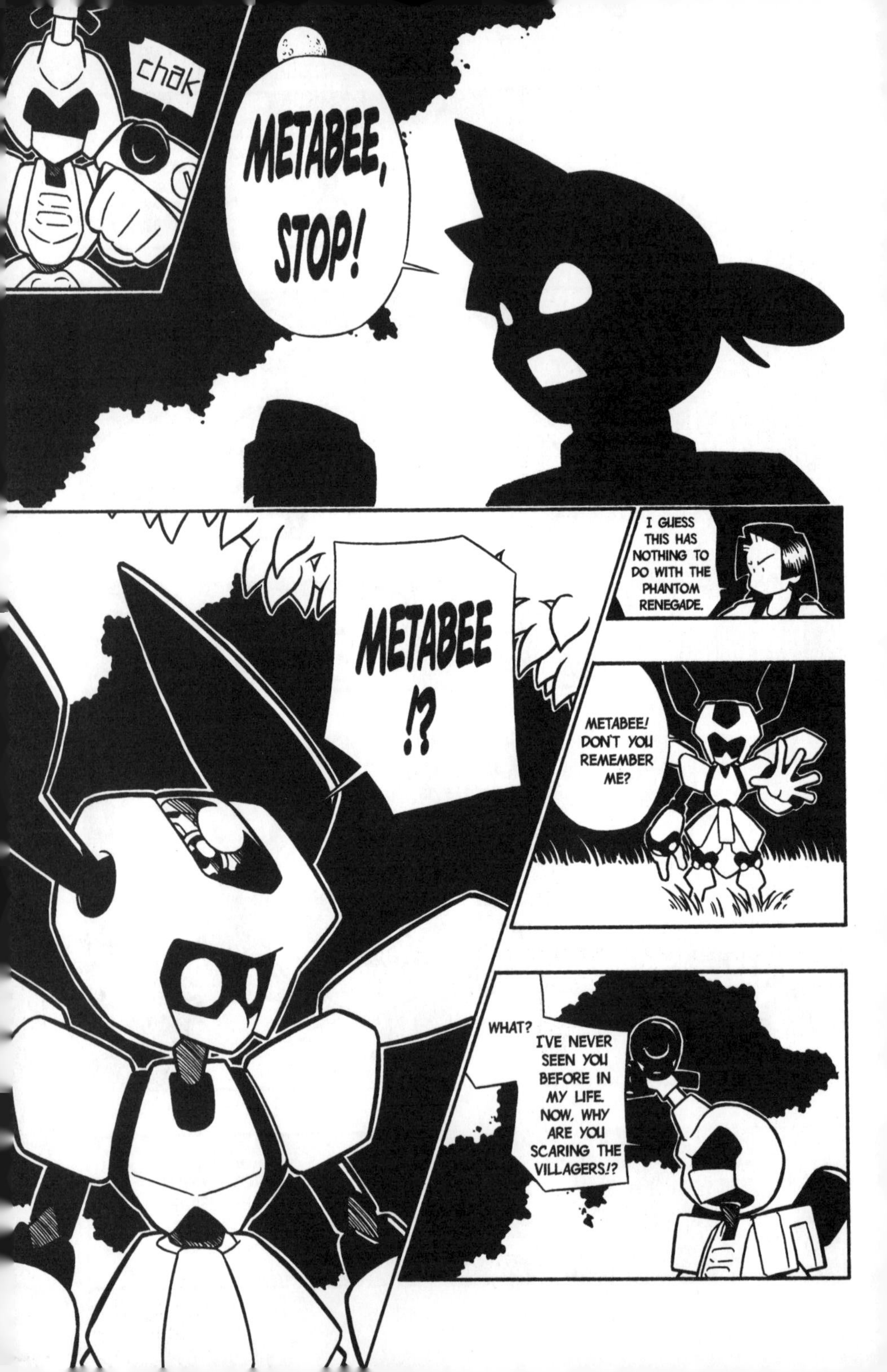
chak
METABEE, STOP!
METABEE !?
I GUESS THIS HAS NOTHING TO DO WITH THE PHANTOM RENEGADE.
METABEE! DON'T YOU REMEMBER ME?
WHAT?
I'VE NEVER SEEN YOU BEFORE IN MY LIFE. NOW, WHY ARE YOU SCARING THE VILLAGERS!?

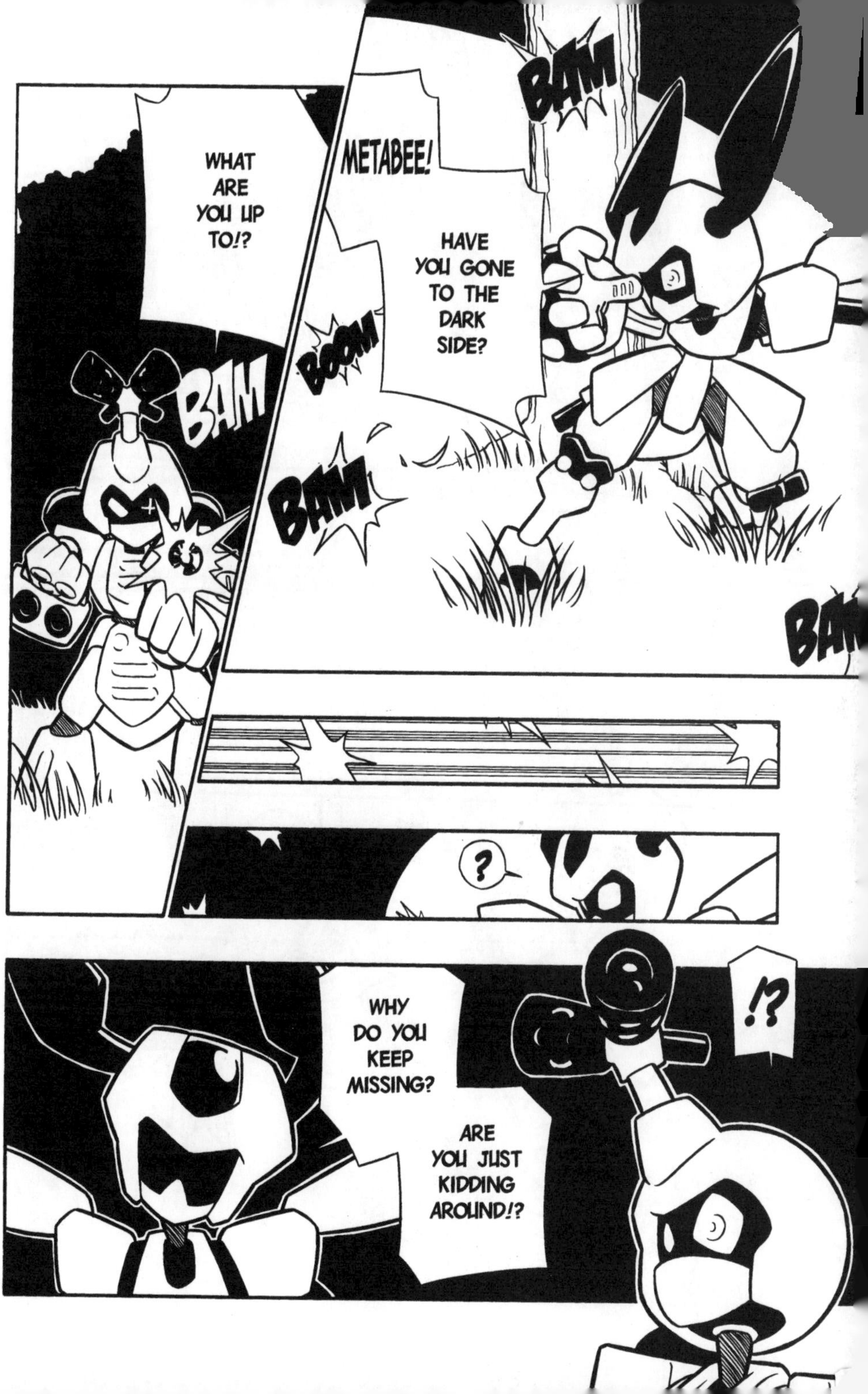
WHAT ARE YOU UP TO!?
BAM
METABEE!
BAM
HAVE YOU GONE TO THE DARK SIDE?
BOOM
BAM
BAM
?
WHY DO YOU KEEP MISSING?
ARE YOU JUST KIDDING AROUND!?
!?

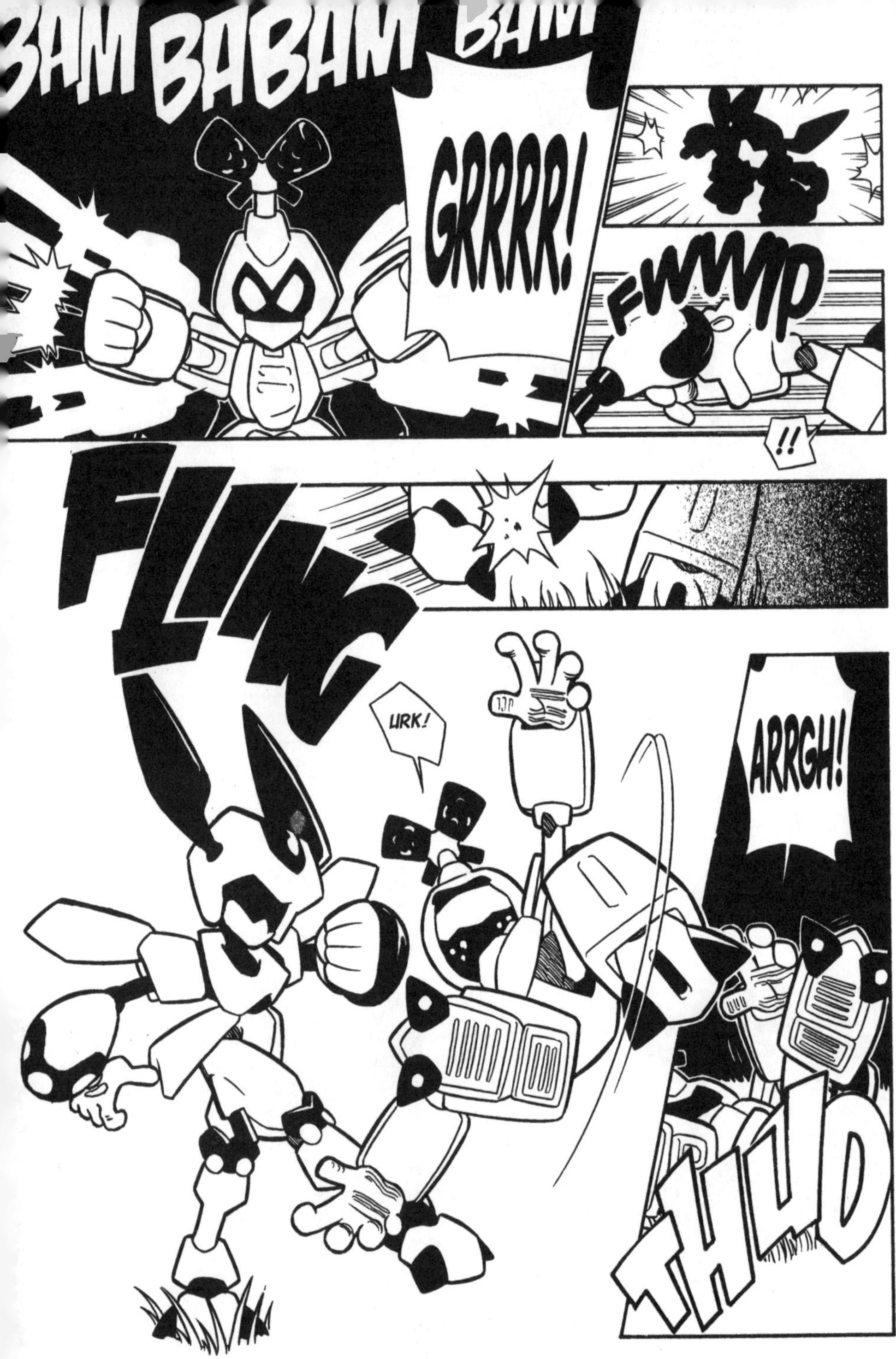
BAM BABAM BAM
GRRRR!
FWWIP
!!
FLING
URK!
ARRGH!
THUD

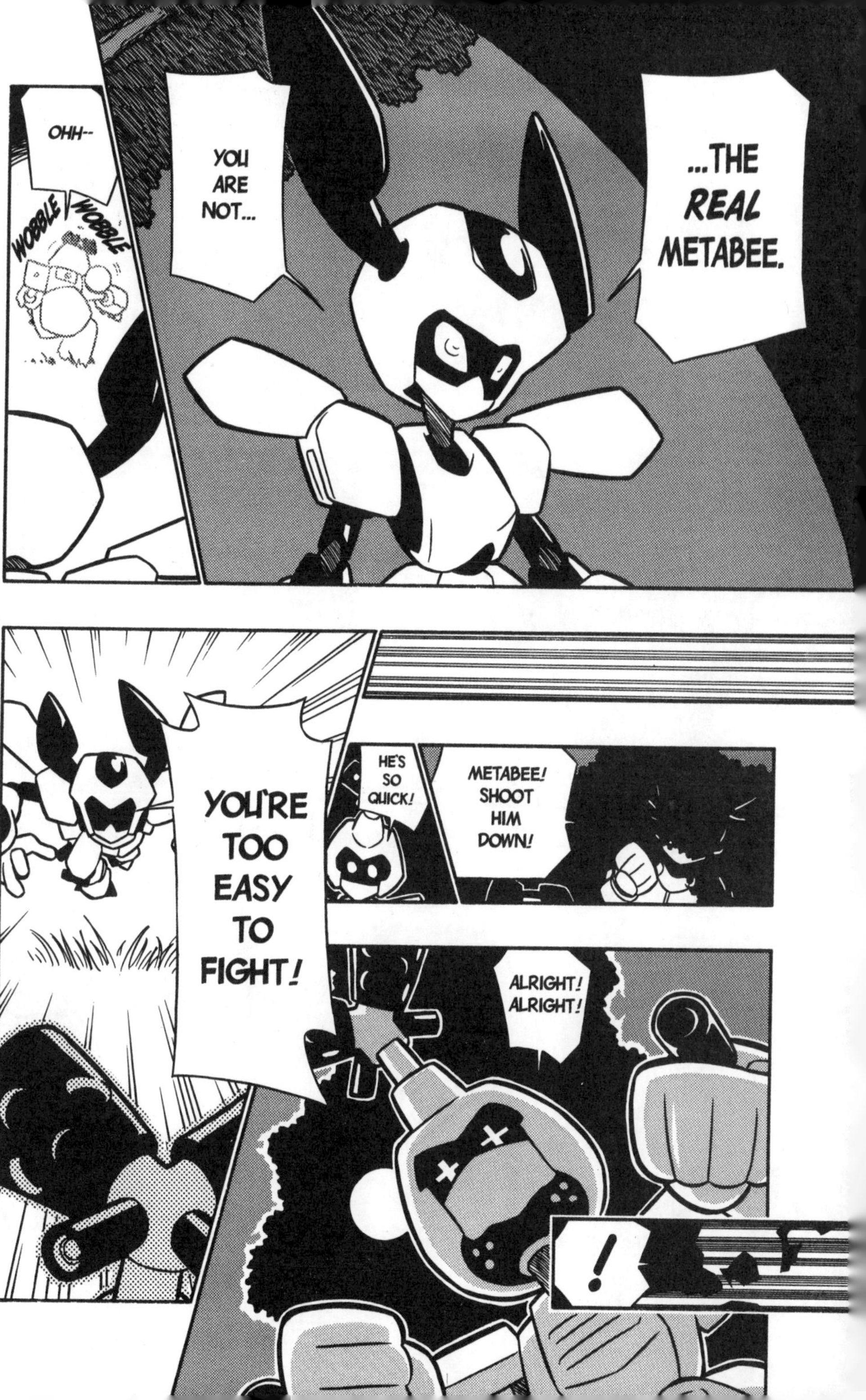

OHH--
WOBBLE WOBBLE
YOU ARE NOT...
...THE *REAL* METABEE.
YOU'RE TOO EASY TO FIGHT!
HE'S SO QUICK!
METABEE! SHOOT HIM DOWN!
ALRIGHT! ALRIGHT!
!

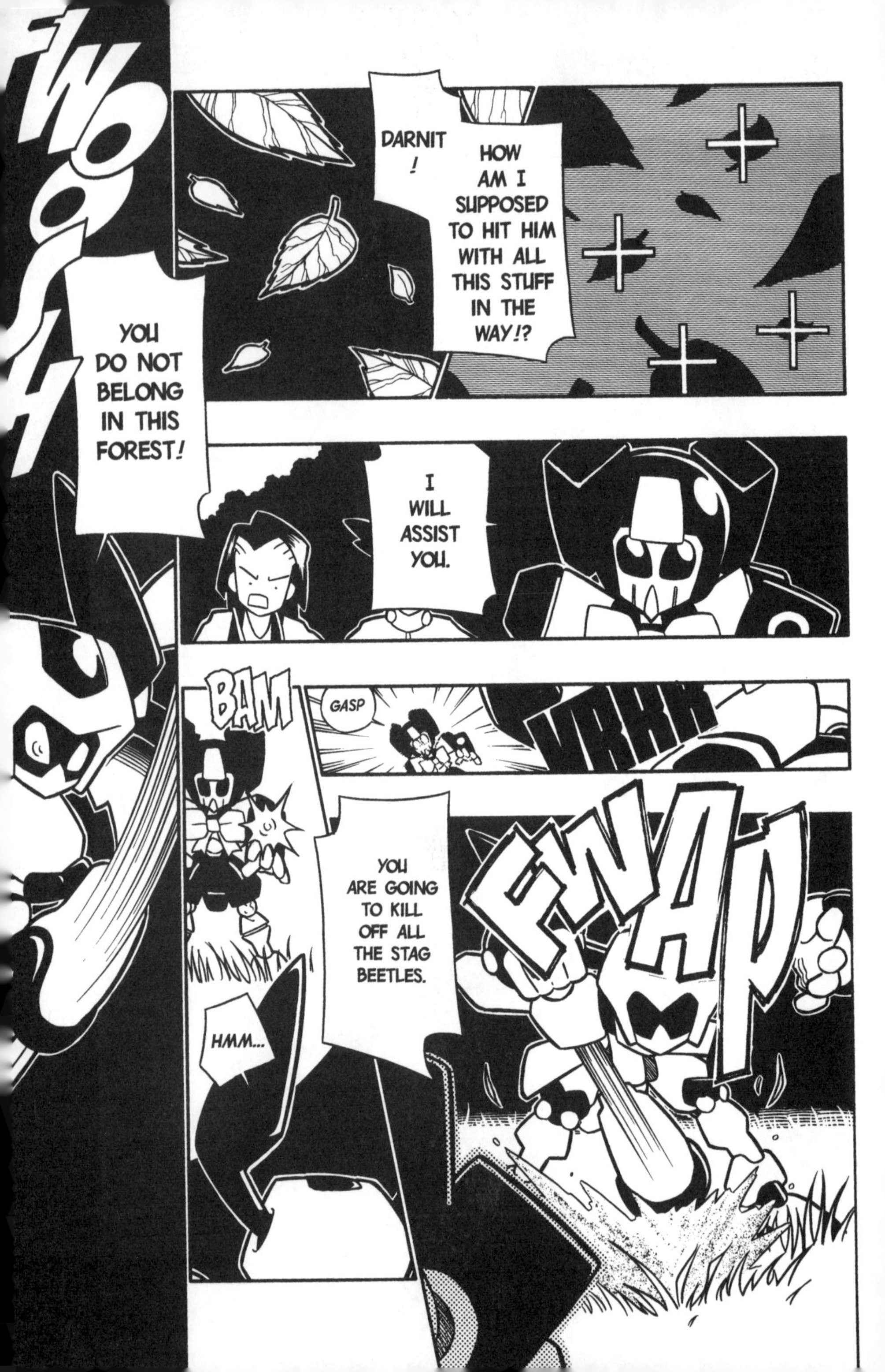
WHOOSH
YOU DO NOT BELONG IN THIS FOREST!
DARNIT!
HOW AM I SUPPOSED TO HIT HIM WITH ALL THIS STUFF IN THE WAY!?
I WILL ASSIST YOU.
BAM
GASP
VRRR
YOU ARE GOING TO KILL OFF ALL THE STAG BEETLES.
HMM...
FWAP

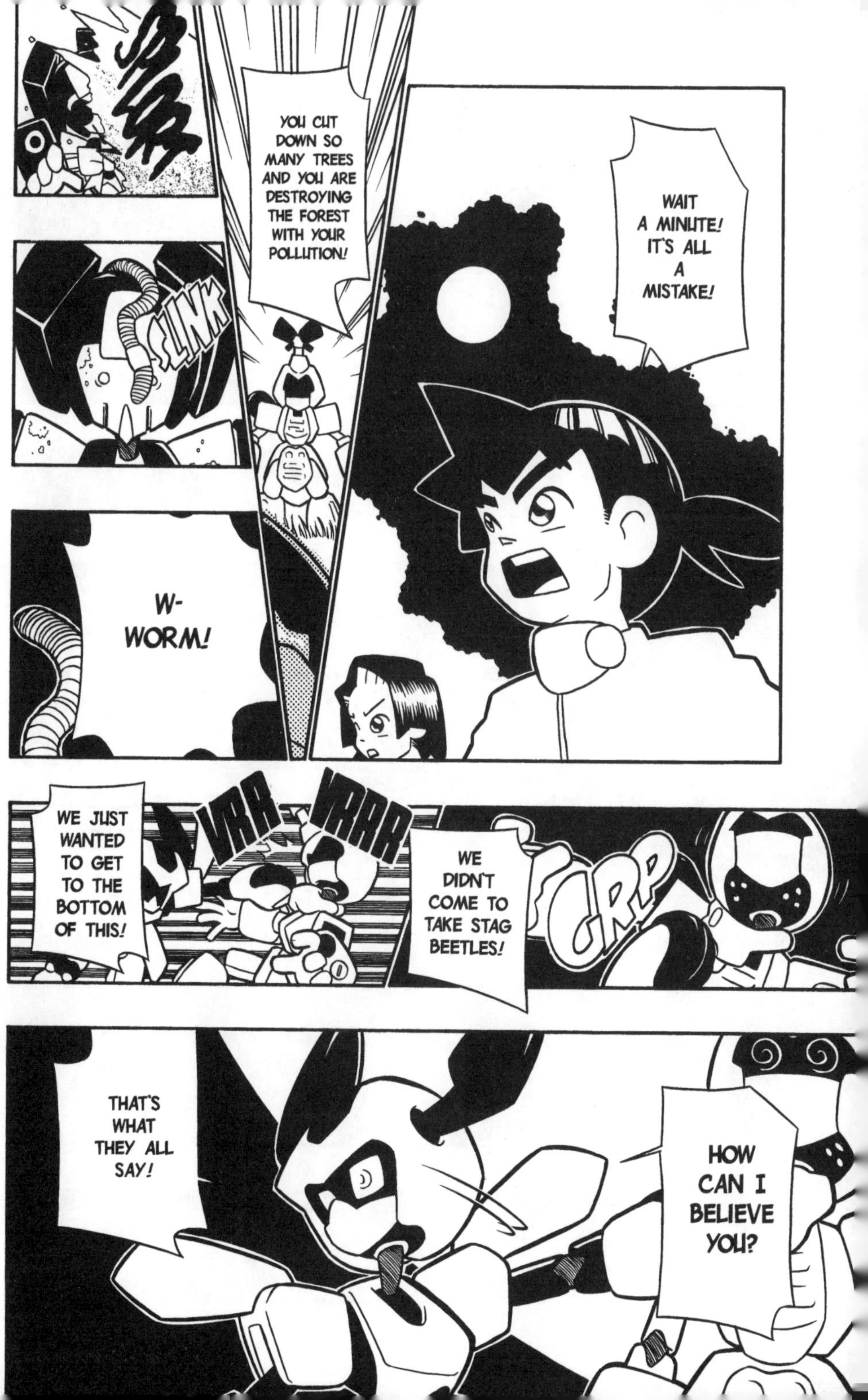
SLINK
W-WORM!
YOU CUT DOWN SO MANY TREES AND YOU ARE DESTROYING THE FOREST WITH YOUR POLLUTION!
WAIT A MINUTE! IT'S ALL A MISTAKE!
WE JUST WANTED TO GET TO THE BOTTOM OF THIS!
VRR VRRR
WE DIDN'T COME TO TAKE STAG BEETLES!
GRP
THAT'S WHAT THEY ALL SAY!
HOW CAN I BELIEVE YOU?

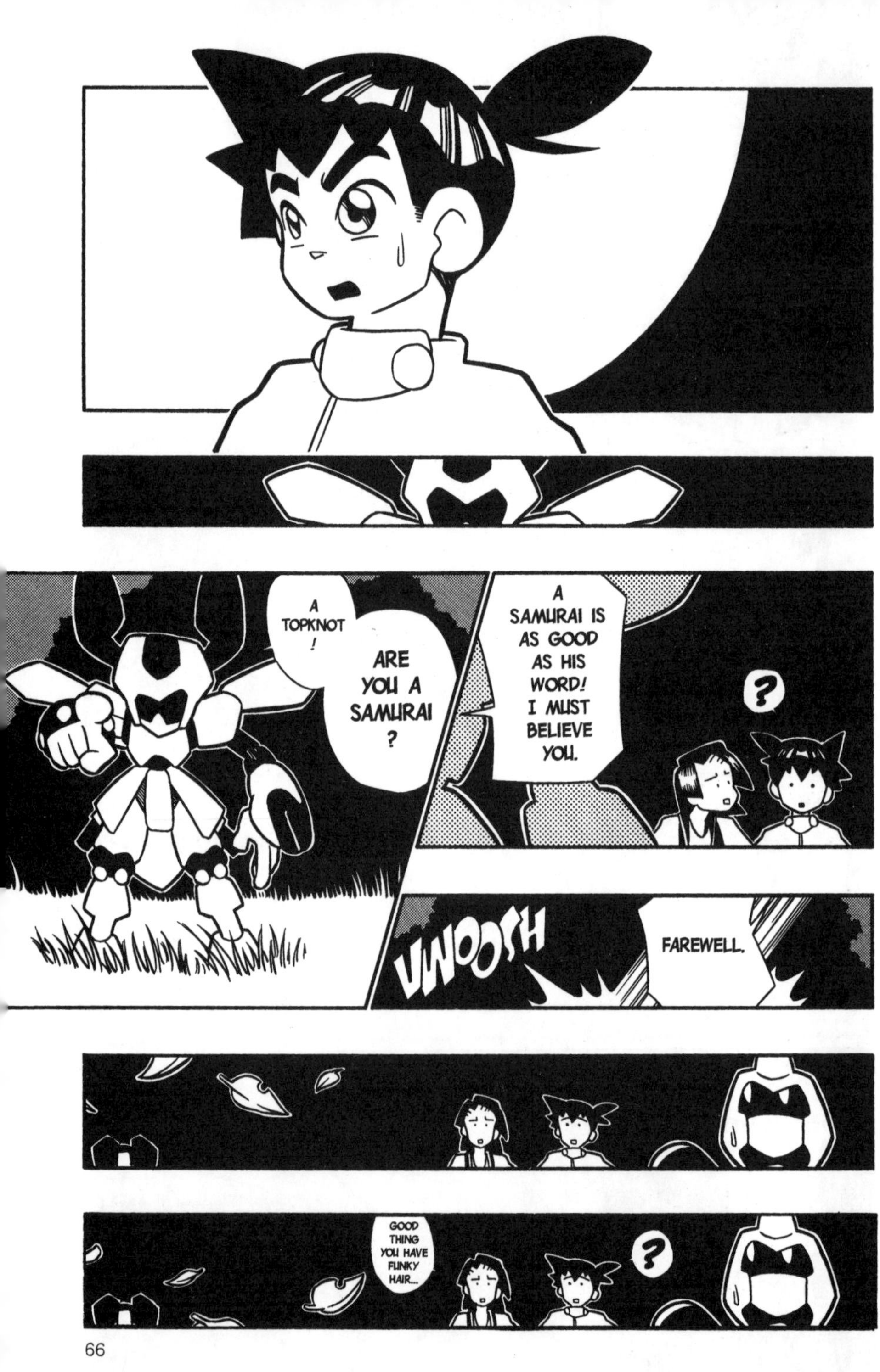
A TOPKNOT!
ARE YOU A SAMURAI?
A SAMURAI IS AS GOOD AS HIS WORD! I MUST BELIEVE YOU.
?
WOOSH
FAREWELL.
GOOD THING YOU HAVE FUNKY HAIR...
?

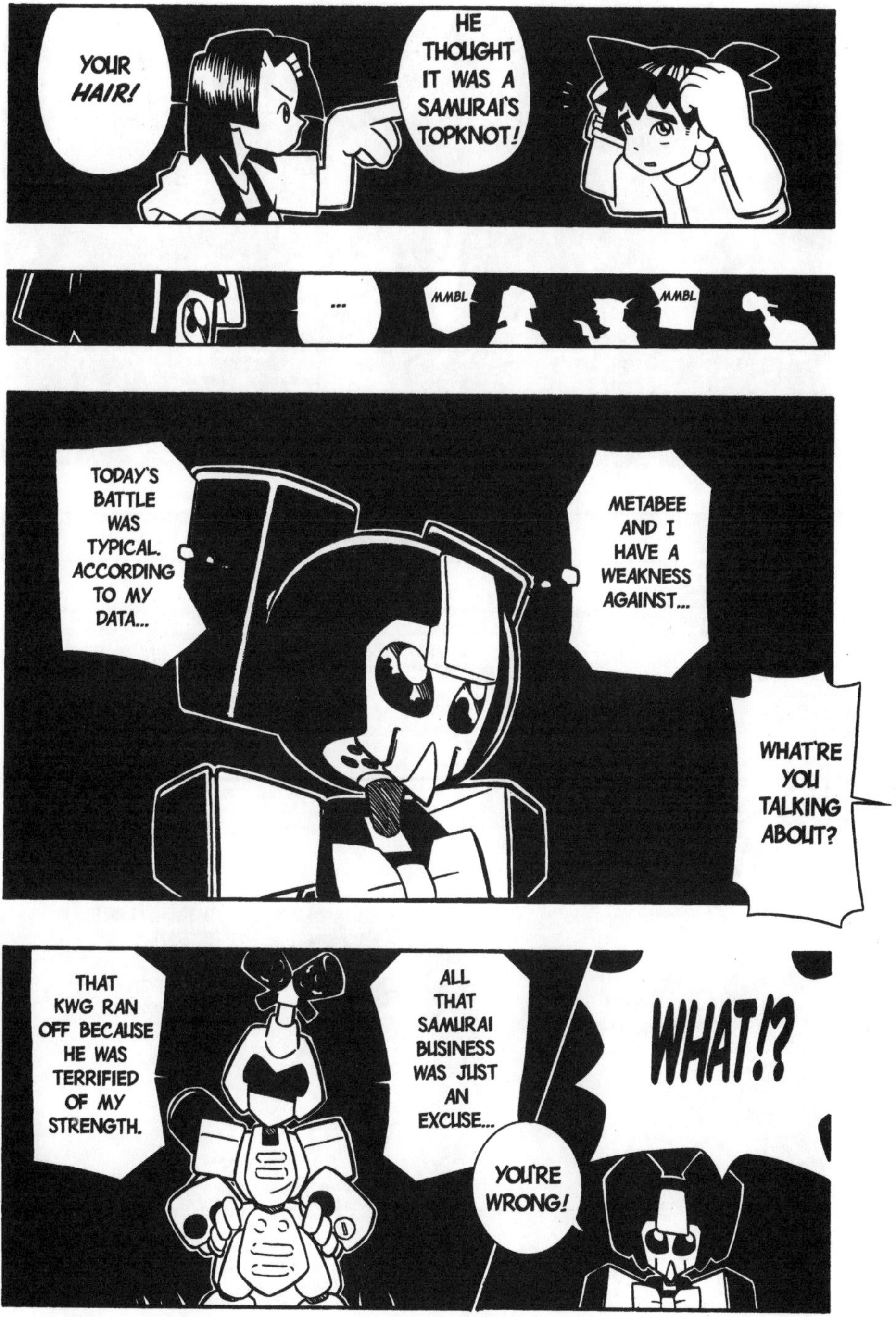
YOUR HAIR!
HE THOUGHT IT WAS A SAMURAI'S TOPKNOT!
...
MMBL
MMBL
TODAY'S BATTLE WAS TYPICAL. ACCORDING TO MY DATA...
METABEE AND I HAVE A WEAKNESS AGAINST...
WHAT'RE YOU TALKING ABOUT?
THAT KWG RAN OFF BECAUSE HE WAS TERRIFIED OF MY STRENGTH.
ALL THAT SAMURAI BUSINESS WAS JUST AN EXCUSE...
YOU'RE WRONG!
WHAT!?

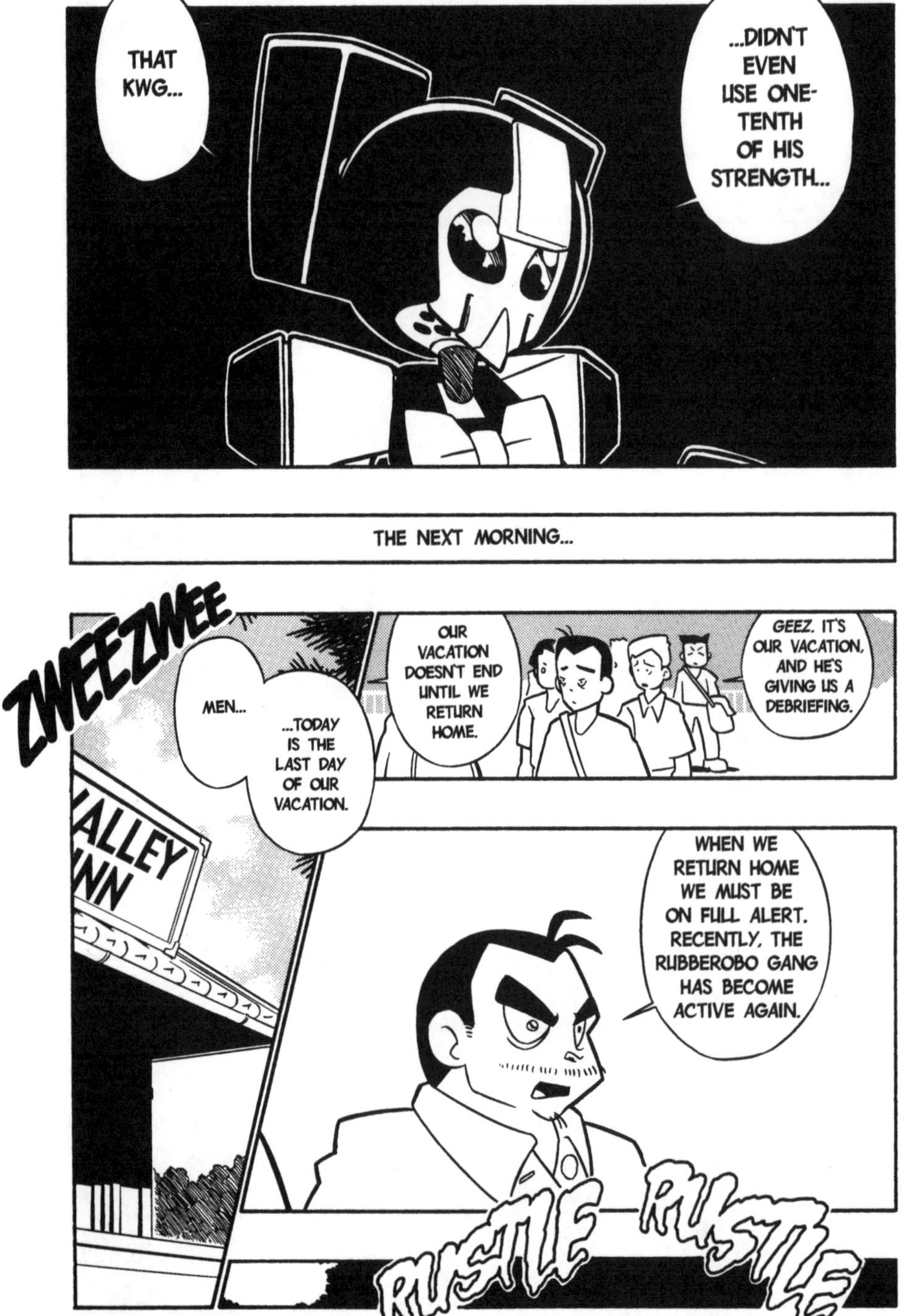
THAT KWG...
...DIDN'T EVEN USE ONE-TENTH OF HIS STRENGTH...
THE NEXT MORNING...
ZWEEZWEE
MEN...
...TODAY IS THE LAST DAY OF OUR VACATION.
OUR VACATION DOESN'T END UNTIL WE RETURN HOME.
GEEZ. IT'S OUR VACATION, AND HE'S GIVING US A DEBRIEFING.
WHEN WE RETURN HOME WE MUST BE ON FULL ALERT. RECENTLY, THE RUBBEROBO GANG HAS BECOME ACTIVE AGAIN.
RUSTLE RUSTLE

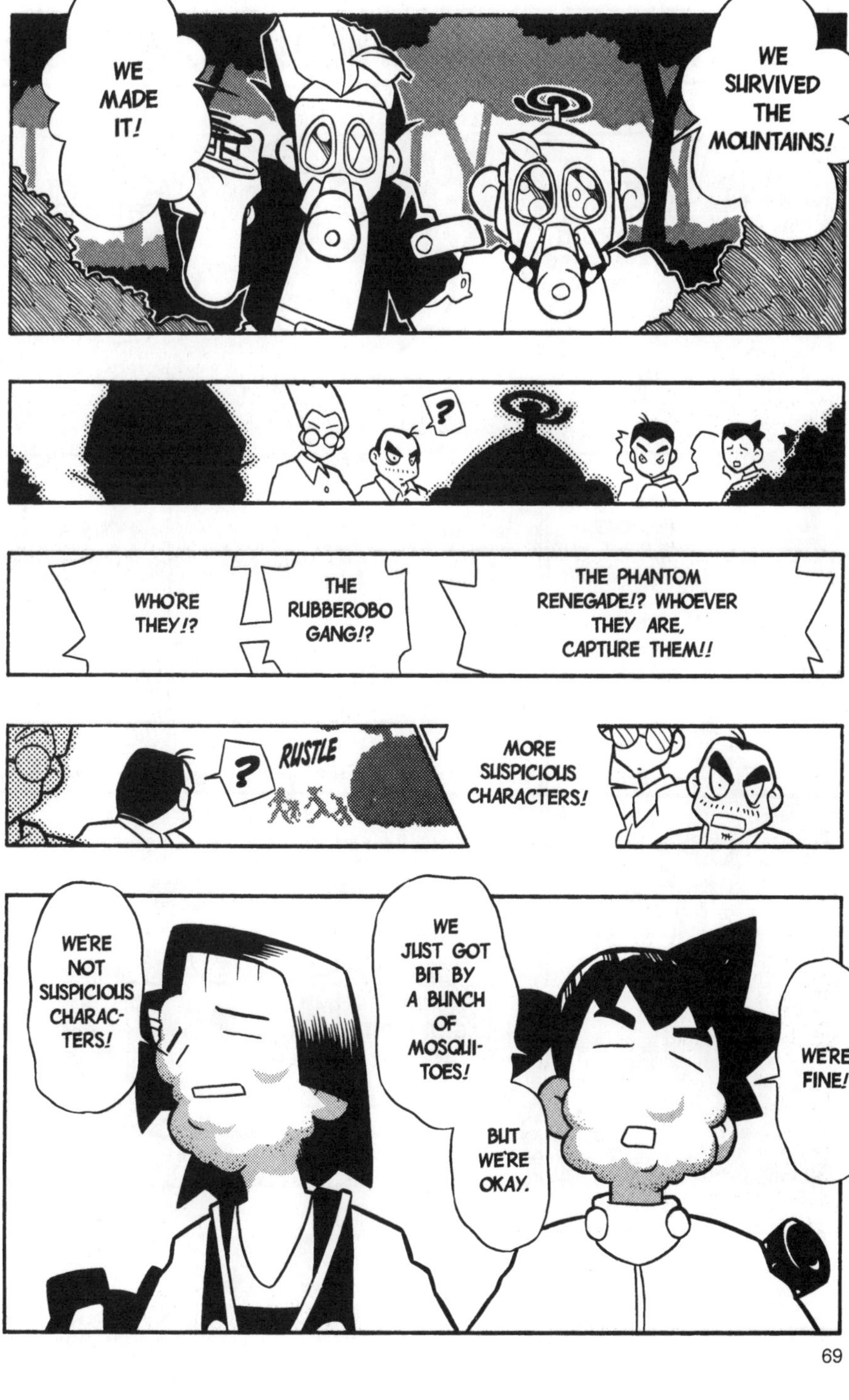
WE MADE IT!
WE SURVIVED THE MOUNTAINS!
?
WHO'RE THEY!?
THE RUBBEROBO GANG!?
THE PHANTOM RENEGADE!? WHOEVER THEY ARE, CAPTURE THEM!!
?
RUSTLE
MORE SUSPICIOUS CHARACTERS!
WE'RE NOT SUSPICIOUS CHARAC-TERS!
WE JUST GOT BIT BY A BUNCH OF MOSQUI-TOES!
BUT WE'RE OKAY.
WE'RE FINE!

BONUS FEATURE! WHAT'S BEEN ON OUR MINDS!

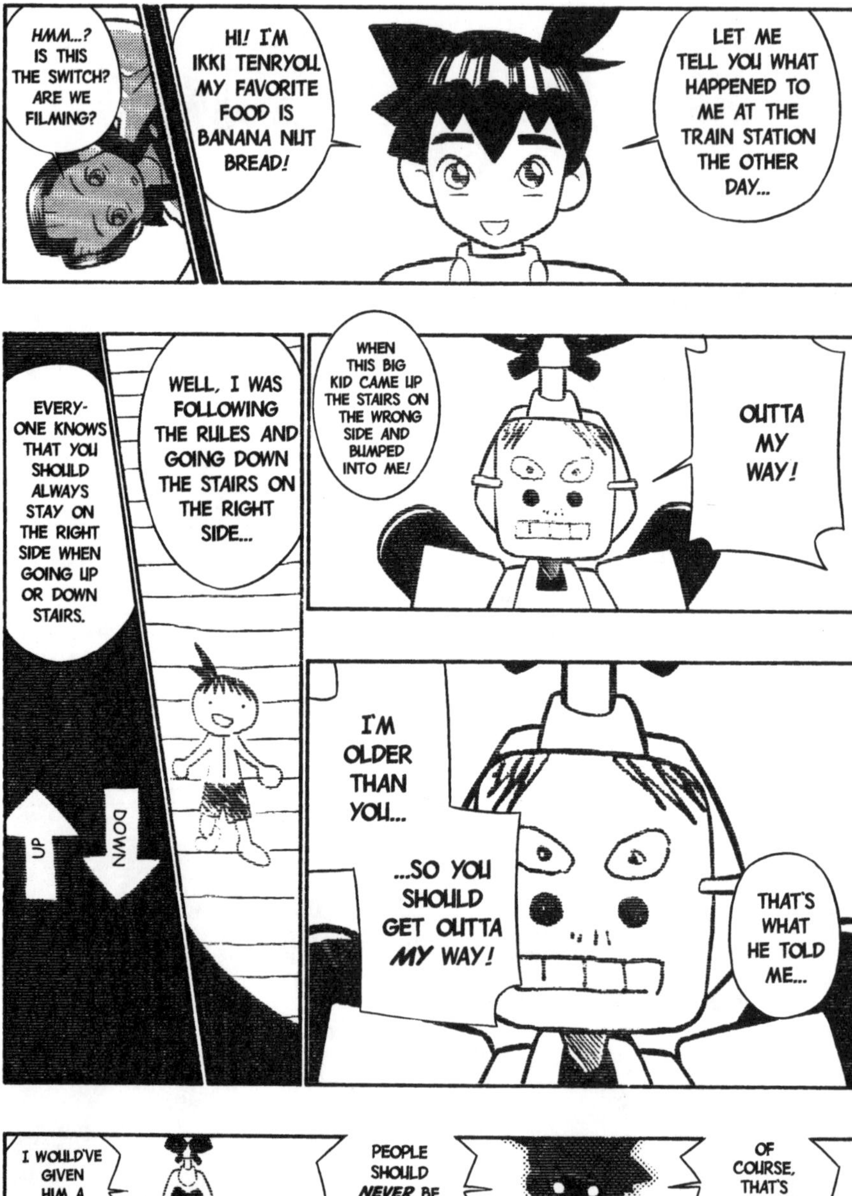
HMM...? IS THIS THE SWITCH? ARE WE FILMING?
HI! I'M IKKI TENRYOU. MY FAVORITE FOOD IS BANANA NUT BREAD!
LET ME TELL YOU WHAT HAPPENED TO ME AT THE TRAIN STATION THE OTHER DAY...
EVERY-ONE KNOWS THAT YOU SHOULD ALWAYS STAY ON THE RIGHT SIDE WHEN GOING UP OR DOWN STAIRS.
WELL, I WAS FOLLOWING THE RULES AND GOING DOWN THE STAIRS ON THE RIGHT SIDE...
UP
DOWN
WHEN THIS BIG KID CAME UP THE STAIRS ON THE WRONG SIDE AND BUMPED INTO ME!
OUTTA MY WAY!
I'M OLDER THAN YOU...
...SO YOU SHOULD GET OUTTA *MY* WAY!
THAT'S WHAT HE TOLD ME...
I WOULD'VE GIVEN HIM A NOOGIE!
PEOPLE SHOULD *NEVER* BE RUDE!
OF COURSE, THAT'S JUST MY OPINION...

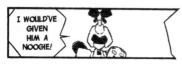

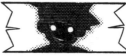

MEDABOTS™

PRESS CONFERENCE ASSAULT!!

AND NOW FOR TODAY'S NEWS FEATURE.
IN RECENT YEARS IN AUSTRALIA, KOALAS ARE NEARING THE POINT OF EXTINCTION...
STUDIO A
HOTEL
...DUE IN PART TO THE DECREASING NUMBER OF EUCALYPTUS TREES...

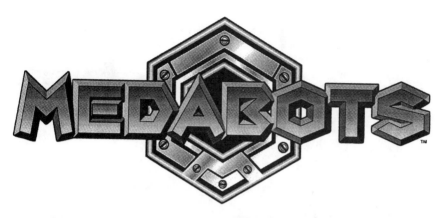

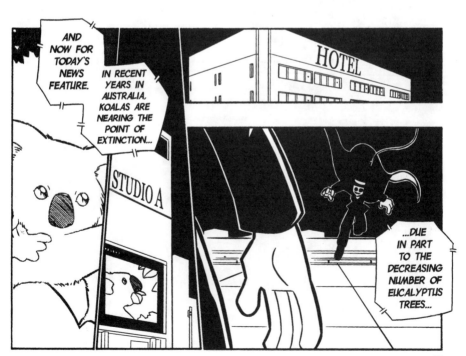

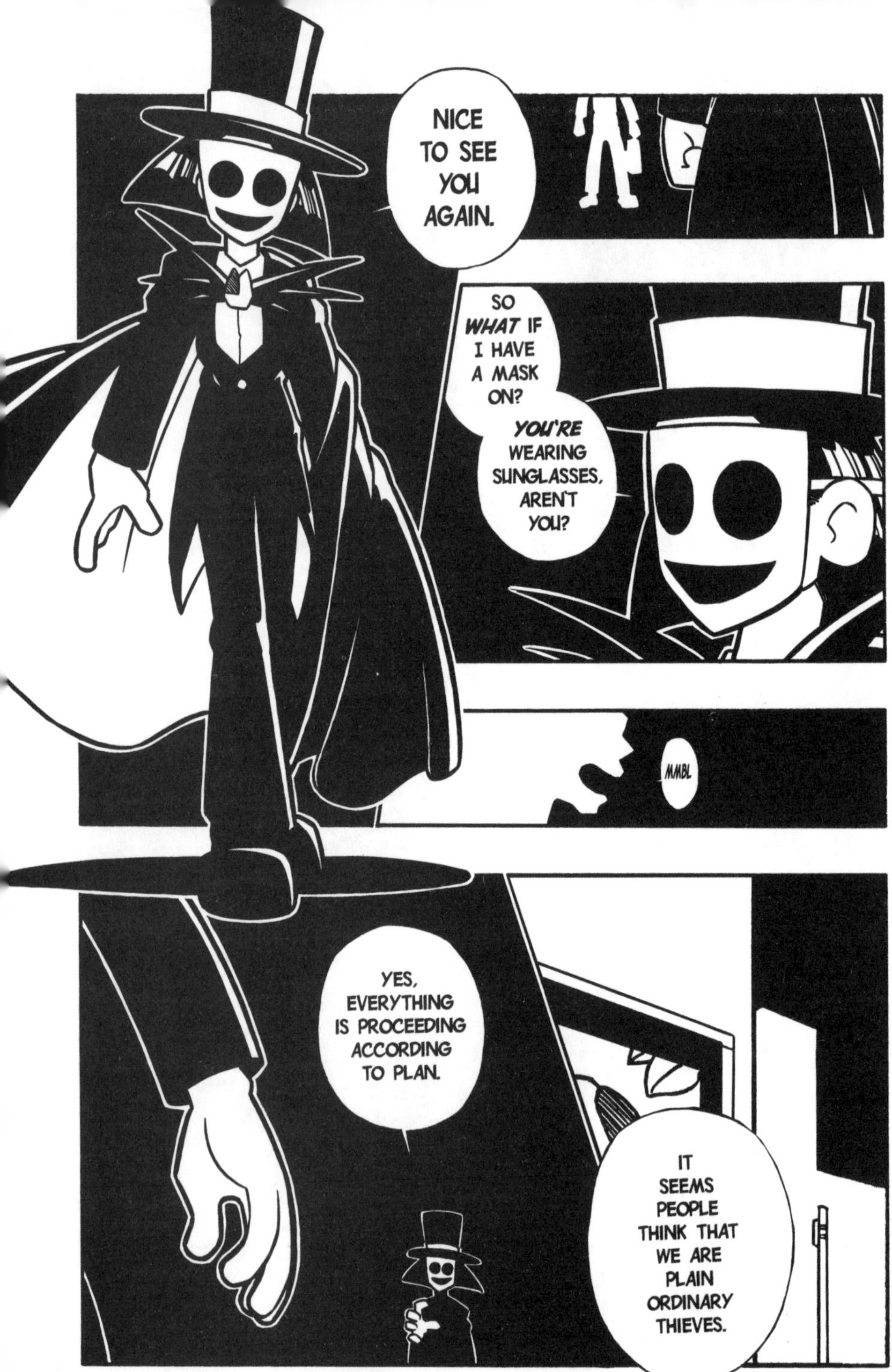
NICE TO SEE YOU AGAIN.
SO *WHAT* IF I HAVE A MASK ON?
YOU'RE WEARING SUNGLASSES, AREN'T YOU?
MMBL
YES, EVERYTHING IS PROCEEDING ACCORDING TO PLAN.
IT SEEMS PEOPLE THINK THAT WE ARE PLAIN ORDINARY THIEVES.

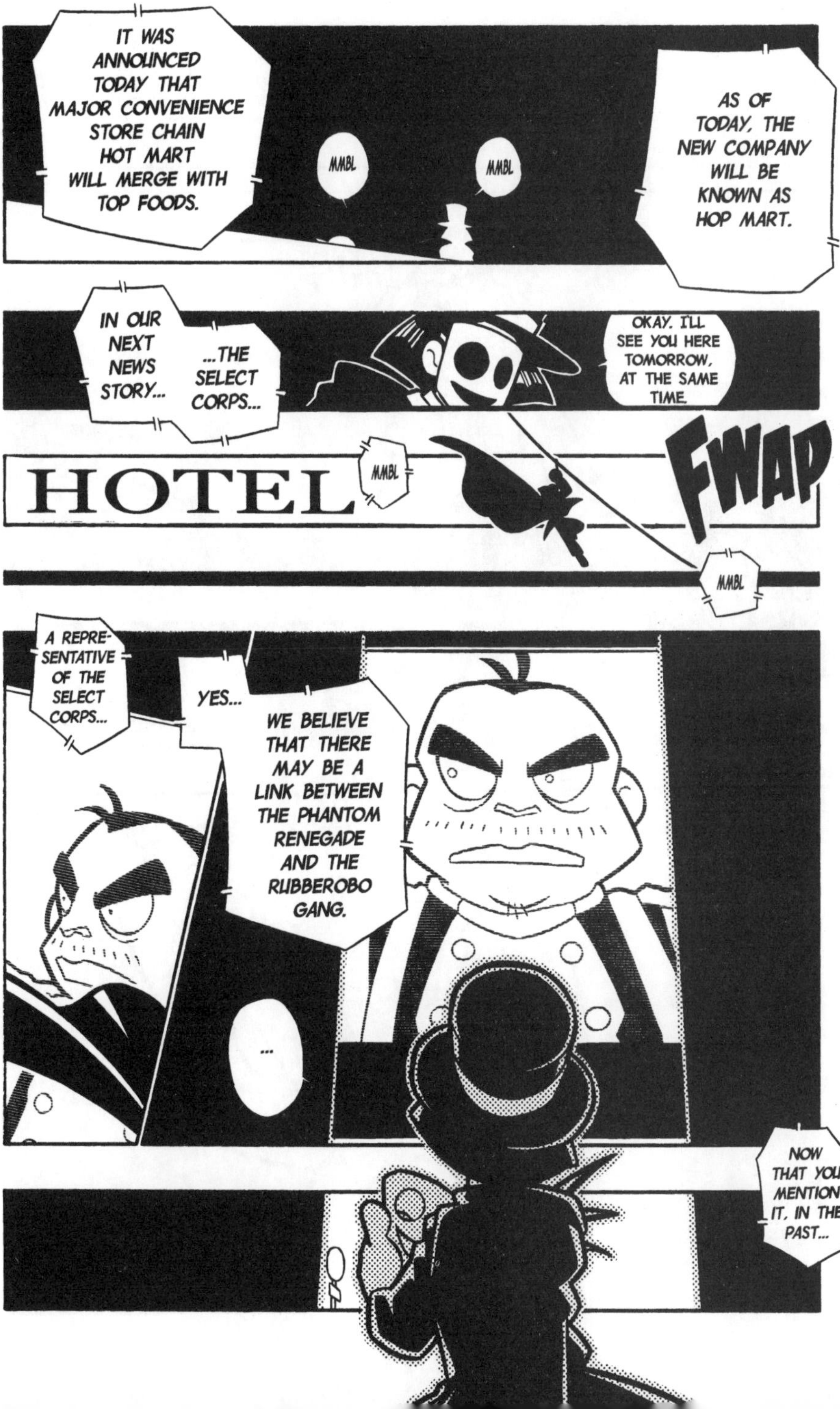
IT WAS ANNOUNCED TODAY THAT MAJOR CONVENIENCE STORE CHAIN HOT MART WILL MERGE WITH TOP FOODS.
MMBL
MMBL
AS OF TODAY, THE NEW COMPANY WILL BE KNOWN AS HOP MART.
IN OUR NEXT NEWS STORY...
...THE SELECT CORPS...
OKAY. I'LL SEE YOU HERE TOMORROW, AT THE SAME TIME.
HOTEL
MMBL
FWAP
MMBL
A REPRESENTATIVE OF THE SELECT CORPS...
YES...
WE BELIEVE THAT THERE MAY BE A LINK BETWEEN THE PHANTOM RENEGADE AND THE RUBBEROBO GANG.
...
NOW THAT YOU MENTION IT, IN THE PAST...

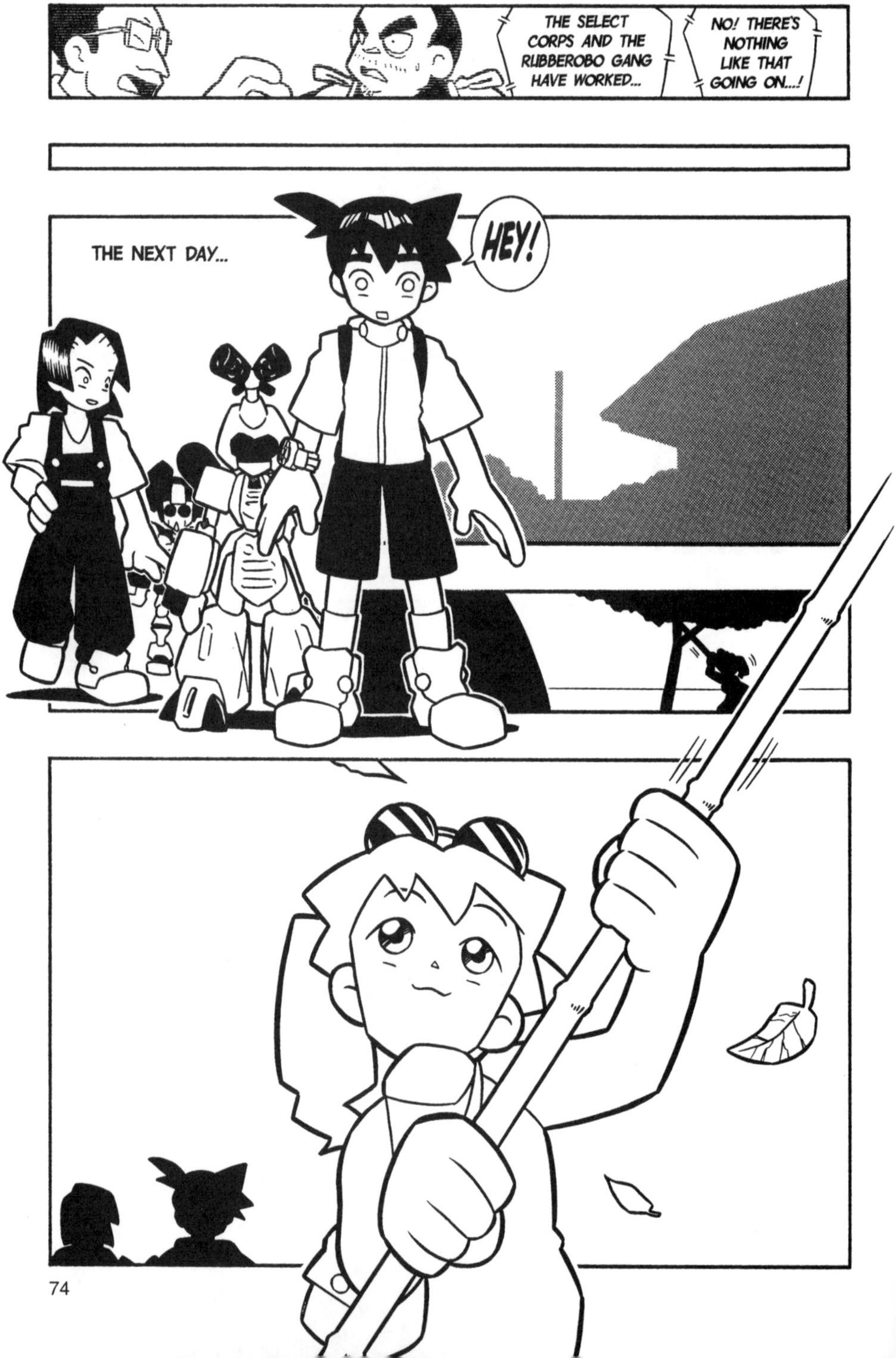

THE SELECT CORPS AND THE RUBBEROBO GANG HAVE WORKED...
NO! THERE'S NOTHING LIKE THAT GOING ON...!
THE NEXT DAY...
HEY!

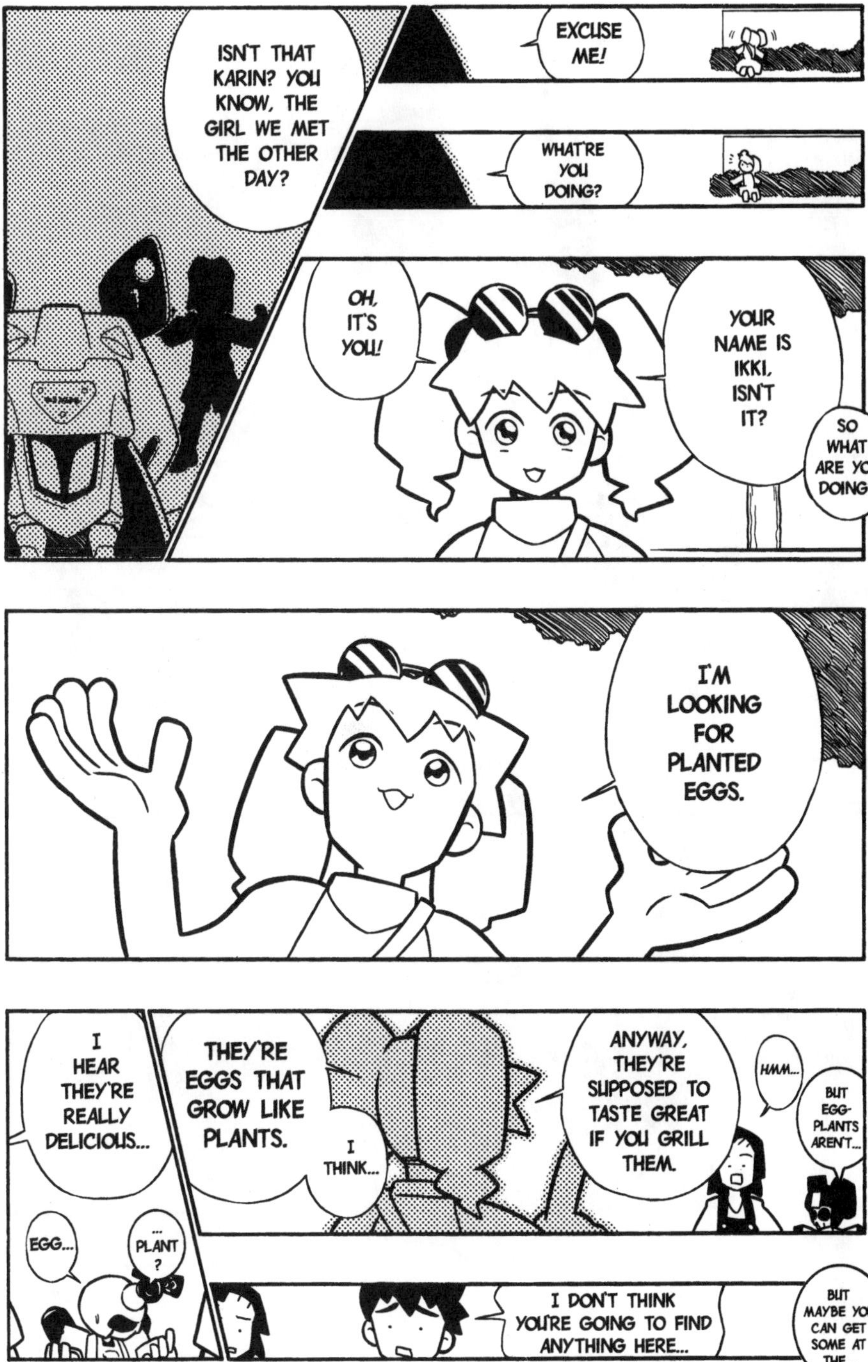
ISN'T THAT KARIN? YOU KNOW, THE GIRL WE MET THE OTHER DAY?
EXCUSE ME!
WHAT'RE YOU DOING?
OH, IT'S YOU!
YOUR NAME IS IKKI, ISN'T IT?
SO WHAT ARE YOU DOING?
I'M LOOKING FOR PLANTED EGGS.
I HEAR THEY'RE REALLY DELICIOUS...
THEY'RE EGGS THAT GROW LIKE PLANTS.
I THINK...
ANYWAY, THEY'RE SUPPOSED TO TASTE GREAT IF YOU GRILL THEM.
HMM...
BUT EGG-PLANTS AREN'T...
EGG...
...PLANT?
I DON'T THINK YOU'RE GOING TO FIND ANYTHING HERE...
BUT MAYBE YOU CAN GET SOME AT THE...

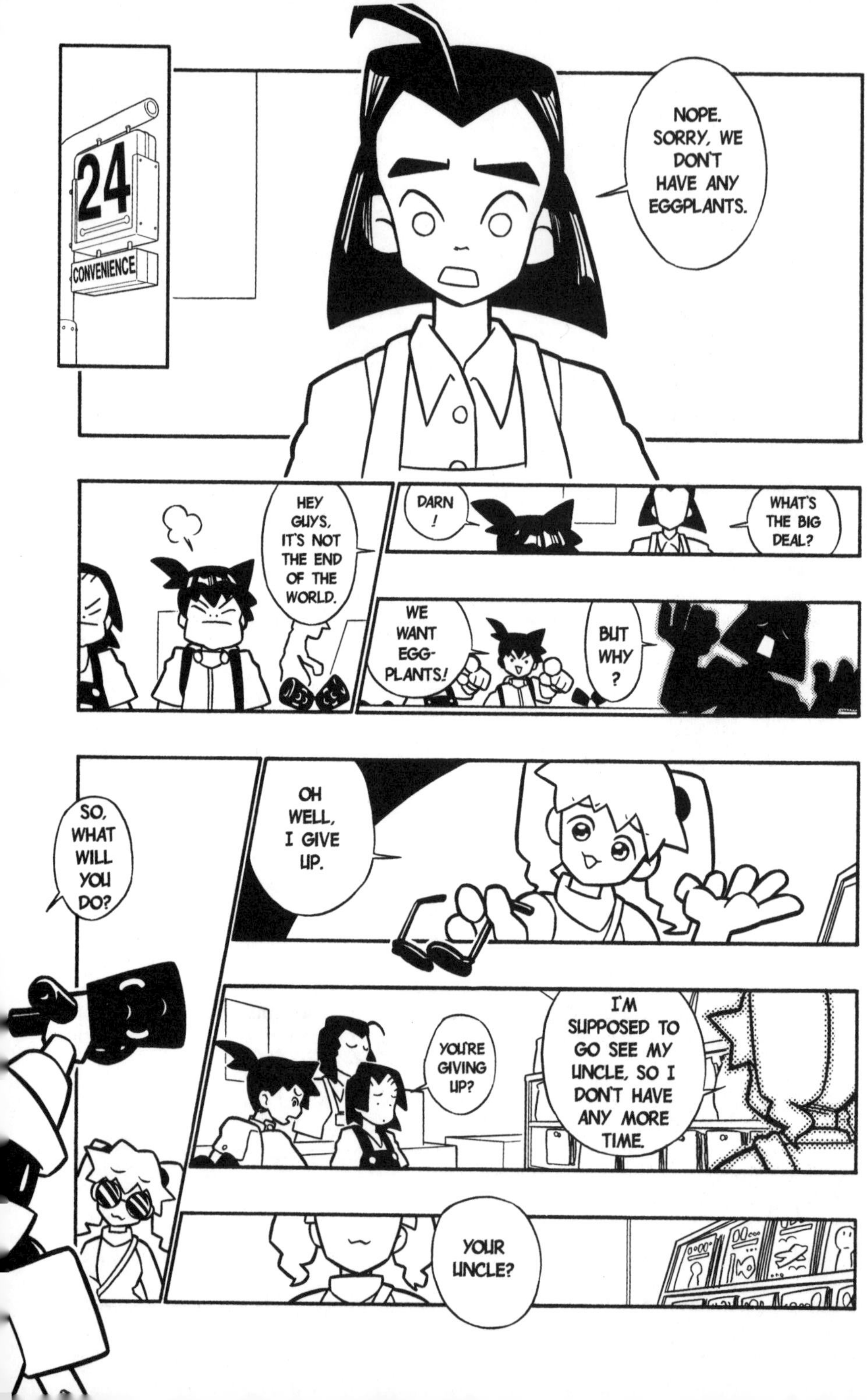
24
CONVENIENCE
NOPE. SORRY, WE DON'T HAVE ANY EGGPLANTS.
HEY GUYS, IT'S NOT THE END OF THE WORLD.
DARN!
WHAT'S THE BIG DEAL?
WE WANT EGG-PLANTS!
BUT WHY?
SO, WHAT WILL YOU DO?
OH WELL, I GIVE UP.
YOU'RE GIVING UP?
I'M SUPPOSED TO GO SEE MY UNCLE, SO I DON'T HAVE ANY MORE TIME.
YOUR UNCLE?

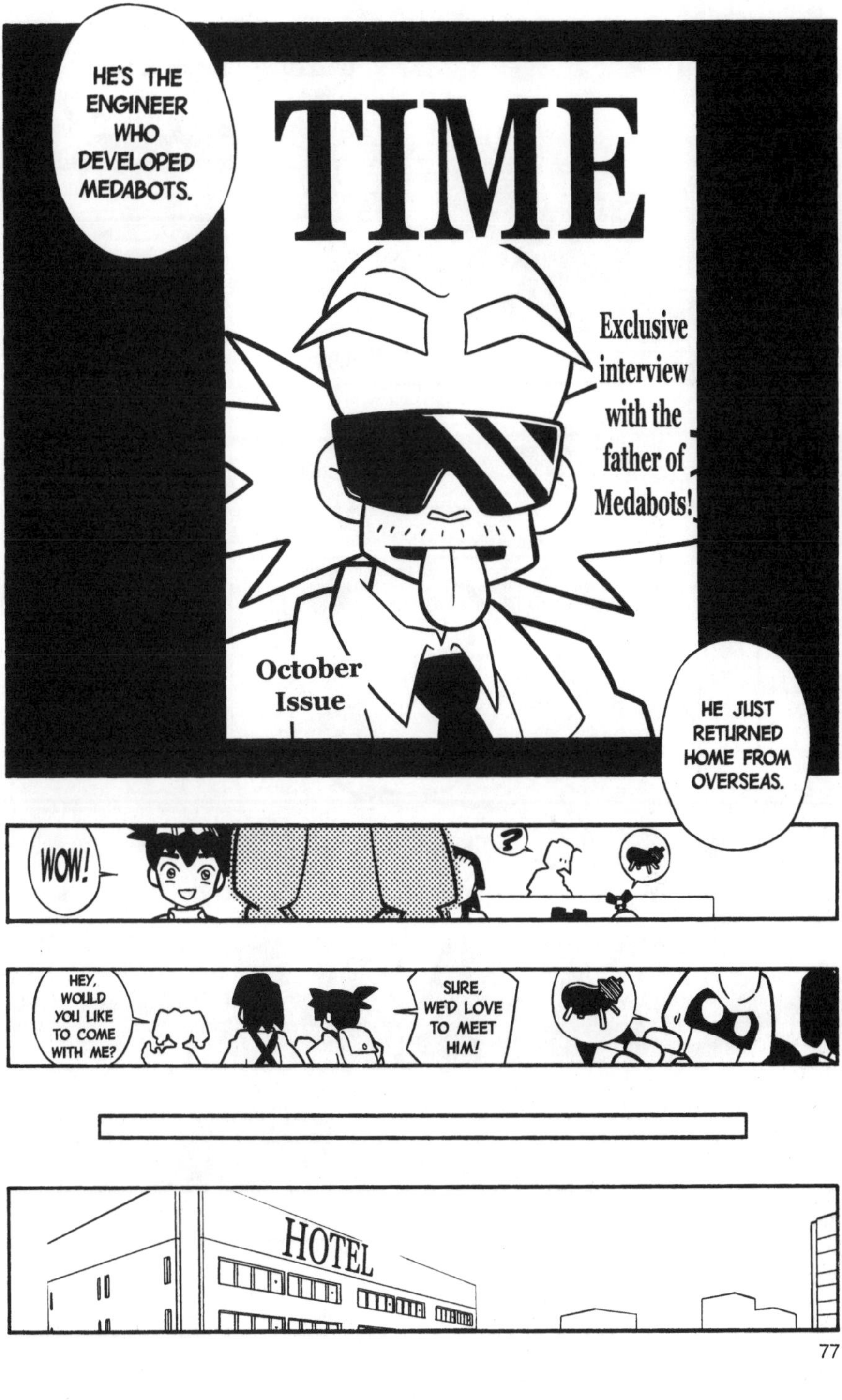
HE'S THE ENGINEER WHO DEVELOPED MEDABOTS.
TIME
Exclusive interview with the father of Medabots!
October Issue
HE JUST RETURNED HOME FROM OVERSEAS.
WOW!
?
HEY, WOULD YOU LIKE TO COME WITH ME?
SURE, WE'D LOVE TO MEET HIM!
HOTEL

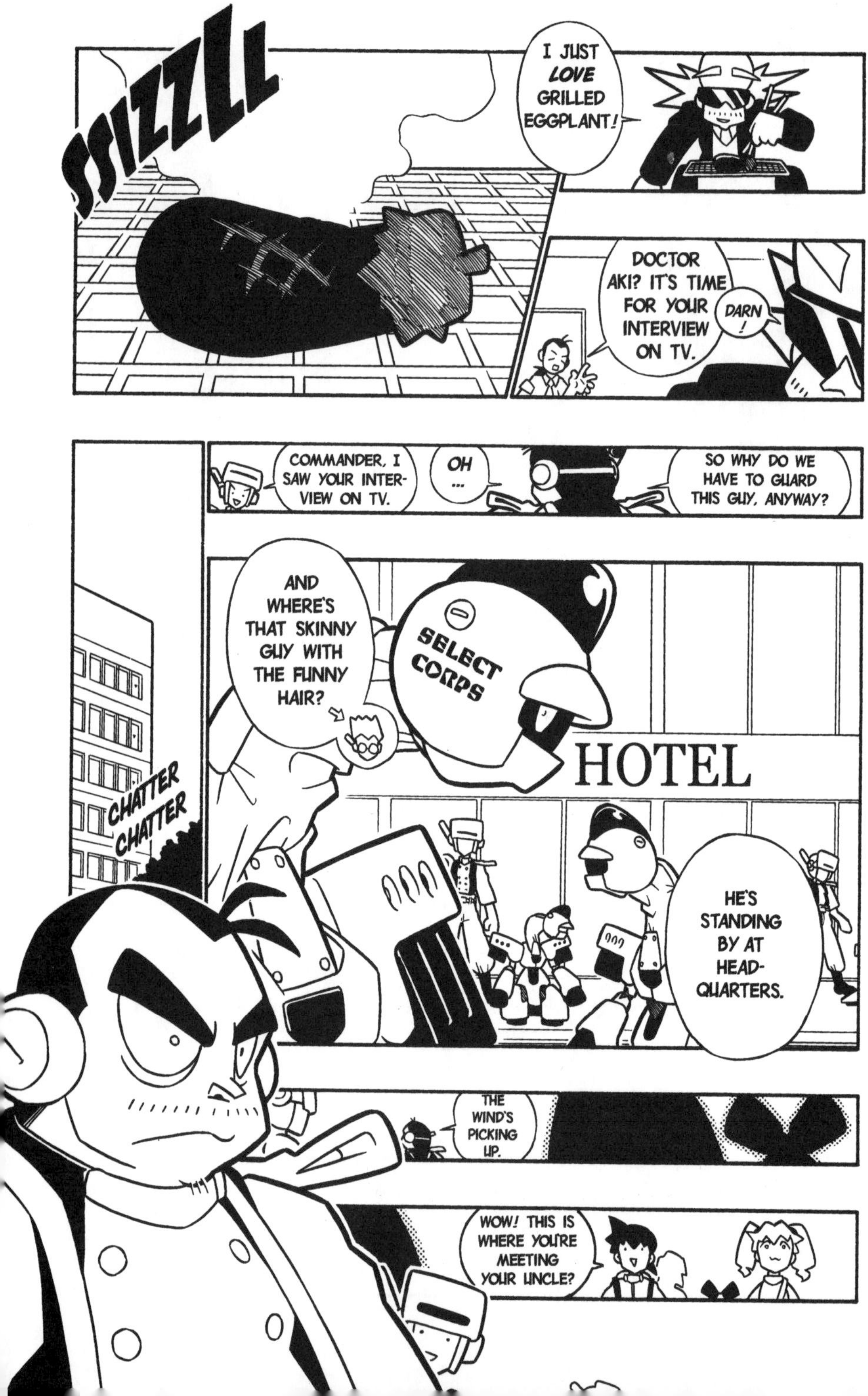
SSIZZLE
I JUST *LOVE* GRILLED EGGPLANT!
DOCTOR AKI? IT'S TIME FOR YOUR INTERVIEW ON TV.
DARN!
COMMANDER, I SAW YOUR INTER-VIEW ON TV.
OH ...
SO WHY DO WE HAVE TO GUARD THIS GUY, ANYWAY?
AND WHERE'S THAT SKINNY GUY WITH THE FUNNY HAIR?
SELECT CORPS
HOTEL
CHATTER CHATTER
HE'S STANDING BY AT HEAD-QUARTERS.
THE WIND'S PICKING UP.
WOW! THIS IS WHERE YOU'RE MEETING YOUR UNCLE?

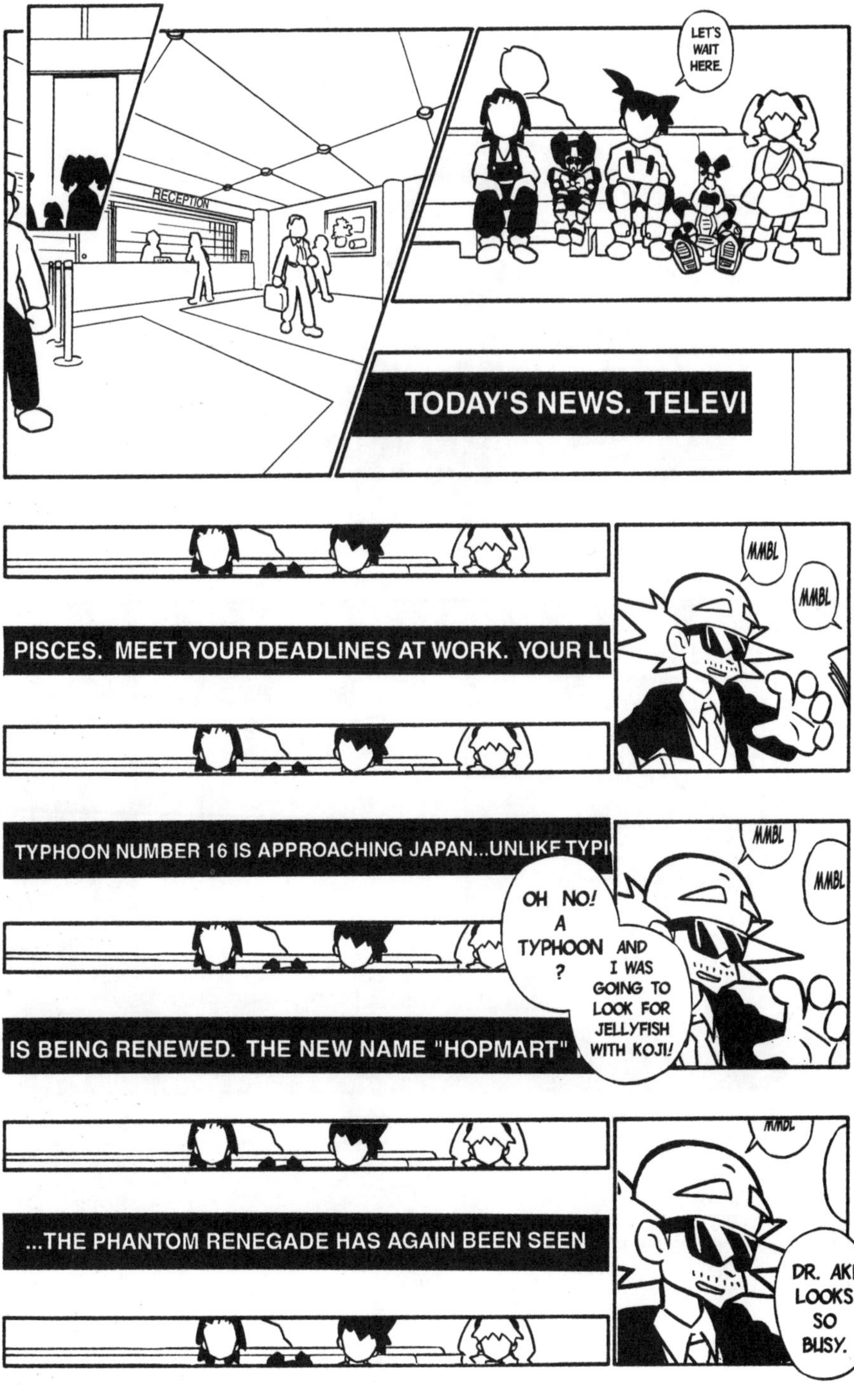
RECEPTION
LET'S WAIT HERE.
TODAY'S NEWS. TELEVI
MMBL
MMBL
PISCES. MEET YOUR DEADLINES AT WORK. YOUR LU
TYPHOON NUMBER 16 IS APPROACHING JAPAN...UNLIKE TYPI
MMBL
MMBL
OH NO! A TYPHOON?
AND I WAS GOING TO LOOK FOR JELLYFISH WITH KOJI!
IS BEING RENEWED. THE NEW NAME "HOPMART"
...THE PHANTOM RENEGADE HAS AGAIN BEEN SEEN
DR. AKI LOOKS SO BUSY.

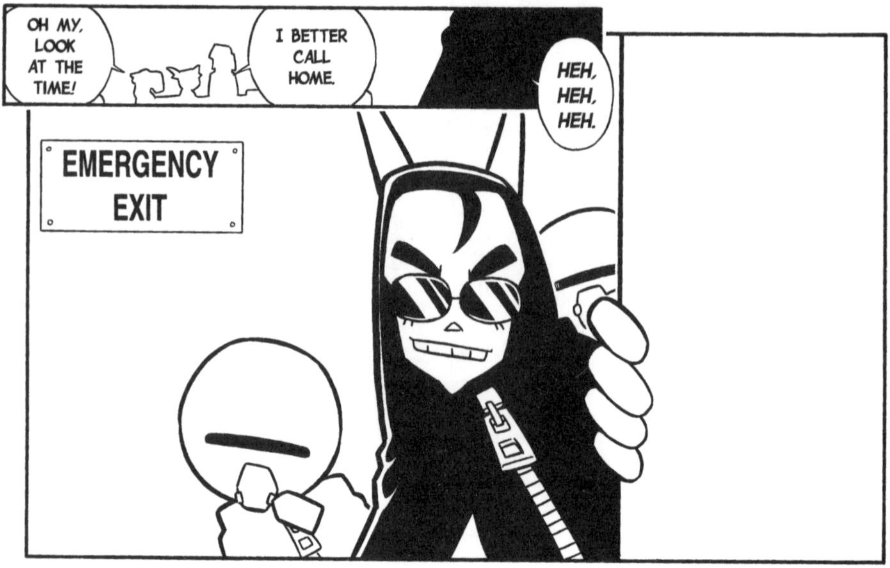
OH MY, LOOK AT THE TIME!
I BETTER CALL HOME.
HEH, HEH, HEH.
EMERGENCY EXIT

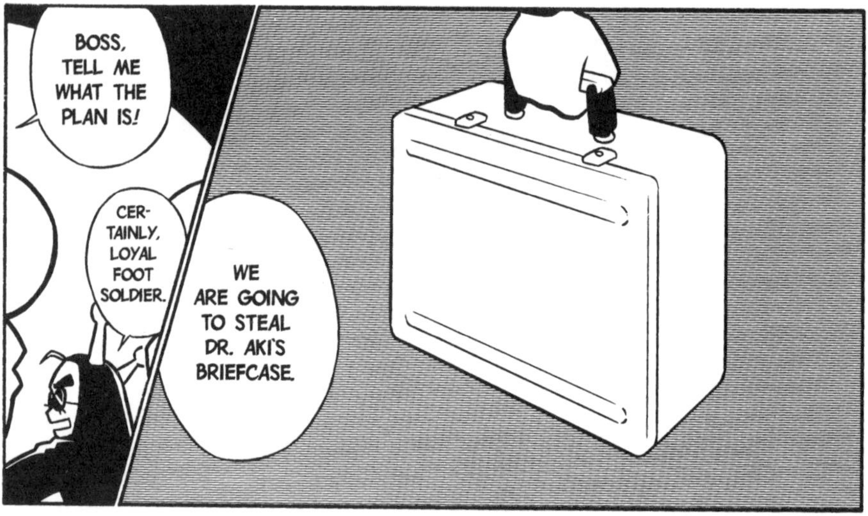
BOSS, TELL ME WHAT THE PLAN IS!
CERTAINLY, LOYAL FOOT SOLDIER.
WE ARE GOING TO STEAL DR. AKI'S BRIEFCASE.

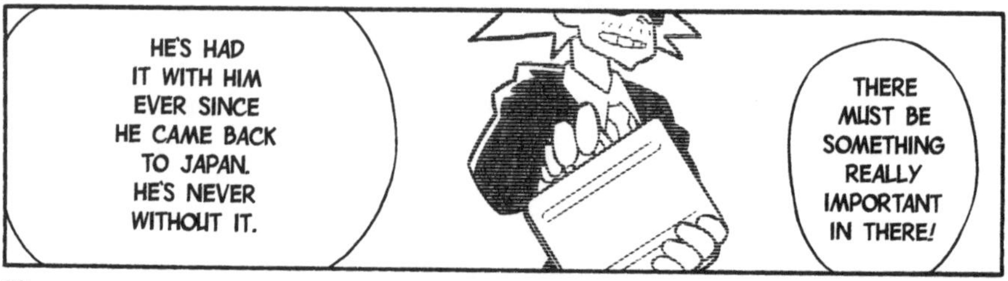
HE'S HAD IT WITH HIM EVER SINCE HE CAME BACK TO JAPAN. HE'S NEVER WITHOUT IT.
THERE MUST BE SOMETHING REALLY IMPORTANT IN THERE!

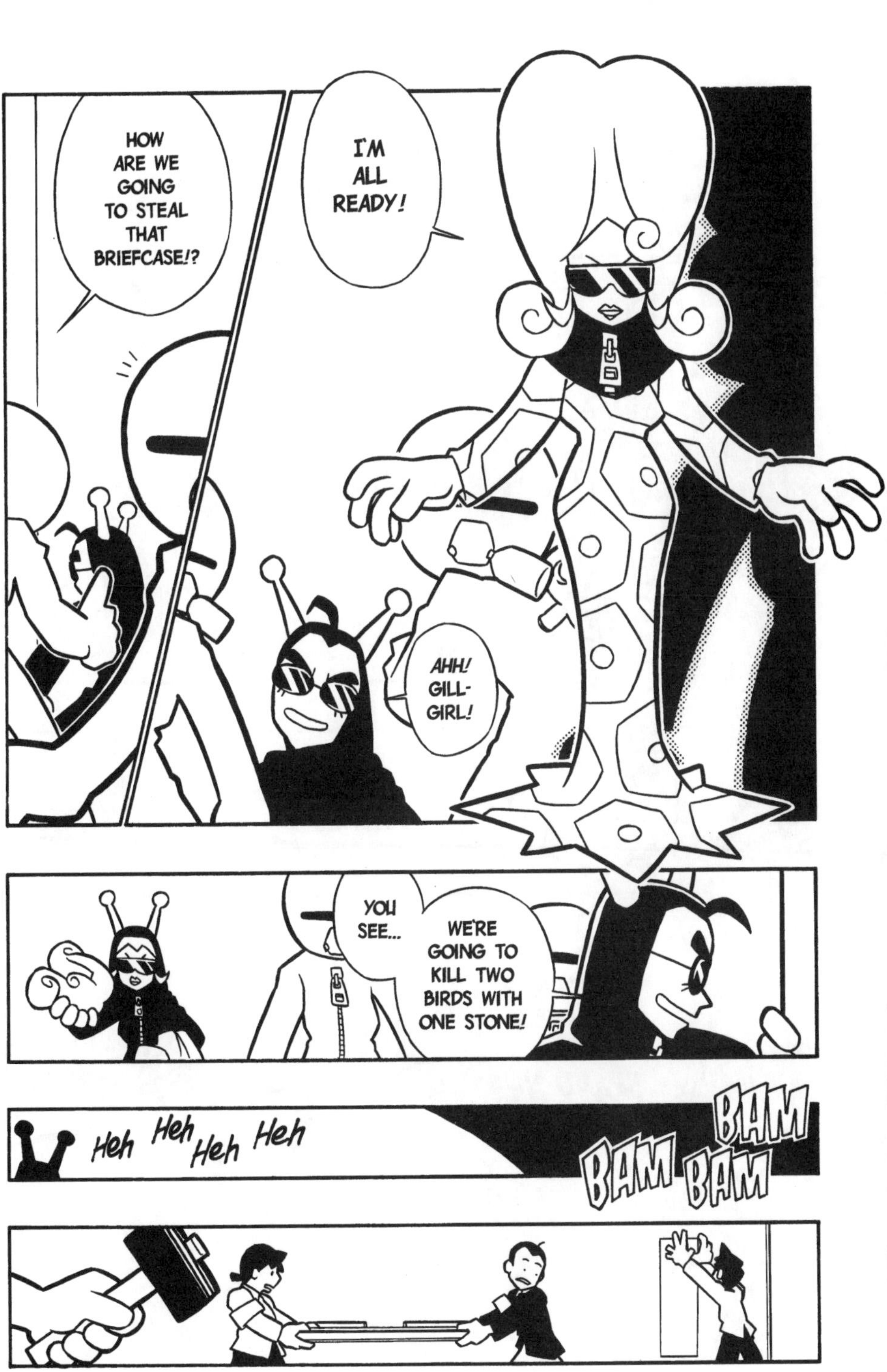
HOW ARE WE GOING TO STEAL THAT BRIEFCASE!?
I'M ALL READY!
AHH! GILL-GIRL!
YOU SEE...
WE'RE GOING TO KILL TWO BIRDS WITH ONE STONE!
Heh Heh Heh Heh
BAM BAM BAM

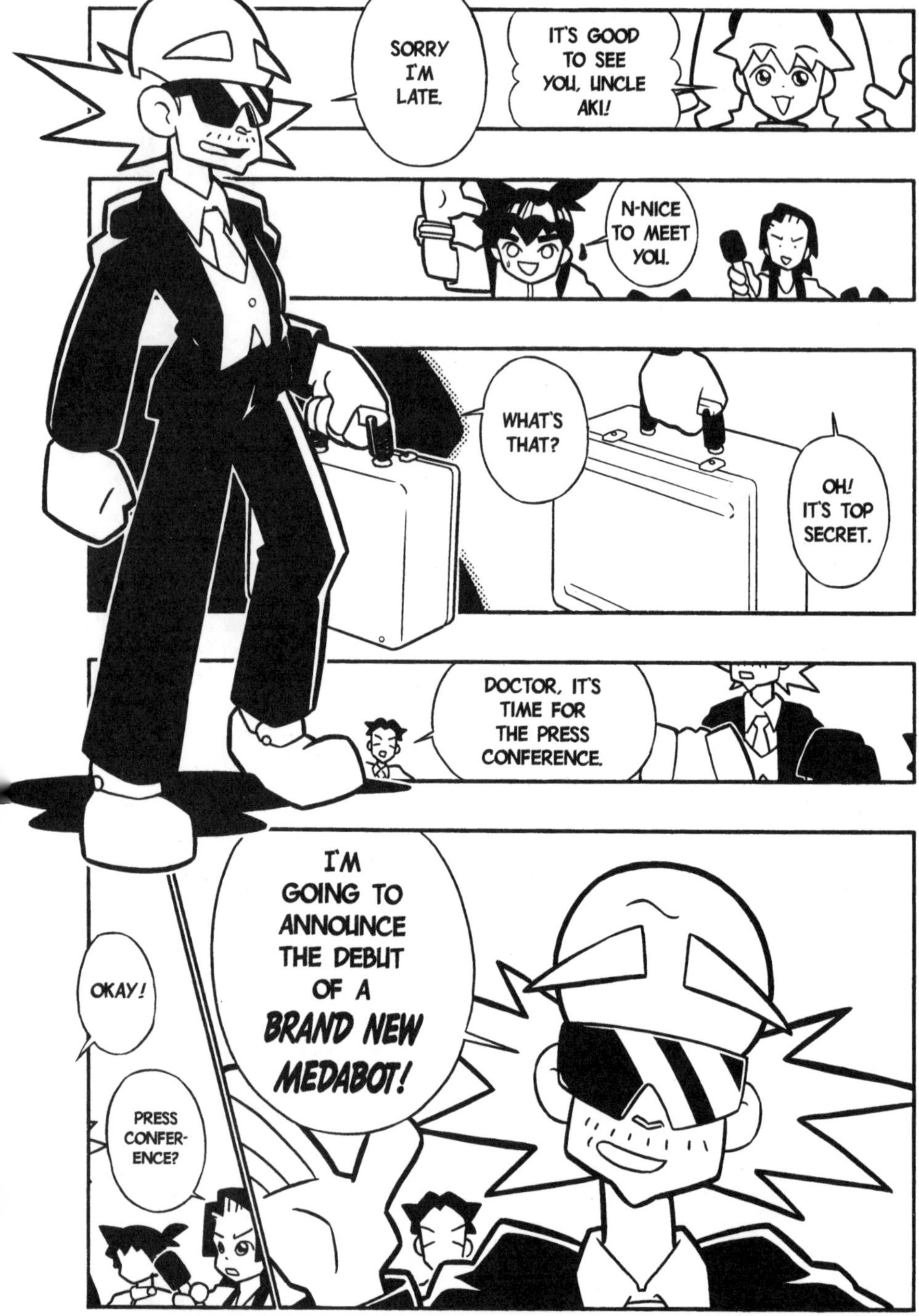
SORRY I'M LATE.
IT'S GOOD TO SEE YOU, UNCLE AKI!
N-NICE TO MEET YOU.
WHAT'S THAT?
OH! IT'S TOP SECRET.
DOCTOR, IT'S TIME FOR THE PRESS CONFERENCE.
OKAY!
PRESS CONFER-ENCE?
I'M GOING TO ANNOUNCE THE DEBUT OF A *BRAND NEW MEDABOT!*

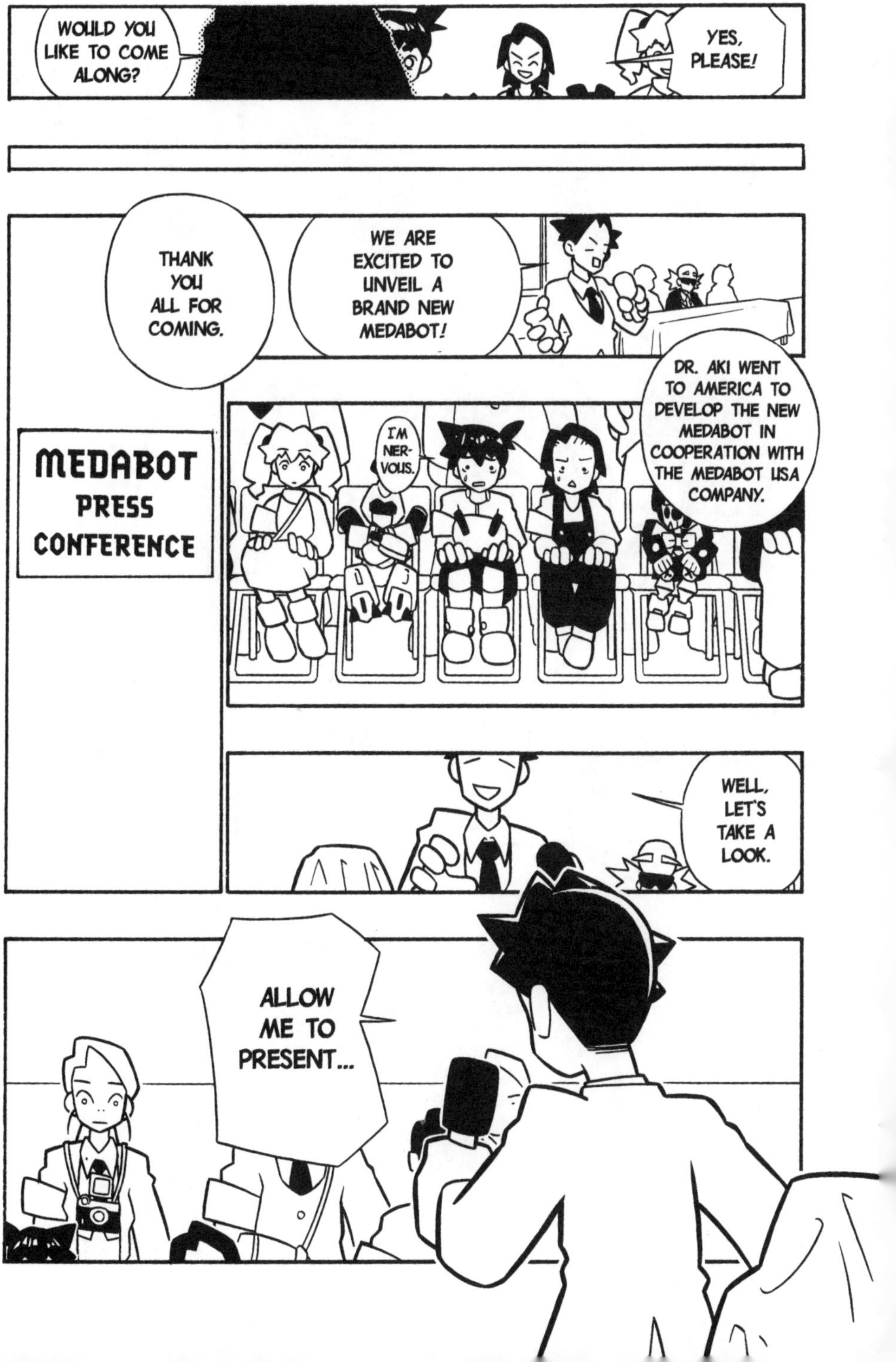
WOULD YOU LIKE TO COME ALONG?
YES, PLEASE!
THANK YOU ALL FOR COMING.
WE ARE EXCITED TO UNVEIL A BRAND NEW MEDABOT!
MEDABOT PRESS CONFERENCE
I'M NER-VOUS.
DR. AKI WENT TO AMERICA TO DEVELOP THE NEW MEDABOT IN COOPERATION WITH THE MEDABOT USA COMPANY.
WELL, LET'S TAKE A LOOK.
ALLOW ME TO PRESENT...

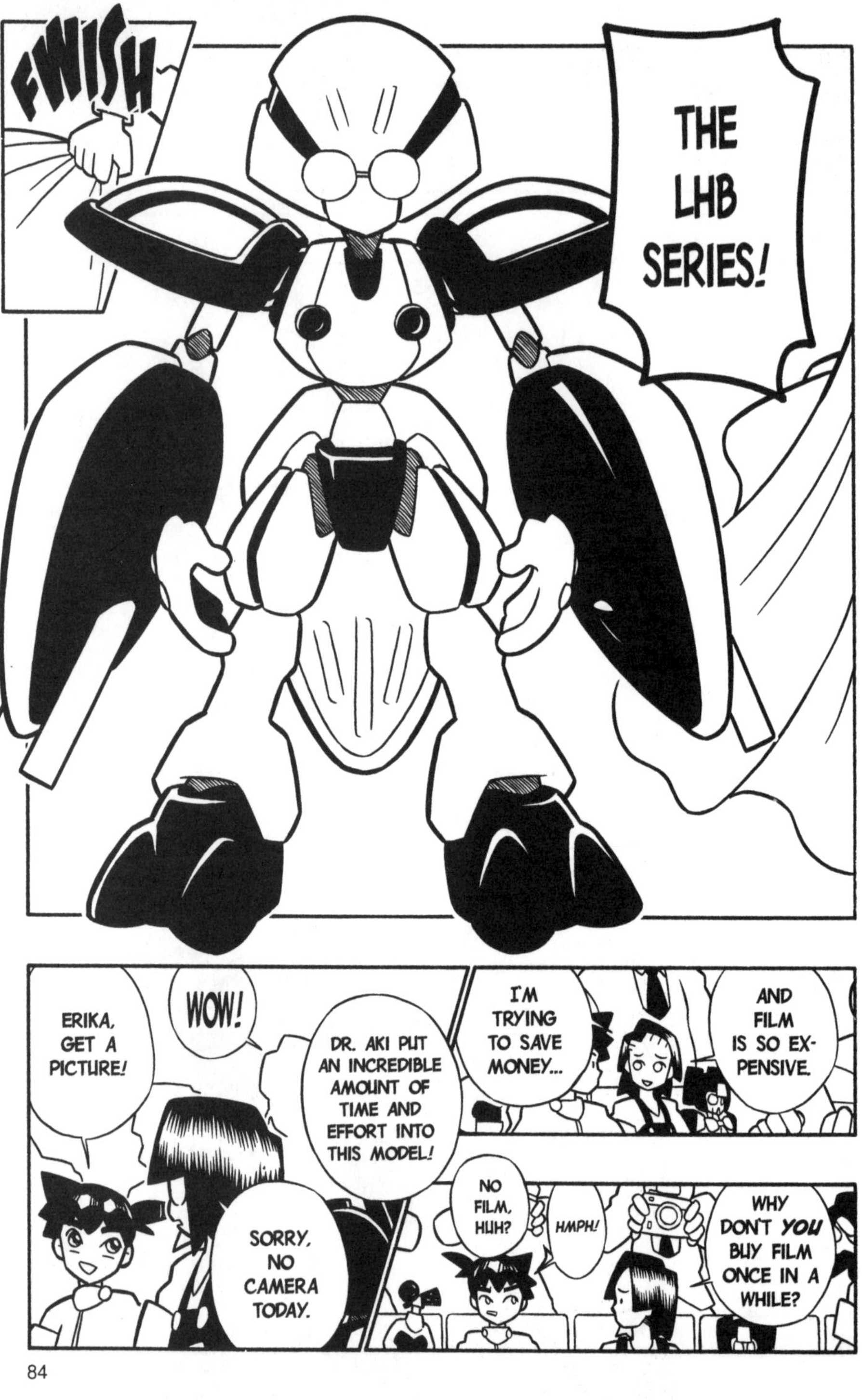
FWISH
THE LHB SERIES!
ERIKA, GET A PICTURE!
WOW!
DR. AKI PUT AN INCREDIBLE AMOUNT OF TIME AND EFFORT INTO THIS MODEL!
SORRY, NO CAMERA TODAY.
I'M TRYING TO SAVE MONEY...
AND FILM IS SO EXPENSIVE.
NO FILM, HUH?
HMPH!
WHY DON'T *YOU* BUY FILM ONCE IN A WHILE?

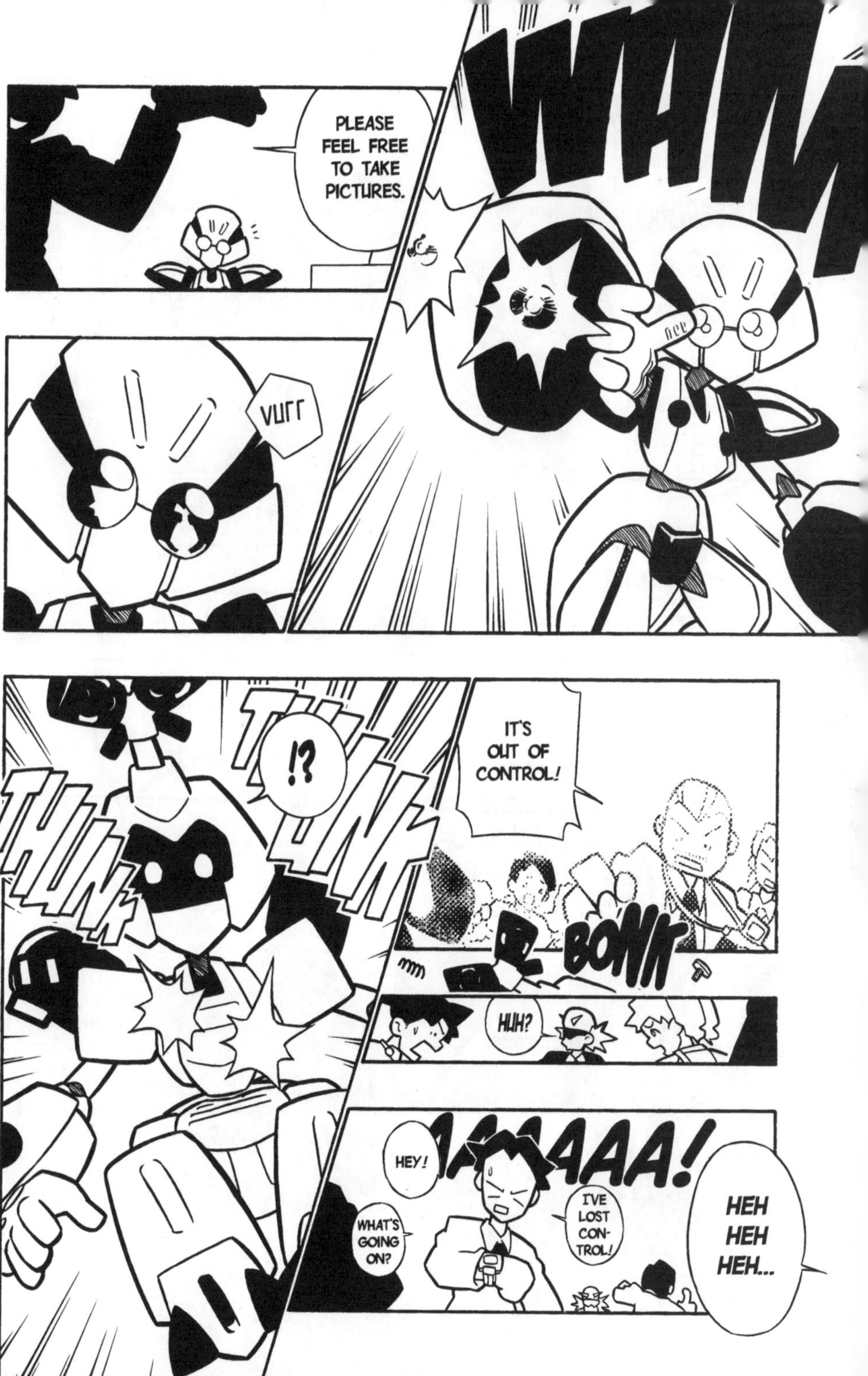
PLEASE FEEL FREE TO TAKE PICTURES.
VURR
WHAM
THUNK
THUNK
!?
IT'S OUT OF CONTROL!
BONK
HUH?
HEY!
AAAAAA!
WHAT'S GOING ON?
I'VE LOST CON-TROL!
HEH HEH HEH...

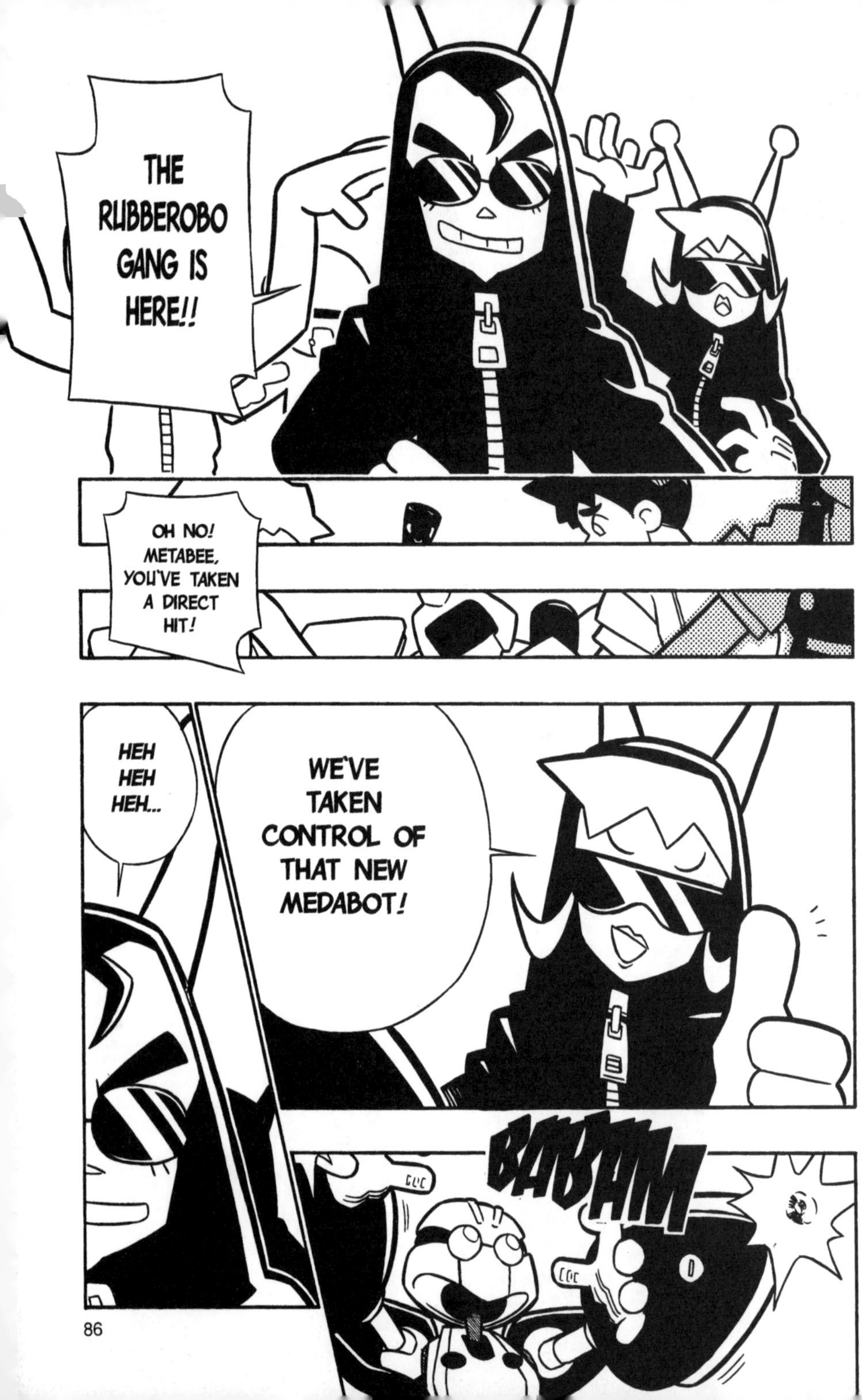
THE RUBBEROBO GANG IS HERE!!
OH NO! METABEE, YOU'VE TAKEN A DIRECT HIT!
HEH HEH HEH...
WE'VE TAKEN CONTROL OF THAT NEW MEDABOT!
BABAM

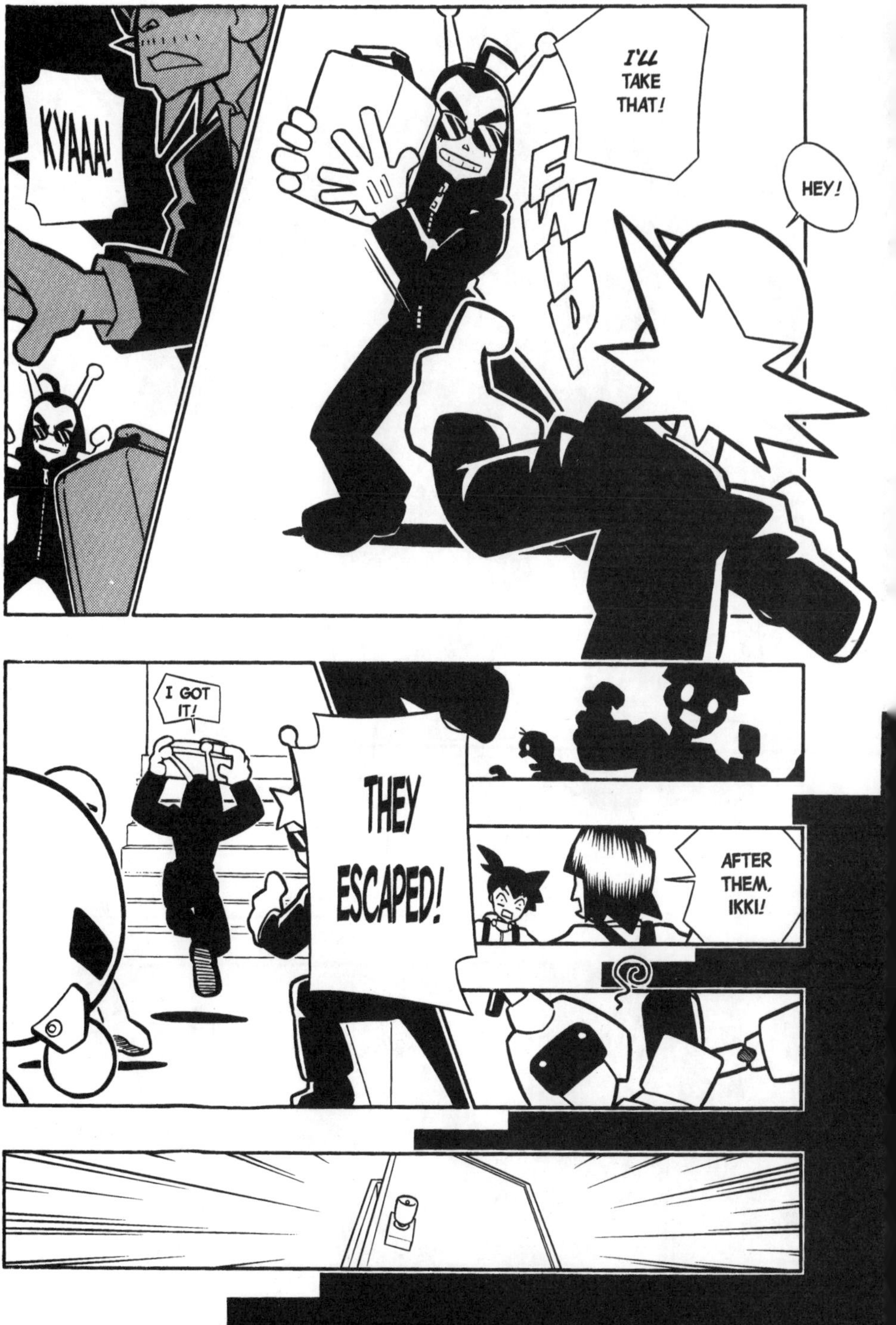
KYAAA!
I'LL TAKE THAT!
FWIP
HEY!
I GOT IT!
THEY ESCAPED!
AFTER THEM, IKKI!

VURR

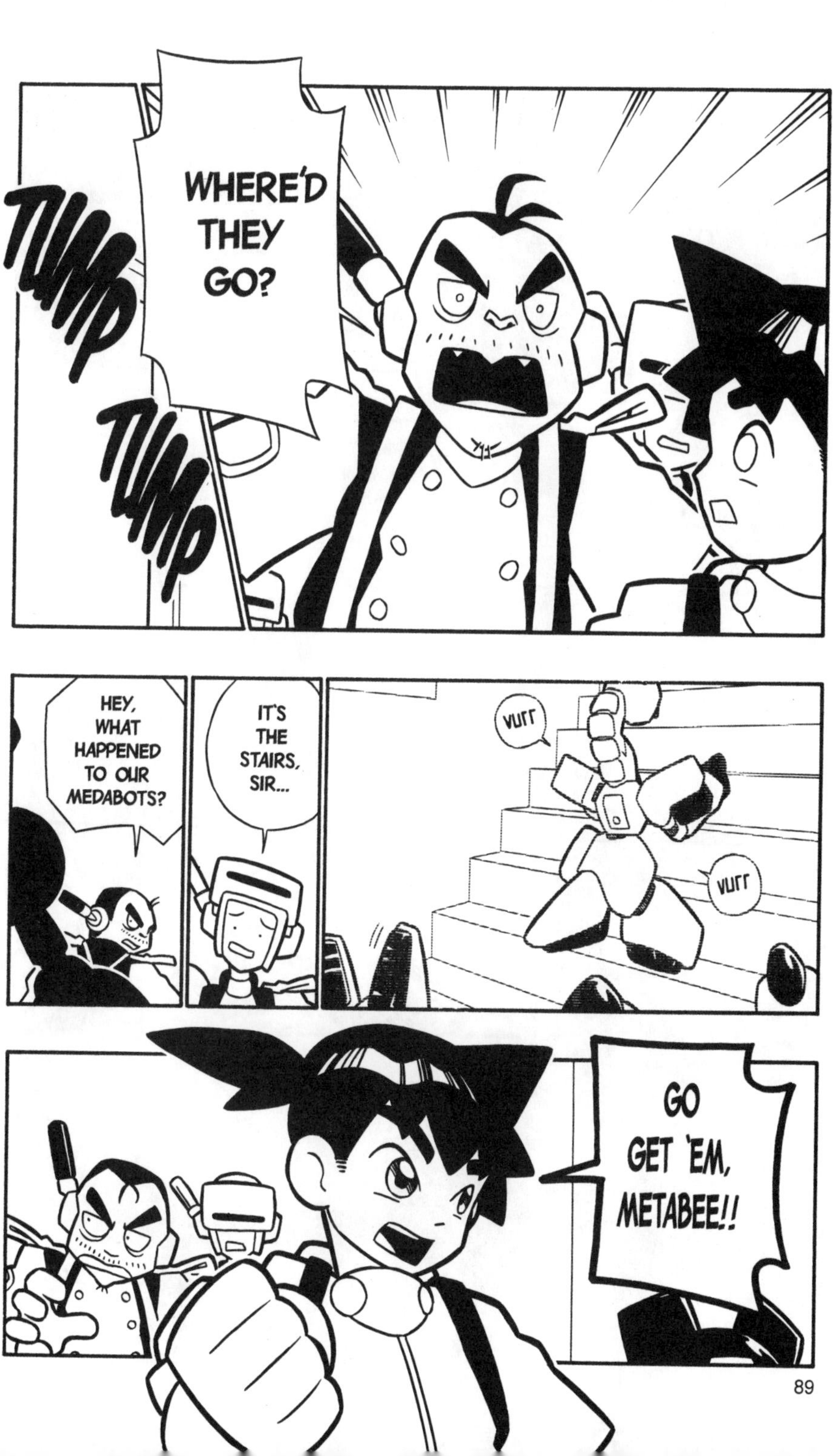
TUMP
WHERE'D THEY GO?
TUMP
HEY, WHAT HAPPENED TO OUR MEDABOTS?
IT'S THE STAIRS, SIR...
VUrr
VUrr
GO GET 'EM, METABEE!!

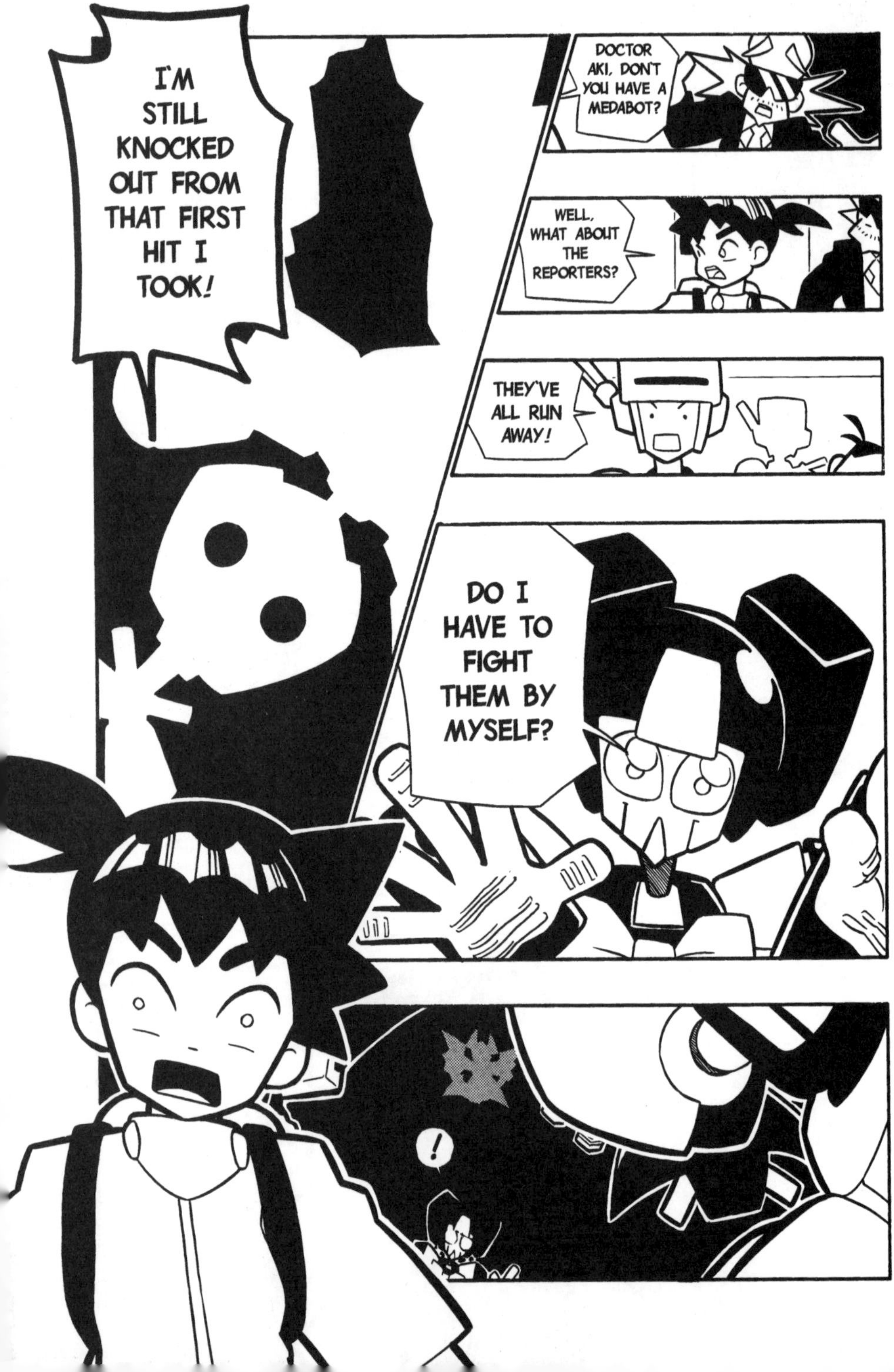
I'M STILL KNOCKED OUT FROM THAT FIRST HIT I TOOK!
DOCTOR AKI, DON'T YOU HAVE A MEDABOT?
WELL, WHAT ABOUT THE REPORTERS?
THEY'VE ALL RUN AWAY!
DO I HAVE TO FIGHT THEM BY MYSELF?
!

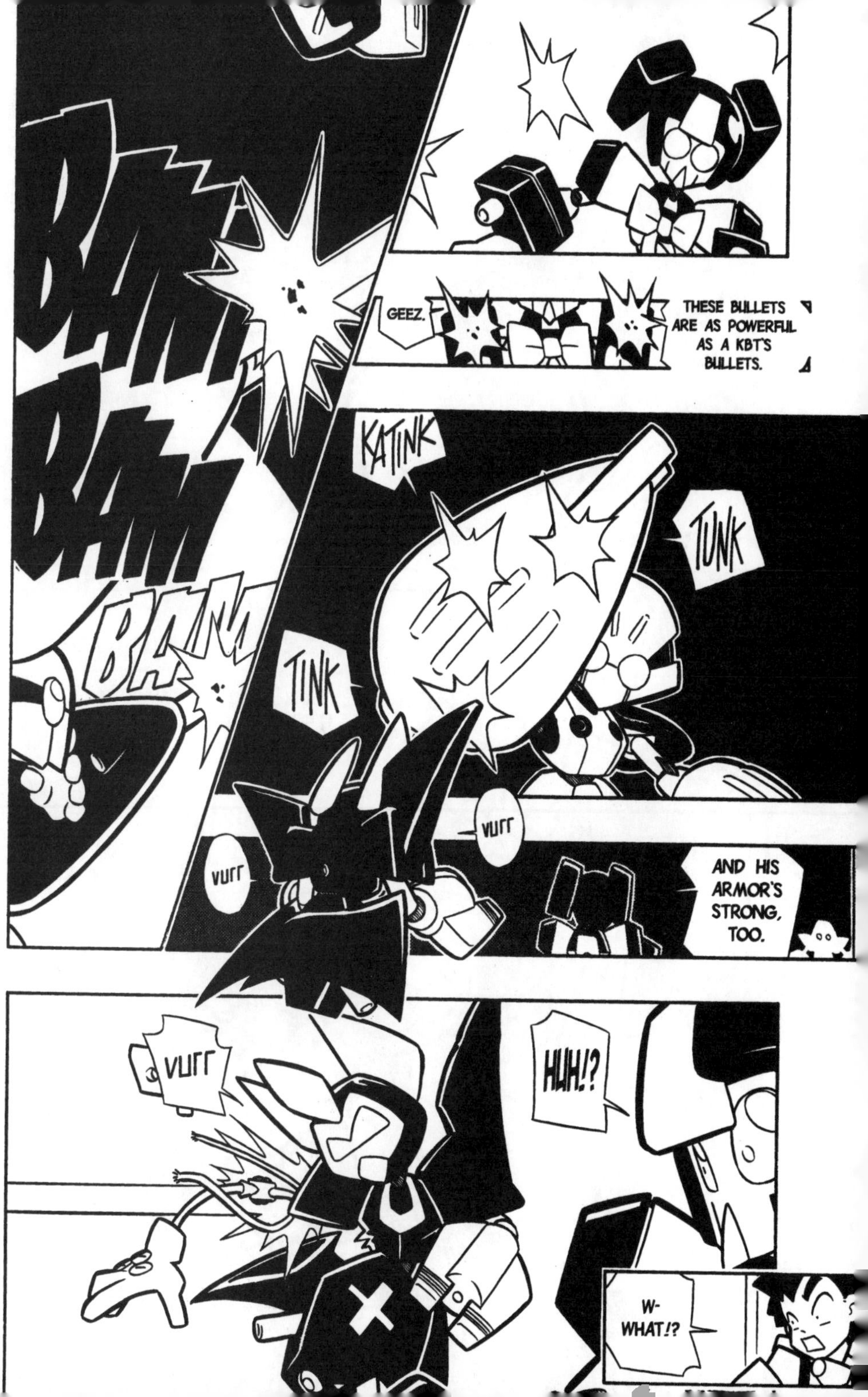
BAM
BAM
BAM
BAM
GEEZ.
THESE BULLETS ARE AS POWERFUL AS A KBT'S BULLETS.
KATINK
TUNK
TINK
VUrr
VUrr
AND HIS ARMOR'S STRONG, TOO.
VUrr
HUH!?
W-WHAT!?

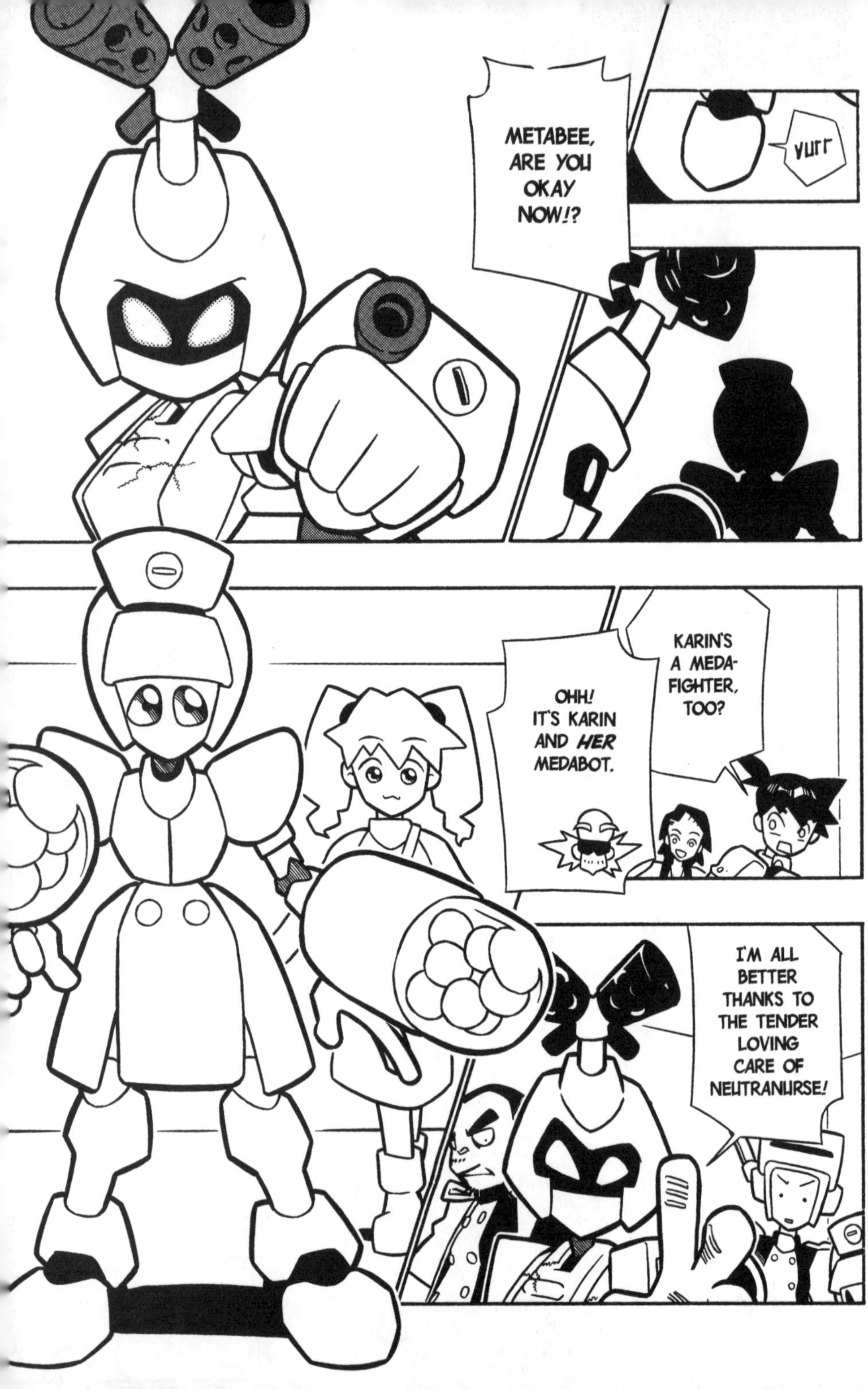
METABEE, ARE YOU OKAY NOW!?
yurr
OHH! IT'S KARIN AND HER MEDABOT.
KARIN'S A MEDA-FIGHTER, TOO?
I'M ALL BETTER THANKS TO THE TENDER LOVING CARE OF NEUTRANURSE!

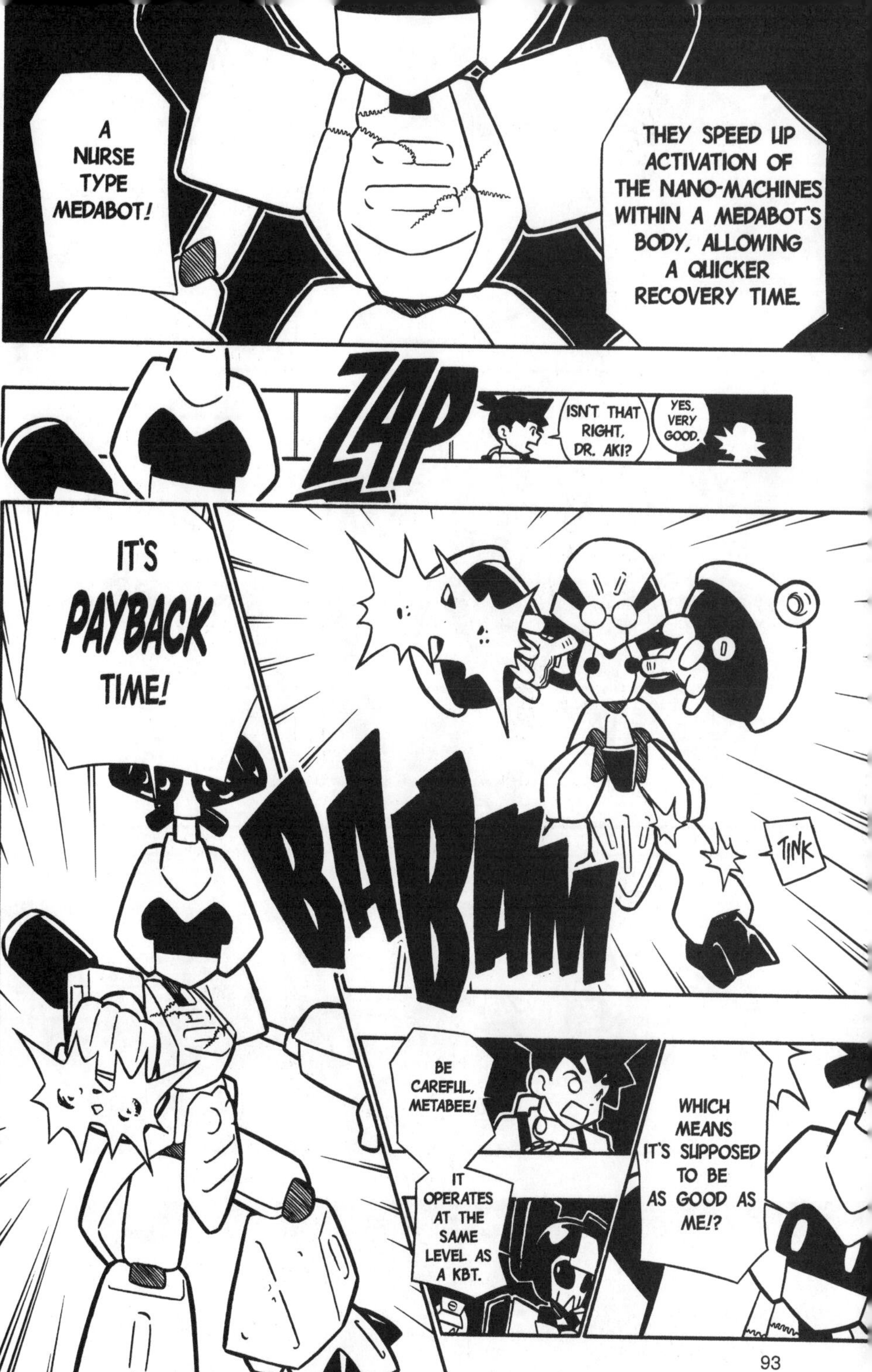
A NURSE TYPE MEDABOT!
THEY SPEED UP ACTIVATION OF THE NANO-MACHINES WITHIN A MEDABOT'S BODY, ALLOWING A QUICKER RECOVERY TIME.
ZAP
ISN'T THAT RIGHT, DR. AKI?
YES, VERY GOOD.
IT'S PAYBACK TIME!
BABAM
TINK
BE CAREFUL, METABEE!
IT OPERATES AT THE SAME LEVEL AS A KBT.
WHICH MEANS IT'S SUPPOSED TO BE AS GOOD AS ME!?

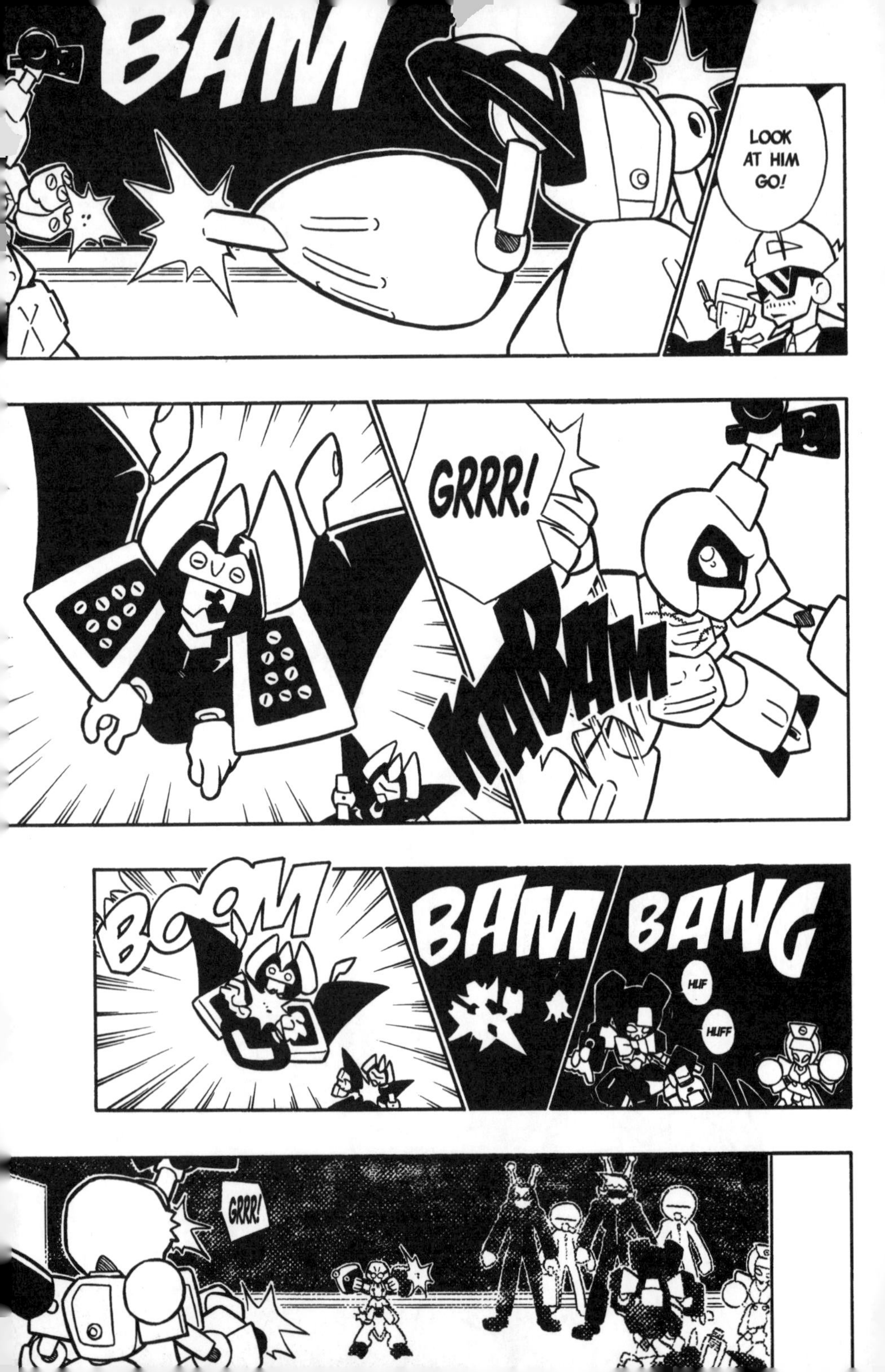
BAM
LOOK AT HIM GO!
GRRR!
KABAM
BOOM
BAM
BANG
HUF
HUFF
GRRR!

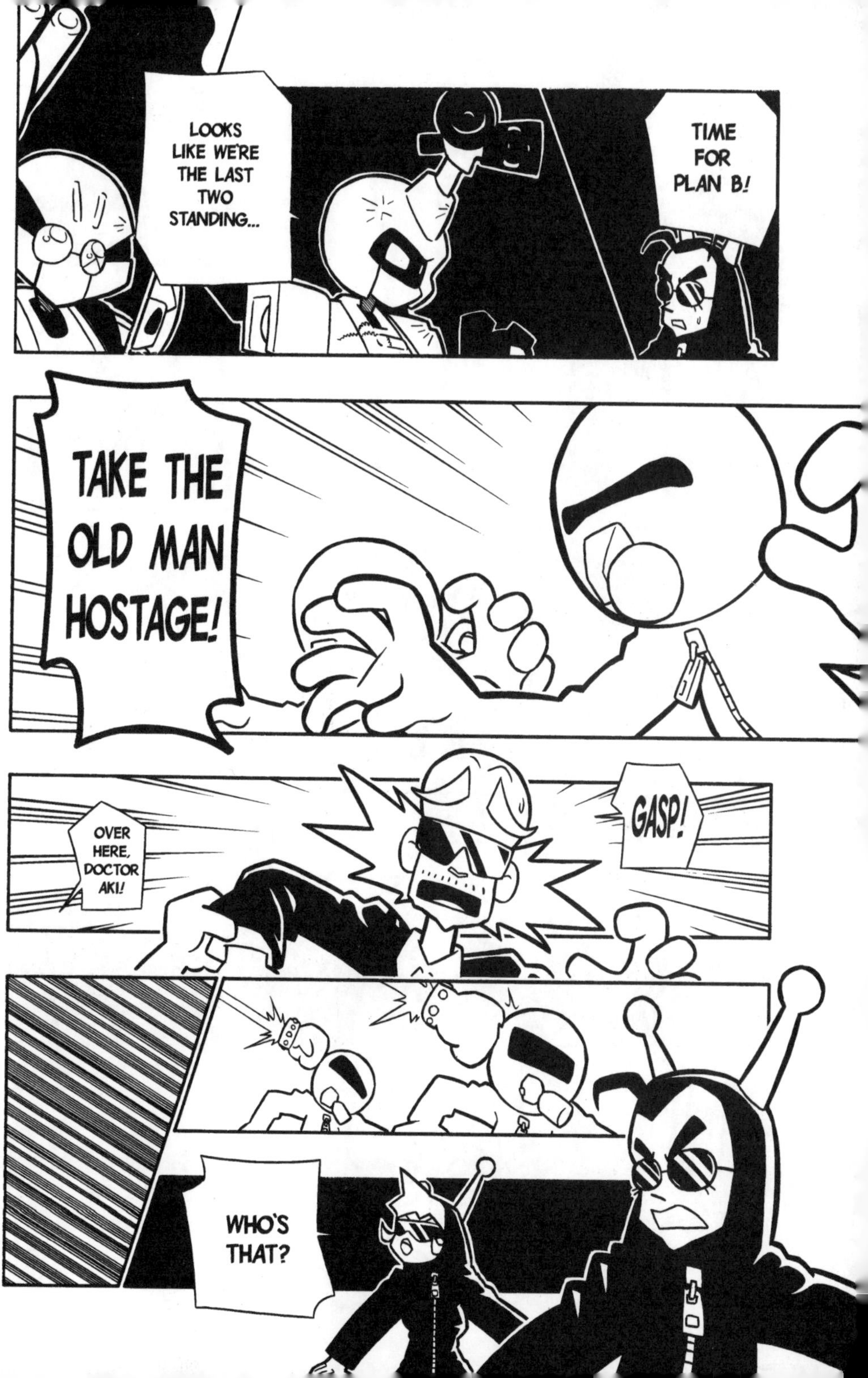
LOOKS LIKE WE'RE THE LAST TWO STANDING...
TIME FOR PLAN B!
TAKE THE OLD MAN HOSTAGE!
OVER HERE, DOCTOR AKI!
GASP!
WHO'S THAT?

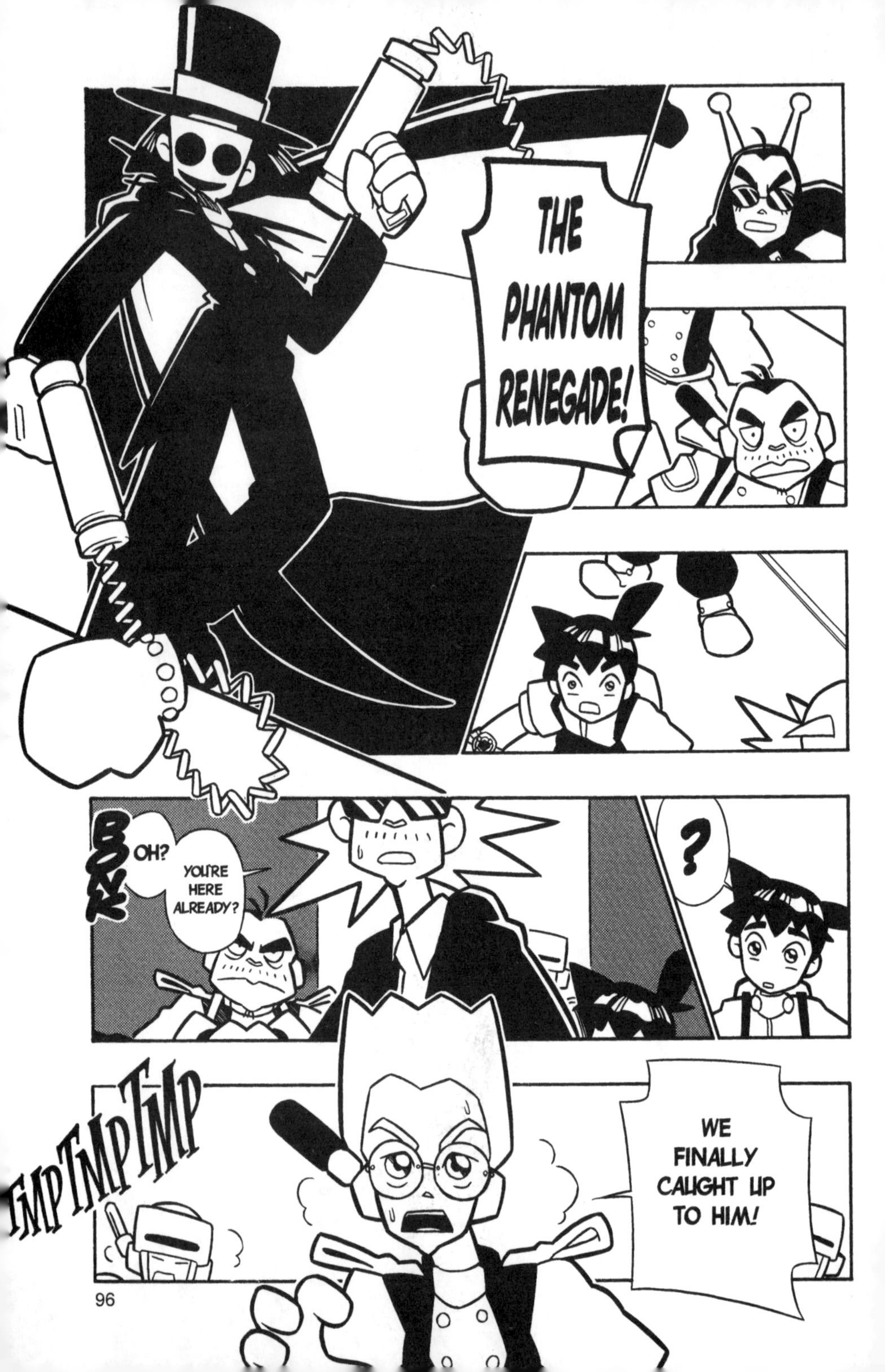
THE PHANTOM RENEGADE!
BONK
OH?
YOU'RE HERE ALREADY?
?
TMP TMP TMP
WE FINALLY CAUGHT UP TO HIM!

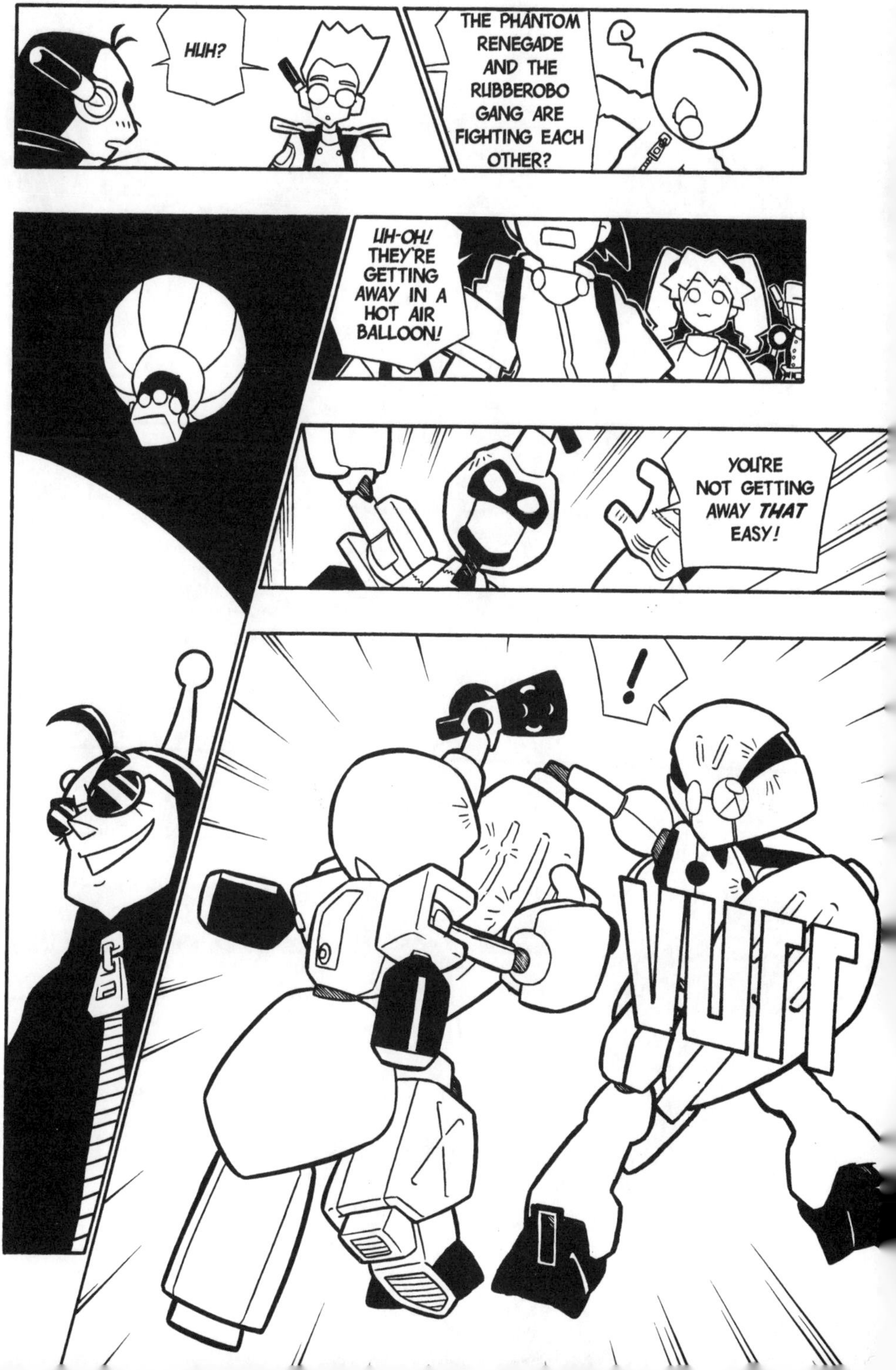
HUH?
THE PHANTOM RENEGADE AND THE RUBBEROBO GANG ARE FIGHTING EACH OTHER?
UH-OH! THEY'RE GETTING AWAY IN A HOT AIR BALLOON!
YOU'RE NOT GETTING AWAY *THAT* EASY!
!
VUTT

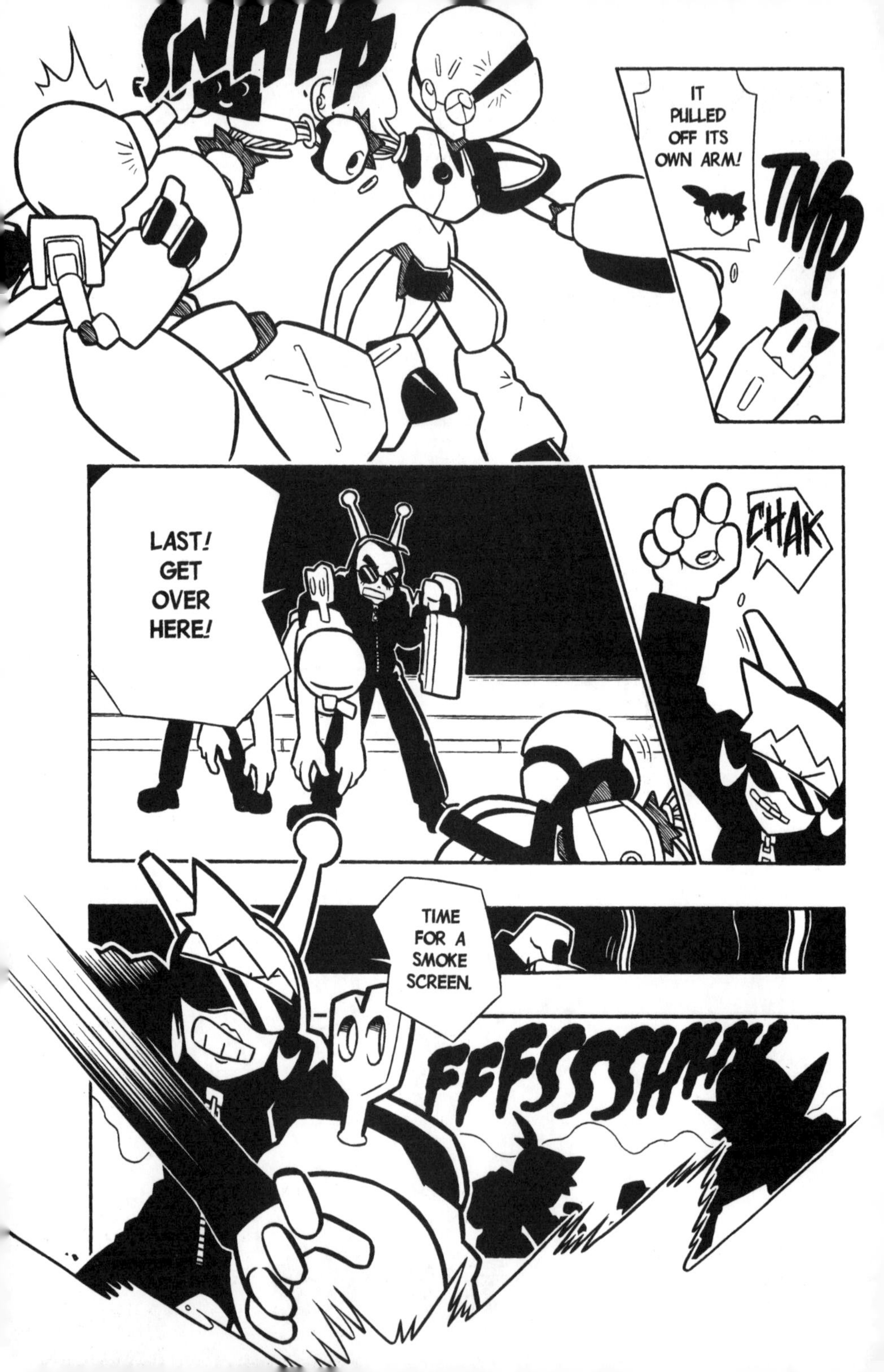
SHHKB
IT PULLED OFF ITS OWN ARM!
TMP
LAST! GET OVER HERE!
CHAK
TIME FOR A SMOKE SCREEN.
FFFSSSHHK

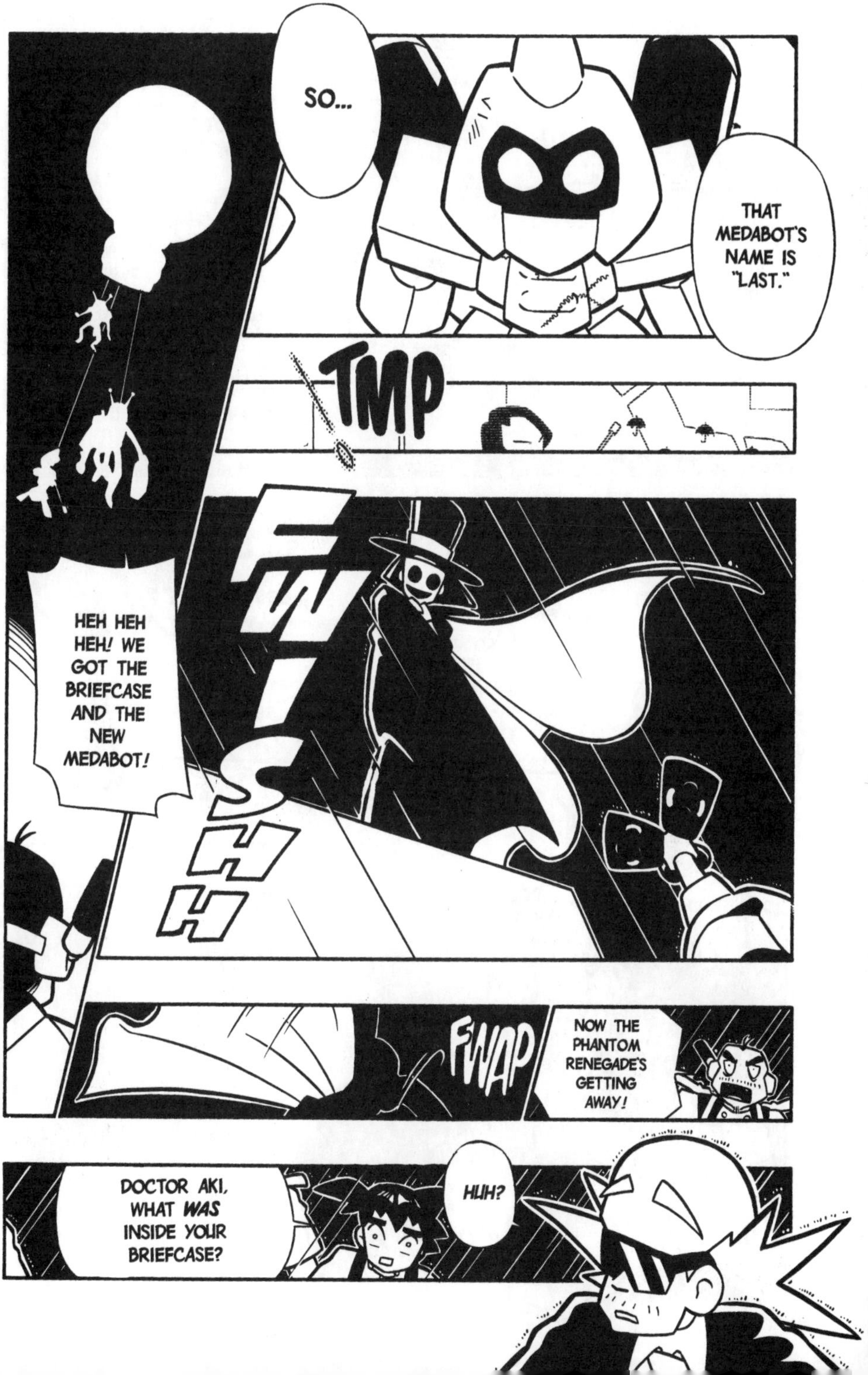
SO...
THAT MEDABOT'S NAME IS "LAST."
TMP
HEH HEH HEH! WE GOT THE BRIEFCASE AND THE NEW MEDABOT!
FWISHHH
FWAP
NOW THE PHANTOM RENEGADE'S GETTING AWAY!
DOCTOR AKI, WHAT WAS INSIDE YOUR BRIEFCASE?
HUH?

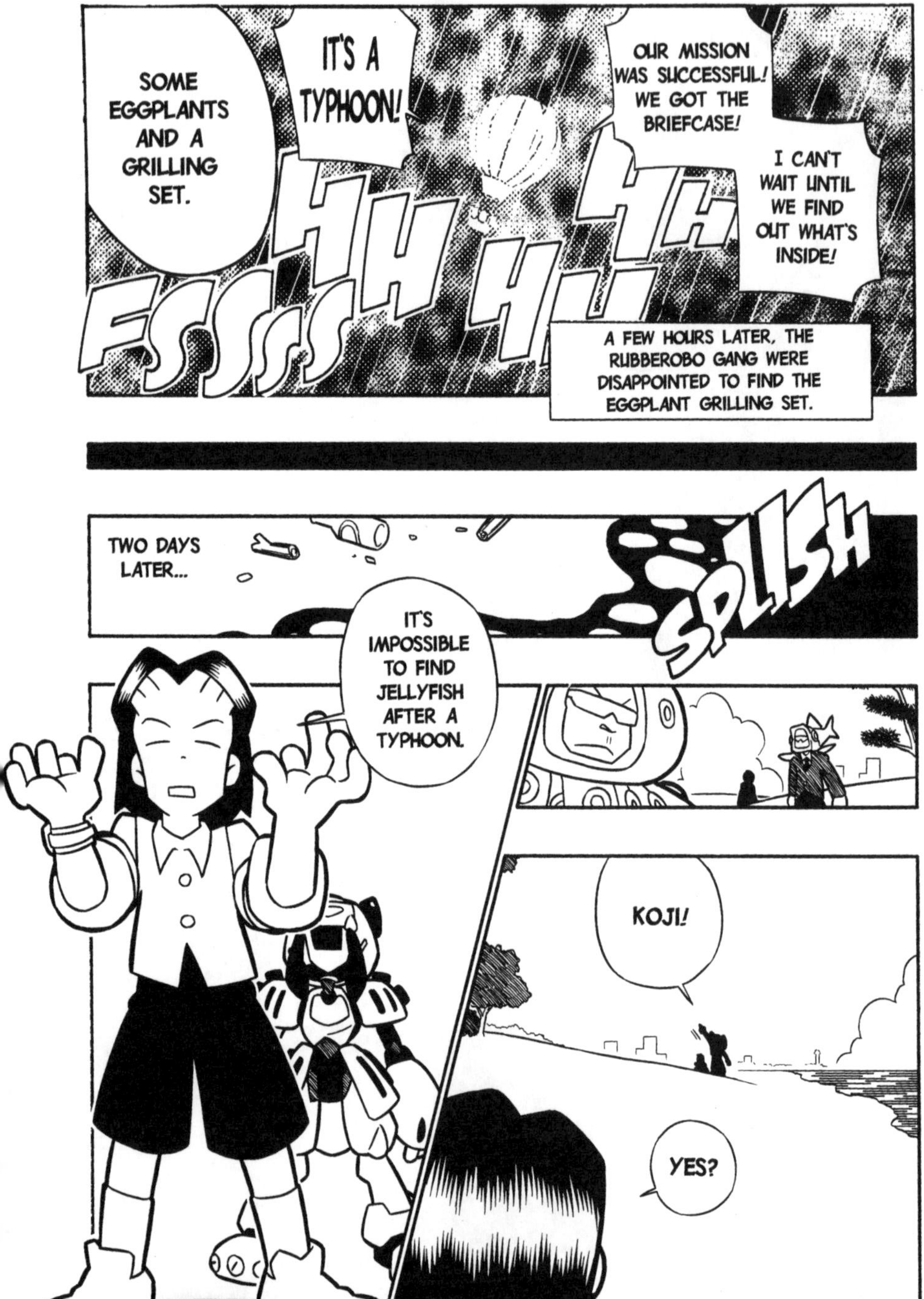
SOME EGGPLANTS AND A GRILLING SET.
IT'S A TYPHOON!
FSSSSSH
OUR MISSION WAS SUCCESSFUL! WE GOT THE BRIEFCASE!
I CAN'T WAIT UNTIL WE FIND OUT WHAT'S INSIDE!
A FEW HOURS LATER, THE RUBBEROBO GANG WERE DISAPPOINTED TO FIND THE EGGPLANT GRILLING SET.
TWO DAYS LATER...
SPLISH
IT'S IMPOSSIBLE TO FIND JELLYFISH AFTER A TYPHOON.
KOJI!
YES?

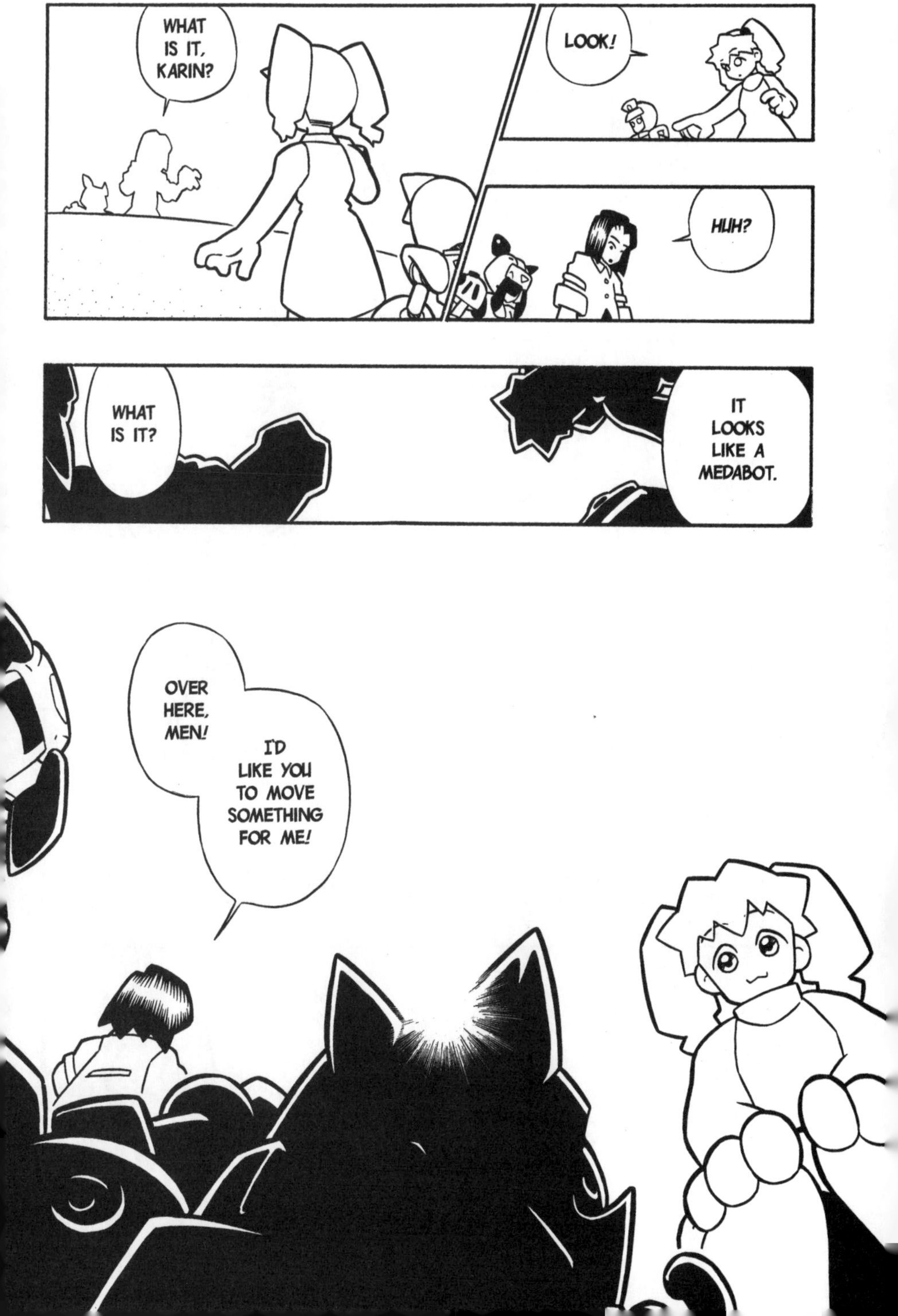
WHAT IS IT, KARIN?
LOOK!
HUH?
WHAT IS IT?
IT LOOKS LIKE A MEDABOT.
OVER HERE, MEN!
I'D LIKE YOU TO MOVE SOMETHING FOR ME!

WHAT'S BEEN ON OUR MINDS!

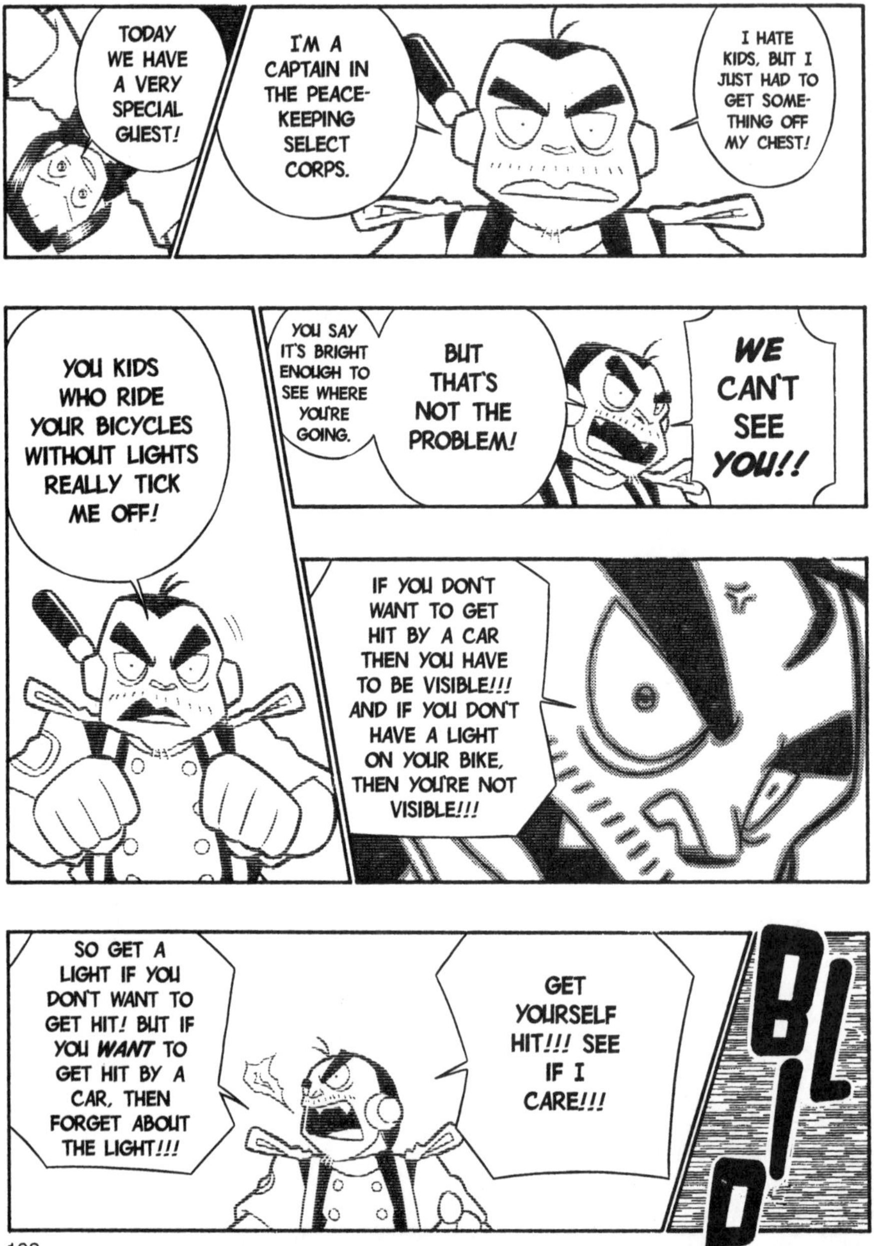
TODAY WE HAVE A VERY SPECIAL GUEST!
I'M A CAPTAIN IN THE PEACE-KEEPING SELECT CORPS.
I HATE KIDS, BUT I JUST HAD TO GET SOME-THING OFF MY CHEST!
YOU KIDS WHO RIDE YOUR BICYCLES WITHOUT LIGHTS REALLY TICK ME OFF!
YOU SAY IT'S BRIGHT ENOUGH TO SEE WHERE YOU'RE GOING.
BUT THAT'S NOT THE PROBLEM!
WE CAN'T SEE YOU!!
IF YOU DON'T WANT TO GET HIT BY A CAR THEN YOU HAVE TO BE VISIBLE!!! AND IF YOU DON'T HAVE A LIGHT ON YOUR BIKE, THEN YOU'RE NOT VISIBLE!!!
SO GET A LIGHT IF YOU DON'T WANT TO GET HIT! BUT IF YOU WANT TO GET HIT BY A CAR, THEN FORGET ABOUT THE LIGHT!!!
GET YOURSELF HIT!!! SEE IF I CARE!!!
BLIP

ROBATTLE ROYALE!!

TOP SECRET MEETING!
OKAY, SO... UMM...
LET'S GET THIS MEETING STARTED!
YOU HAVE THE FLOOR ...
KACHOO
WHAT !?
OH, OKAY!
Shnort
THIS DARN KID!
HE ALWAYS SEEMS TO BE GETTING IN OUR WAY!
I DID A LITTLE CHECKING UP ON HIM...

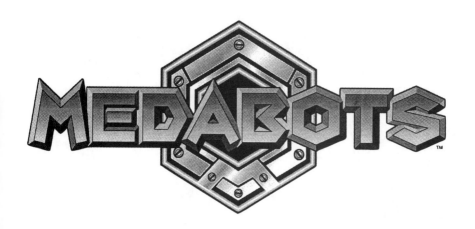

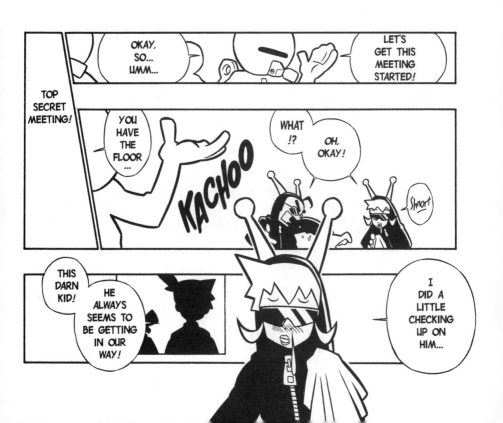

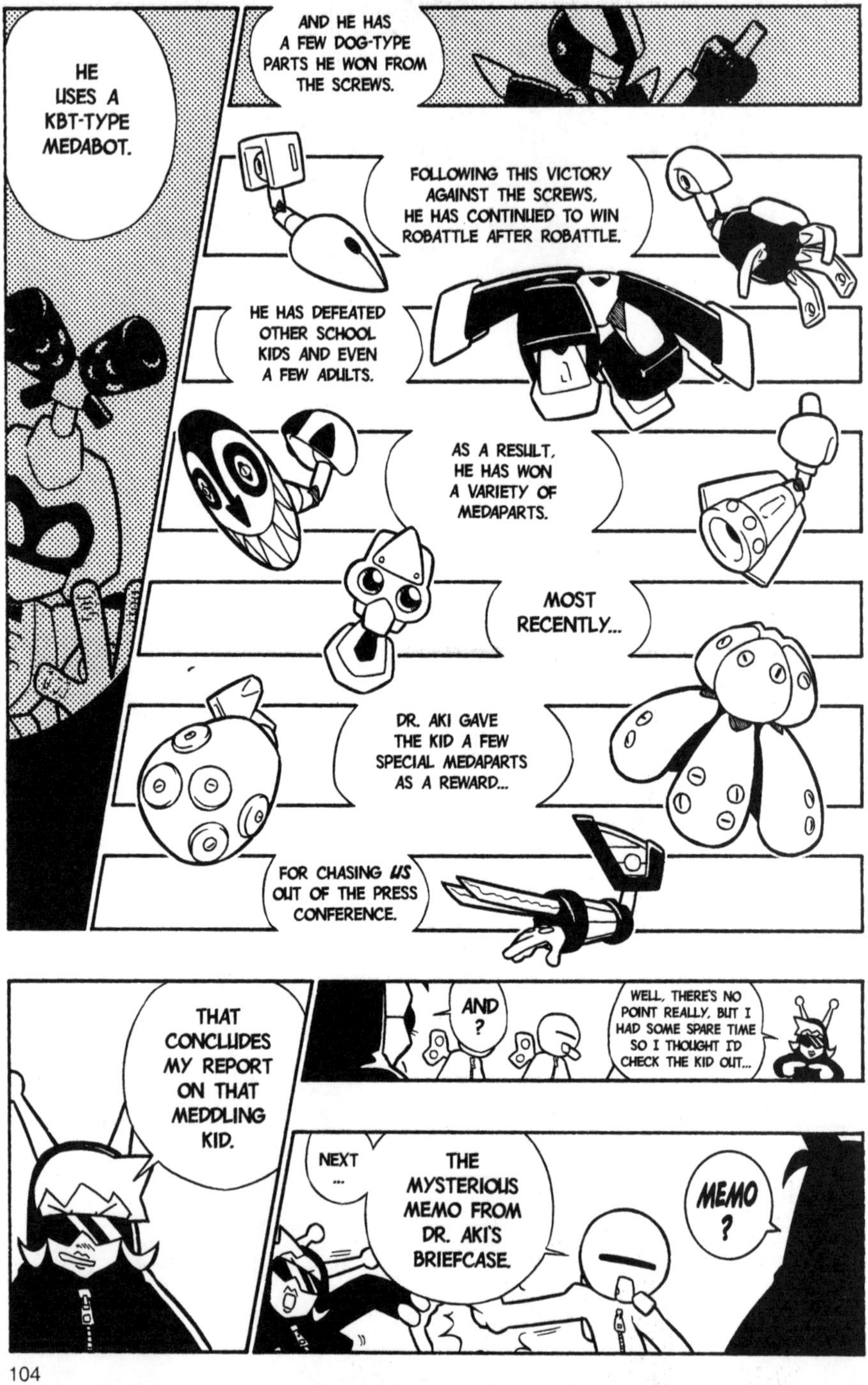
HE USES A KBT-TYPE MEDABOT.
AND HE HAS A FEW DOG-TYPE PARTS HE WON FROM THE SCREWS.
FOLLOWING THIS VICTORY AGAINST THE SCREWS, HE HAS CONTINUED TO WIN ROBATTLE AFTER ROBATTLE.
HE HAS DEFEATED OTHER SCHOOL KIDS AND EVEN A FEW ADULTS.
AS A RESULT, HE HAS WON A VARIETY OF MEDAPARTS.
MOST RECENTLY...
DR. AKI GAVE THE KID A FEW SPECIAL MEDAPARTS AS A REWARD...
FOR CHASING *US* OUT OF THE PRESS CONFERENCE.
THAT CONCLUDES MY REPORT ON THAT MEDDLING KID.
AND ?
WELL, THERE'S NO POINT REALLY, BUT I HAD SOME SPARE TIME SO I THOUGHT I'D CHECK THE KID OUT...
NEXT ...
THE MYSTERIOUS MEMO FROM DR. AKI'S BRIEFCASE.
MEMO ?

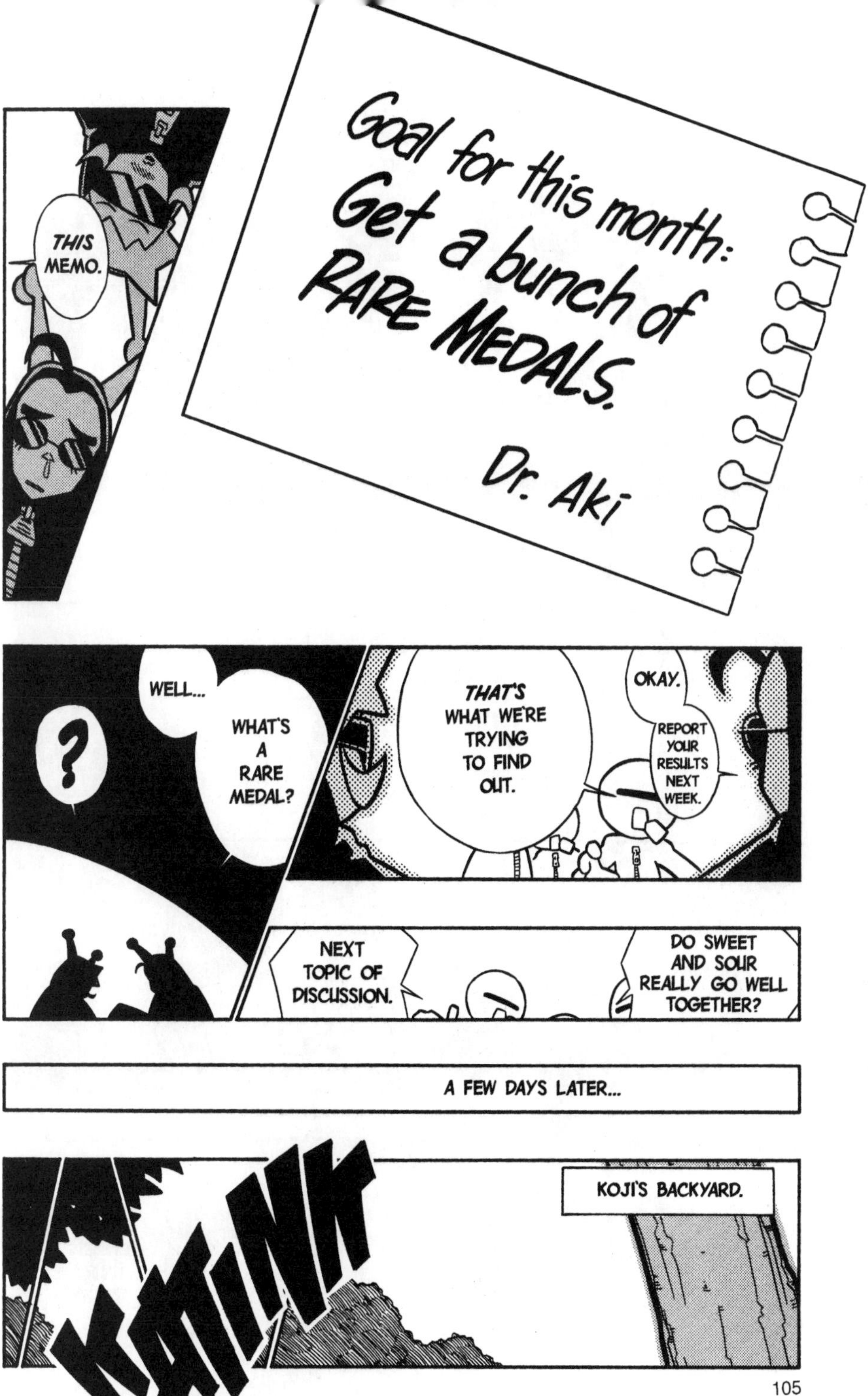
THIS MEMO.
Goal for this month:
Get a bunch of RARE MEDALS.
Dr. Aki
WELL...
?
WHAT'S A RARE MEDAL?
THAT'S WHAT WE'RE TRYING TO FIND OUT.
OKAY.
REPORT YOUR RESULTS NEXT WEEK.
NEXT TOPIC OF DISCUSSION.
DO SWEET AND SOUR REALLY GO WELL TOGETHER?
A FEW DAYS LATER...
KATINK
KOJI'S BACKYARD.

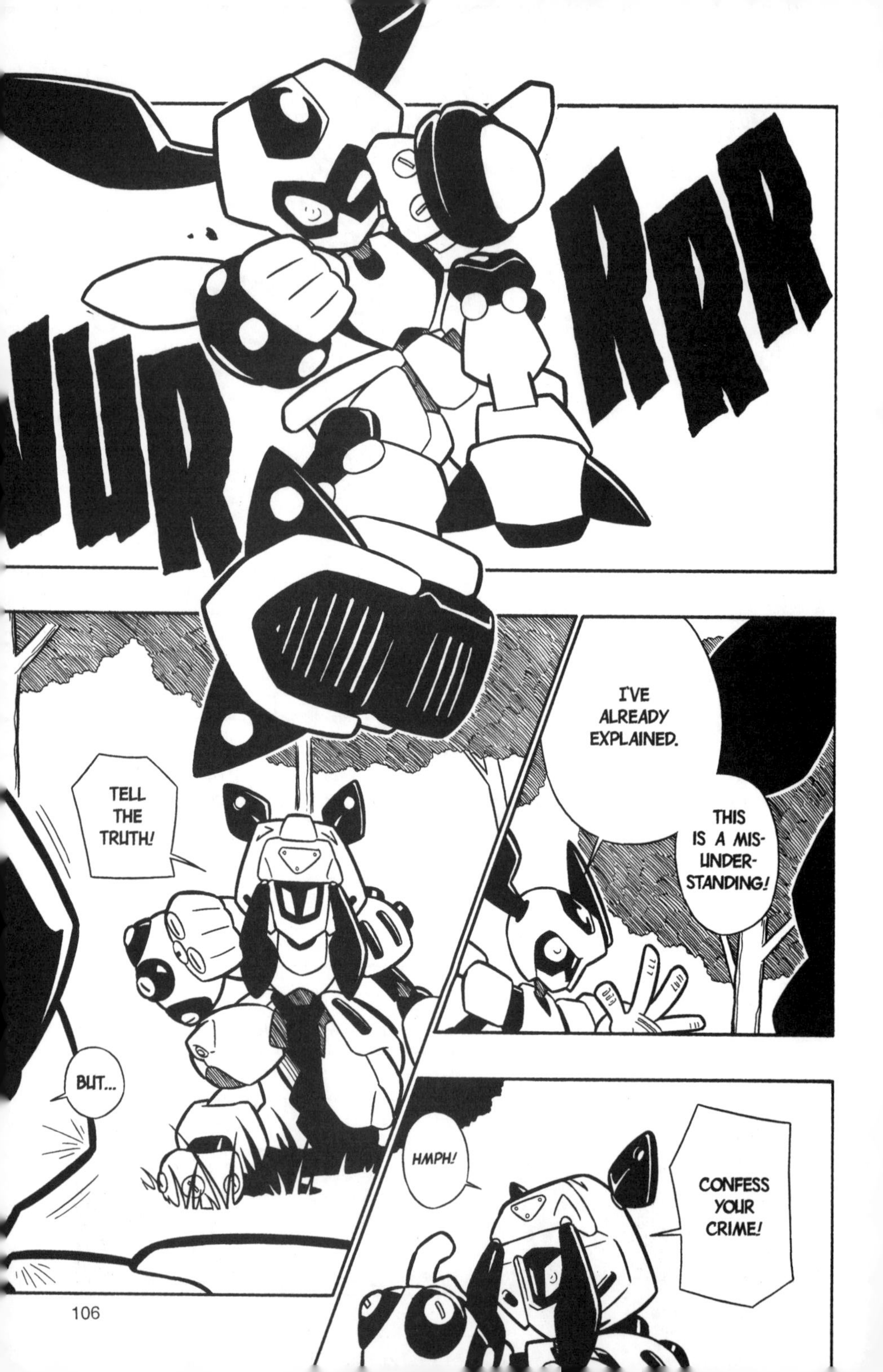
VUURRRR
TELL THE TRUTH!
BUT...
I'VE ALREADY EXPLAINED.
THIS IS A MIS-UNDER-STANDING!
HMPH!
CONFESS YOUR CRIME!

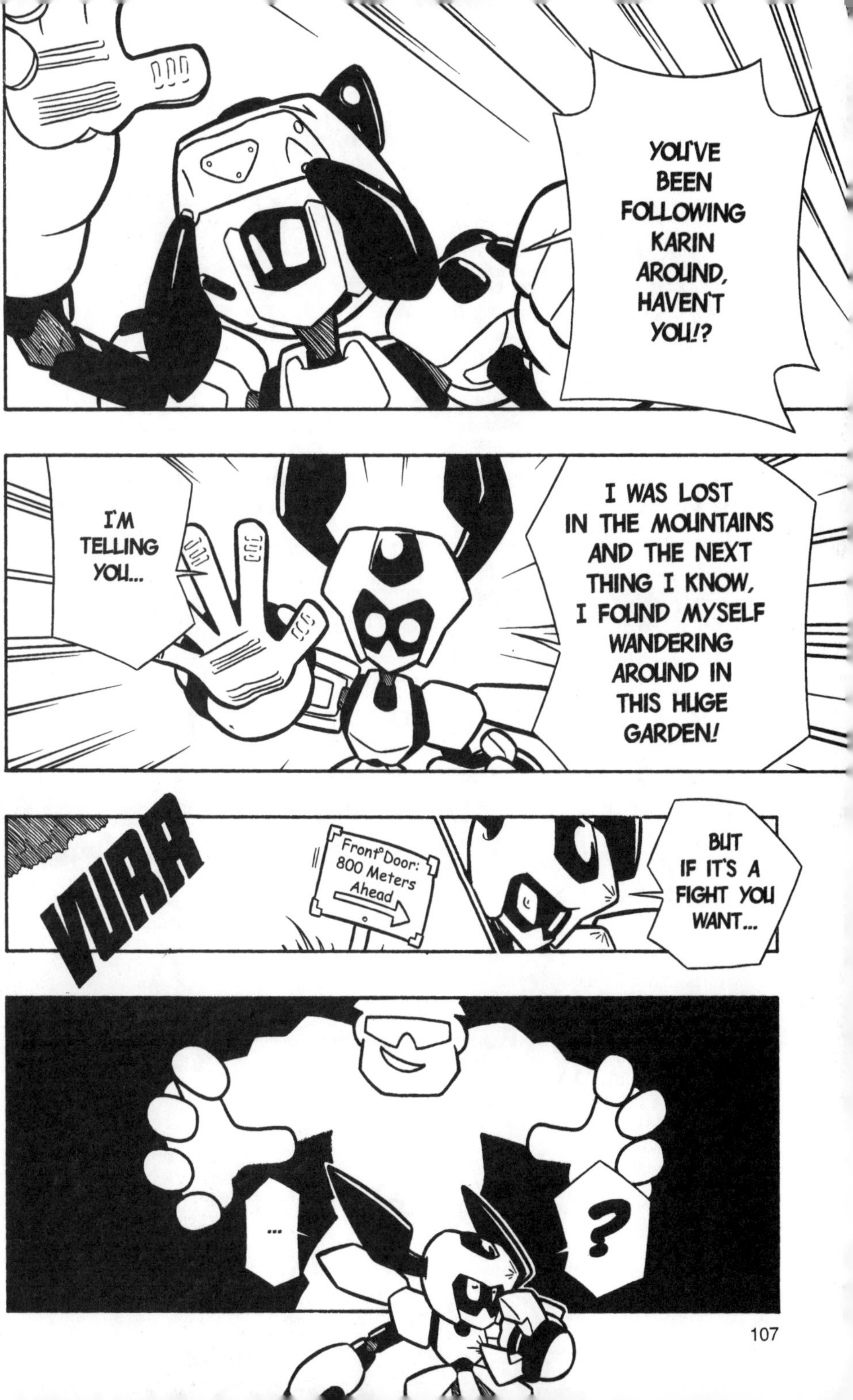
YOU'VE BEEN FOLLOWING KARIN AROUND, HAVEN'T YOU!?
I'M TELLING YOU...
I WAS LOST IN THE MOUNTAINS AND THE NEXT THING I KNOW, I FOUND MYSELF WANDERING AROUND IN THIS HUGE GARDEN!
VURR
Front Door: 800 Meters Ahead
BUT IF IT'S A FIGHT YOU WANT...
...
?

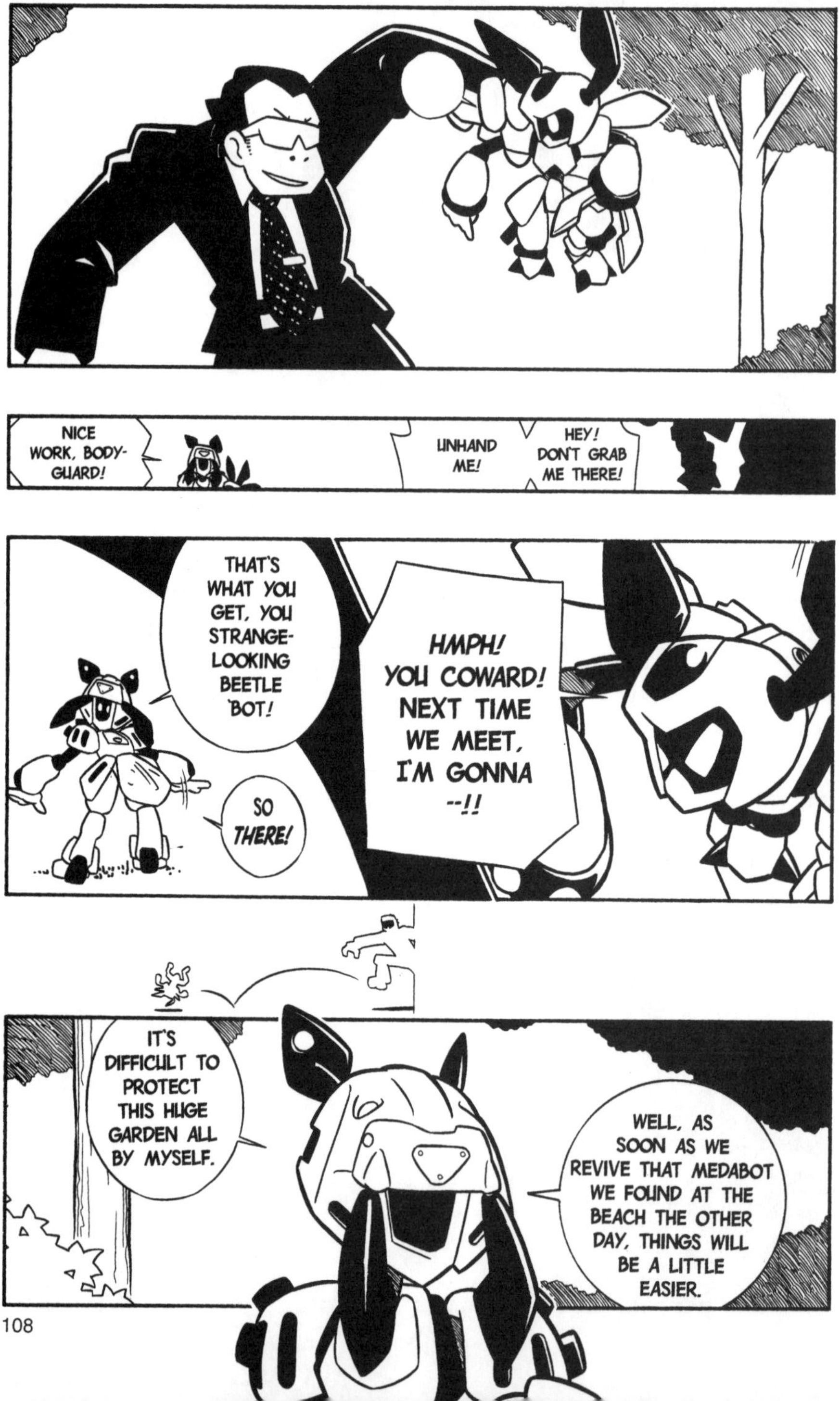
NICE WORK, BODY-GUARD!
UNHAND ME!
HEY! DON'T GRAB ME THERE!
THAT'S WHAT YOU GET, YOU STRANGE-LOOKING BEETLE 'BOT!
SO THERE!
HMPH! YOU COWARD! NEXT TIME WE MEET, I'M GONNA --!!
IT'S DIFFICULT TO PROTECT THIS HUGE GARDEN ALL BY MYSELF.
WELL, AS SOON AS WE REVIVE THAT MEDABOT WE FOUND AT THE BEACH THE OTHER DAY, THINGS WILL BE A LITTLE EASIER.

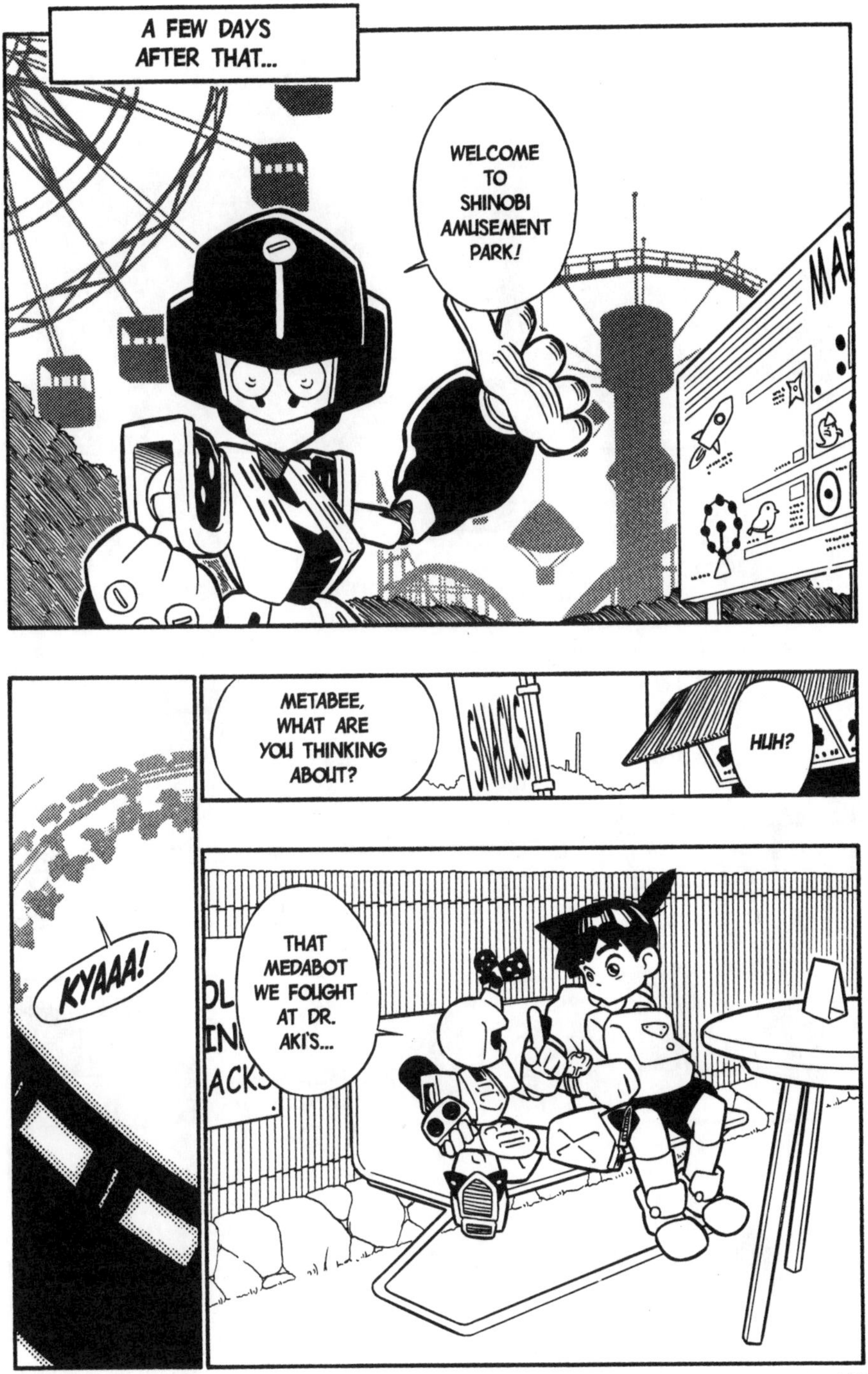

A FEW DAYS AFTER THAT...
WELCOME TO SHINOBI AMUSEMENT PARK!
MAI
KYAAA!
METABEE, WHAT ARE YOU THINKING ABOUT?
SNACKS
HUH?
THAT MEDABOT WE FOUGHT AT DR. AKI'S...

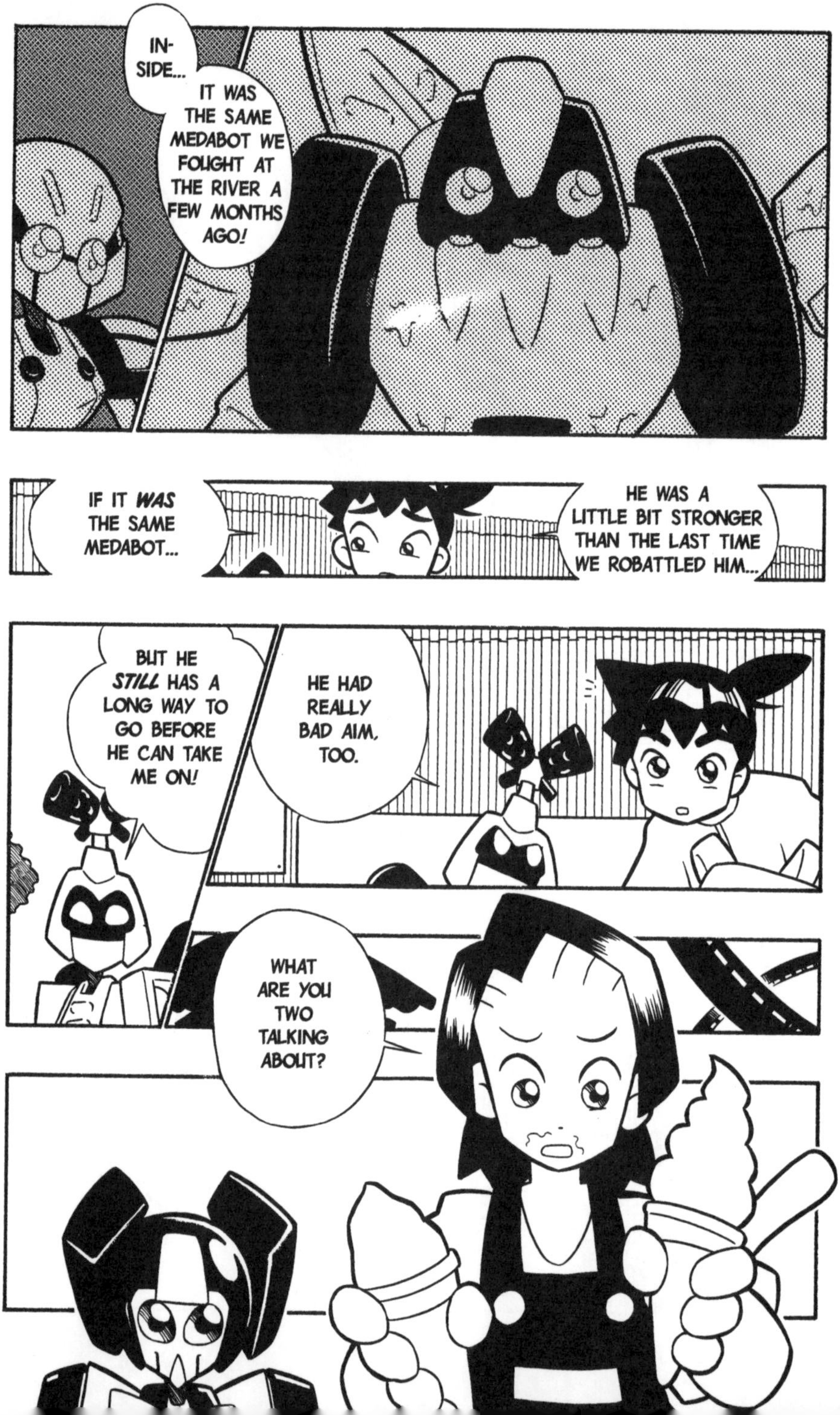
INSIDE...
IT WAS THE SAME MEDABOT WE FOUGHT AT THE RIVER A FEW MONTHS AGO!
IF IT WAS THE SAME MEDABOT...
HE WAS A LITTLE BIT STRONGER THAN THE LAST TIME WE ROBATTLED HIM...
BUT HE STILL HAS A LONG WAY TO GO BEFORE HE CAN TAKE ME ON!
HE HAD REALLY BAD AIM, TOO.
WHAT ARE YOU TWO TALKING ABOUT?

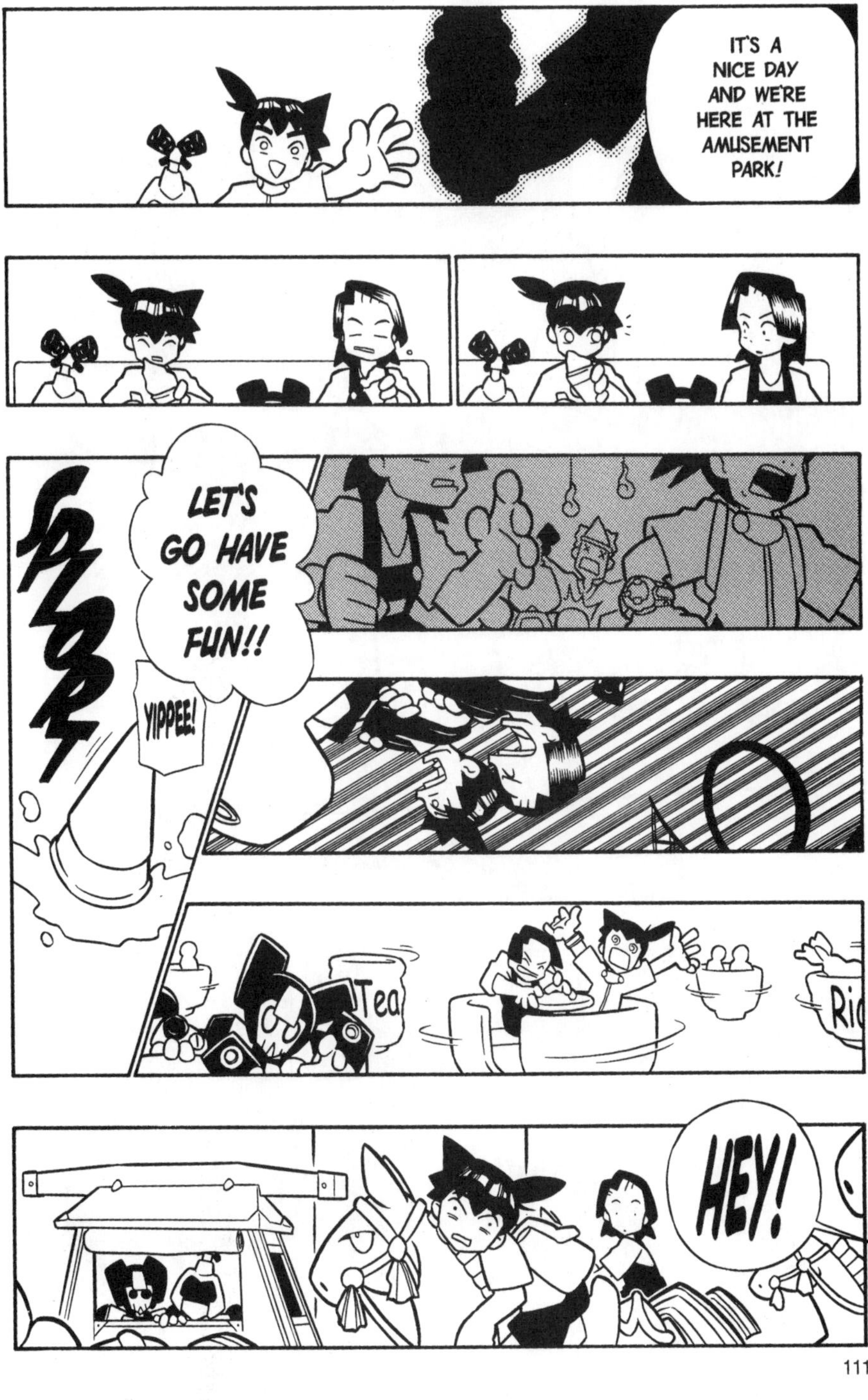
IT'S A NICE DAY AND WE'RE HERE AT THE AMUSEMENT PARK!
LET'S GO HAVE SOME FUN!!
SPLORT
YIPPEE!
Tea
Ri
HEY!

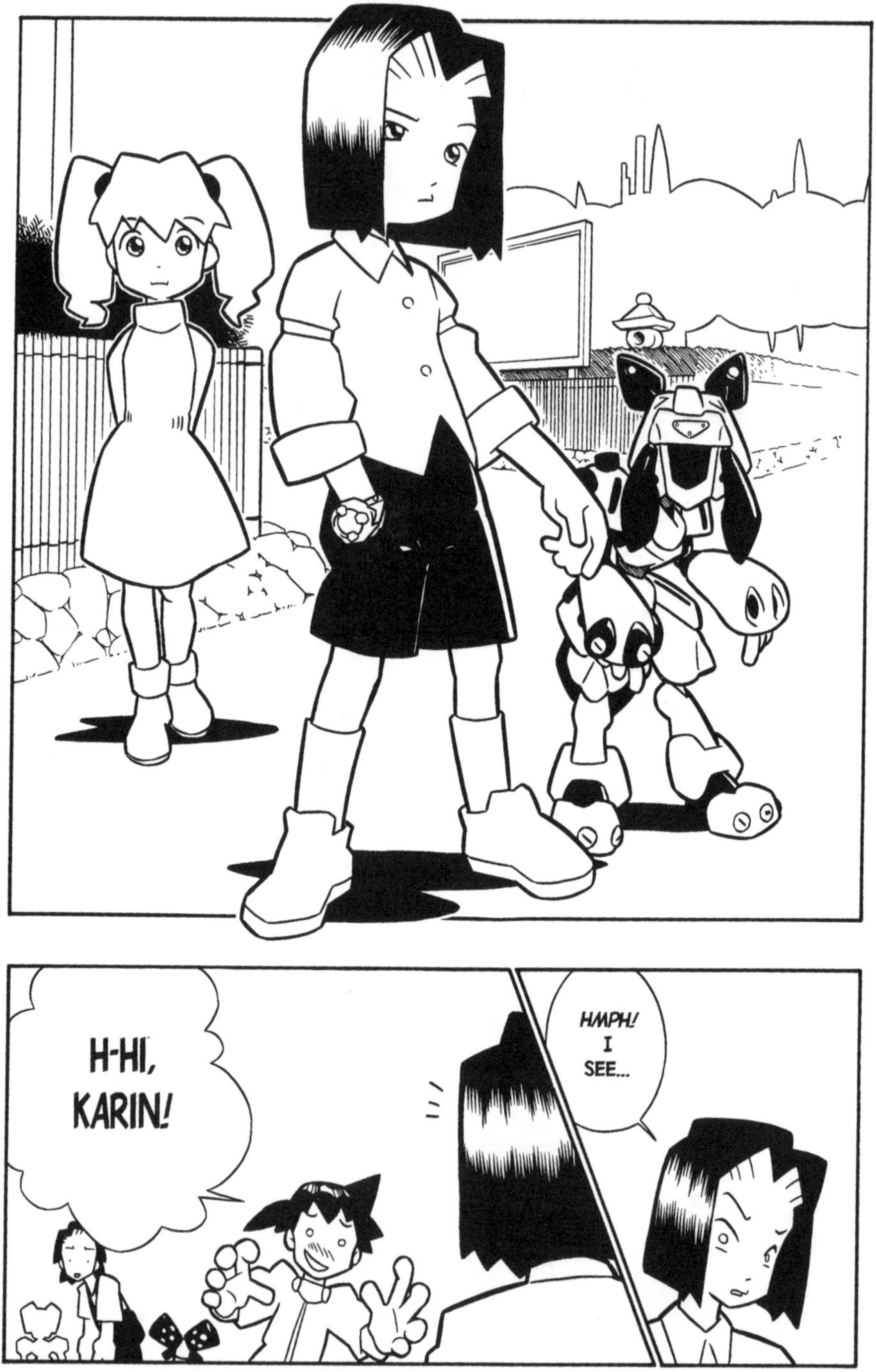
H-HI, KARIN!
HMPH! I SEE...

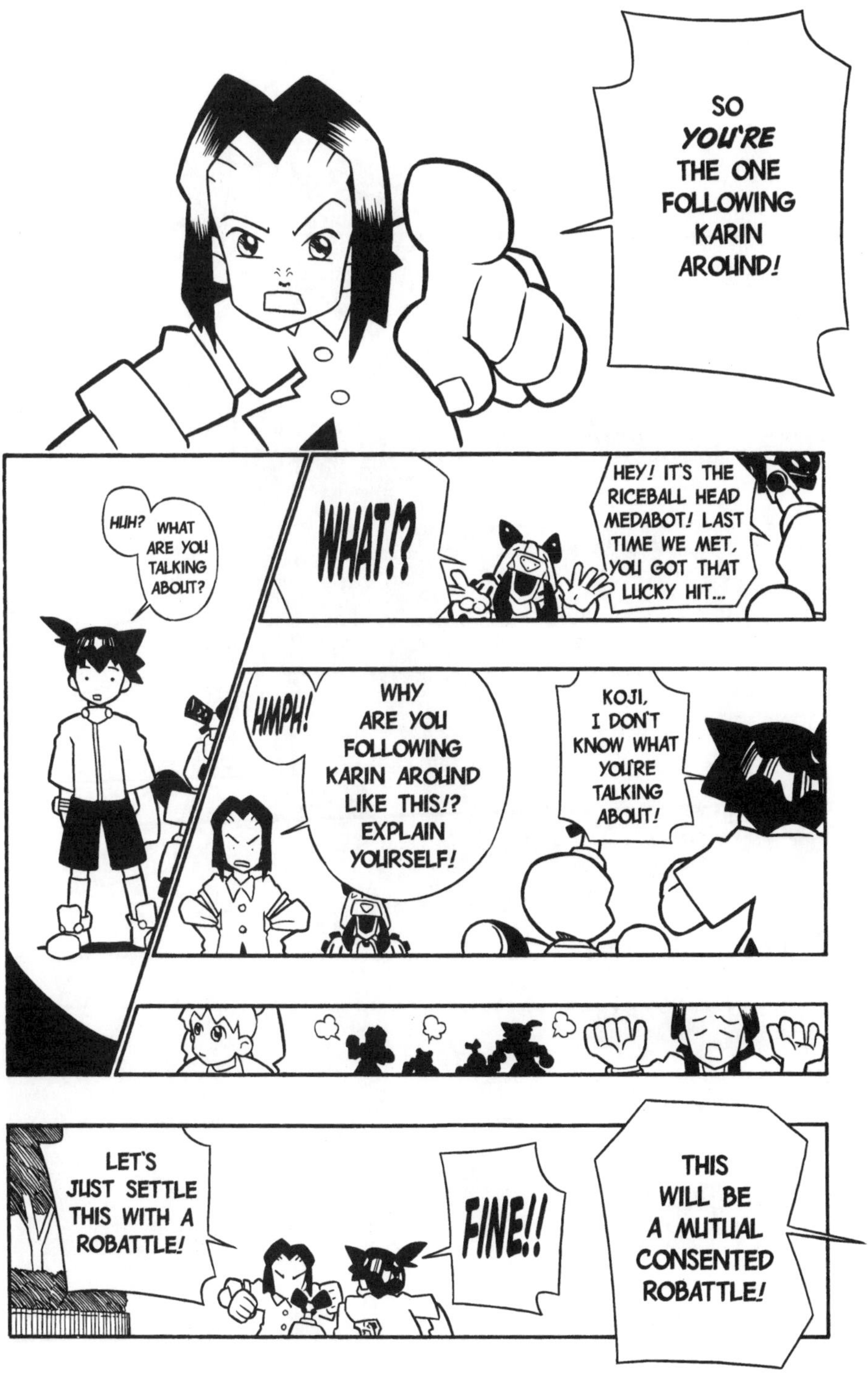
SO YOU'RE THE ONE FOLLOWING KARIN AROUND!
HUH? WHAT ARE YOU TALKING ABOUT?
WHAT!?
HEY! IT'S THE RICEBALL HEAD MEDABOT! LAST TIME WE MET, YOU GOT THAT LUCKY HIT...
HMPH!
WHY ARE YOU FOLLOWING KARIN AROUND LIKE THIS!? EXPLAIN YOURSELF!
KOJI, I DON'T KNOW WHAT YOU'RE TALKING ABOUT!
LET'S JUST SETTLE THIS WITH A ROBATTLE!
FINE!!
THIS WILL BE A MUTUAL CONSENTED ROBATTLE!

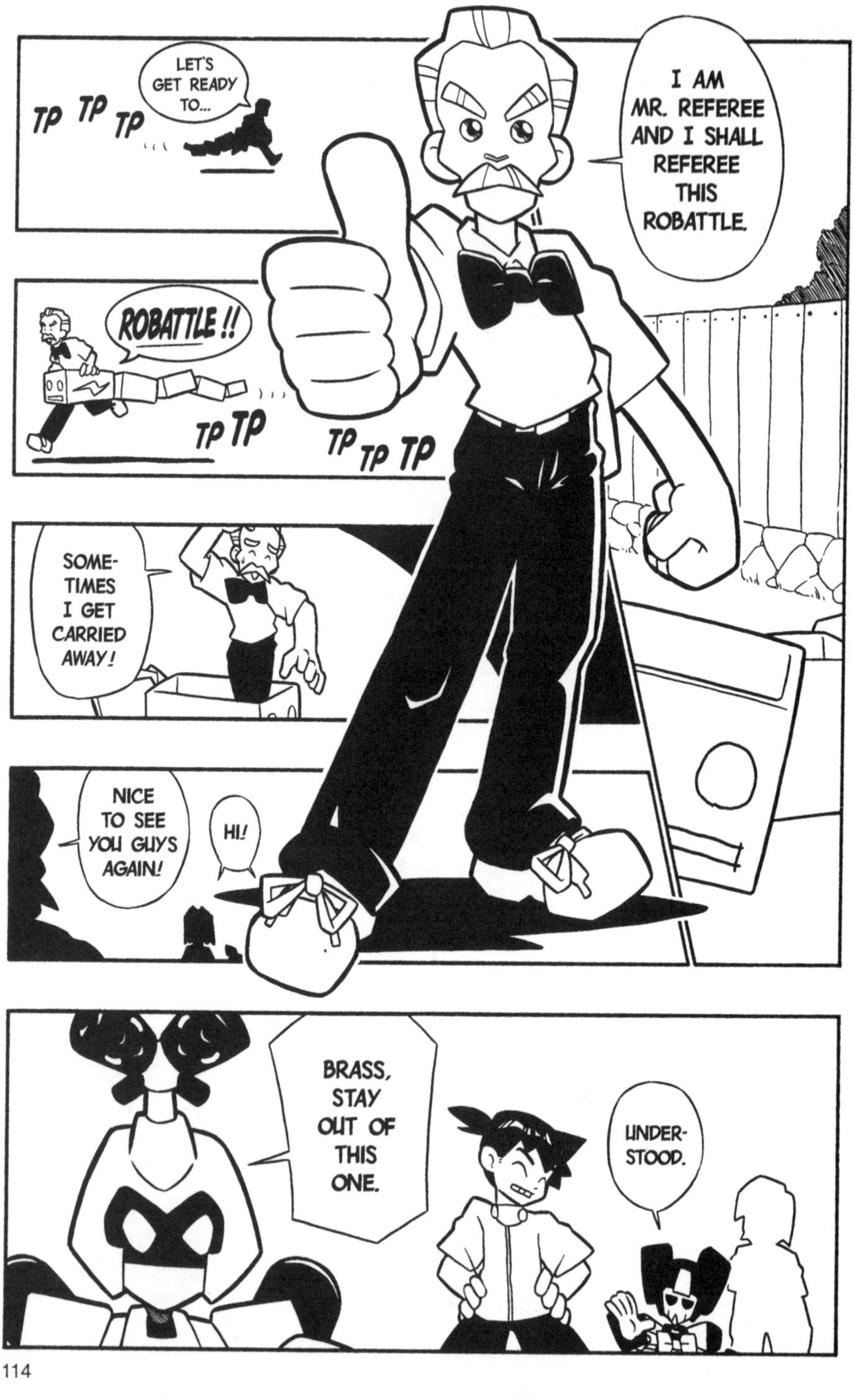
TP TP TP
LET'S GET READY TO...
I AM MR. REFEREE AND I SHALL REFEREE THIS ROBATTLE.
ROBATTLE !!
TP TP
TP TP TP
SOME-TIMES I GET CARRIED AWAY!
NICE TO SEE YOU GUYS AGAIN!
HI!
BRASS, STAY OUT OF THIS ONE.
UNDER-STOOD.

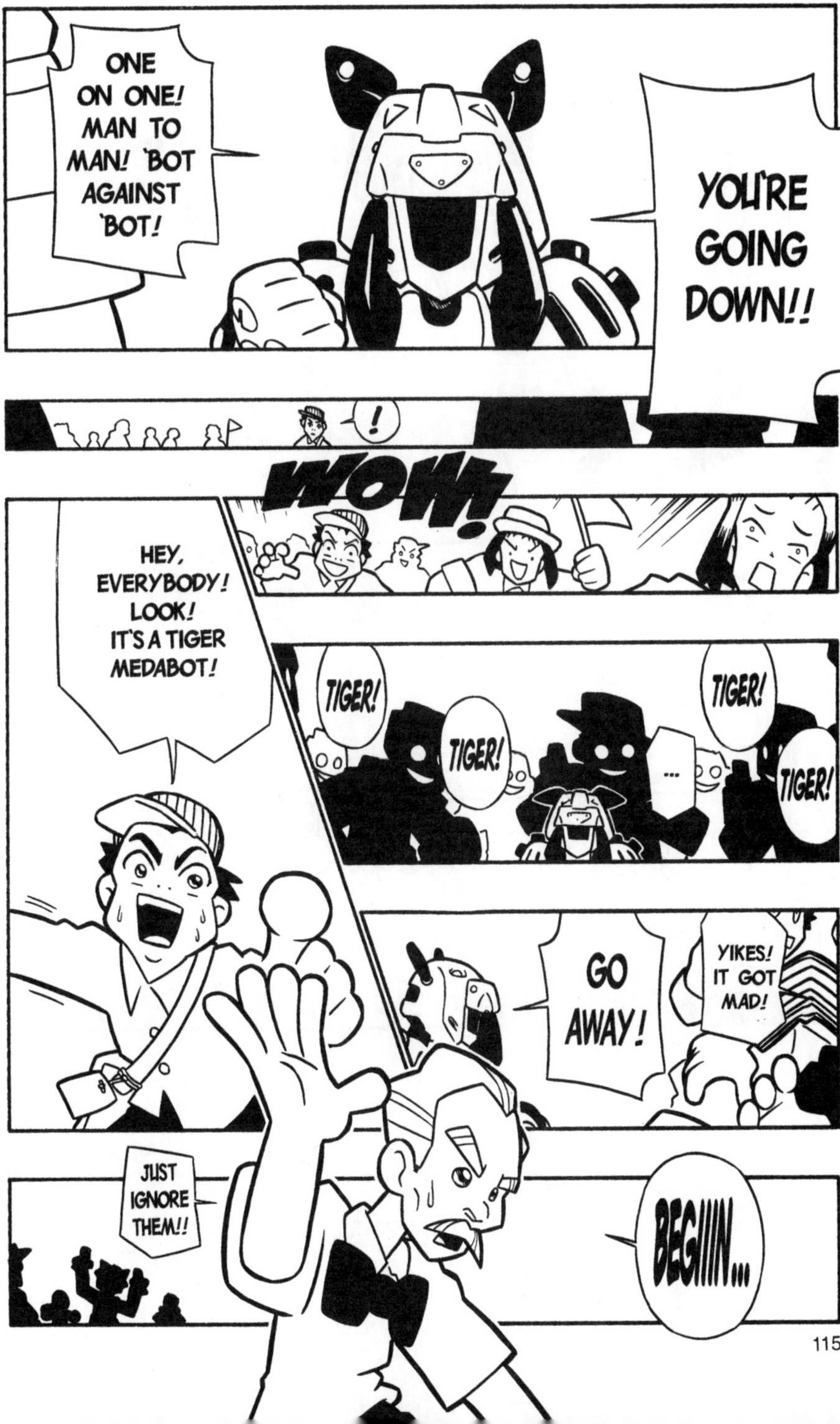
ONE ON ONE! MAN TO MAN! 'BOT AGAINST 'BOT!
YOU'RE GOING DOWN!!
!
WOW!
HEY, EVERYBODY! LOOK! IT'S A TIGER MEDABOT!
TIGER!
TIGER!
...
TIGER!
TIGER!
GO AWAY!
YIKES! IT GOT MAD!
JUST IGNORE THEM!!
BEGIIIN...

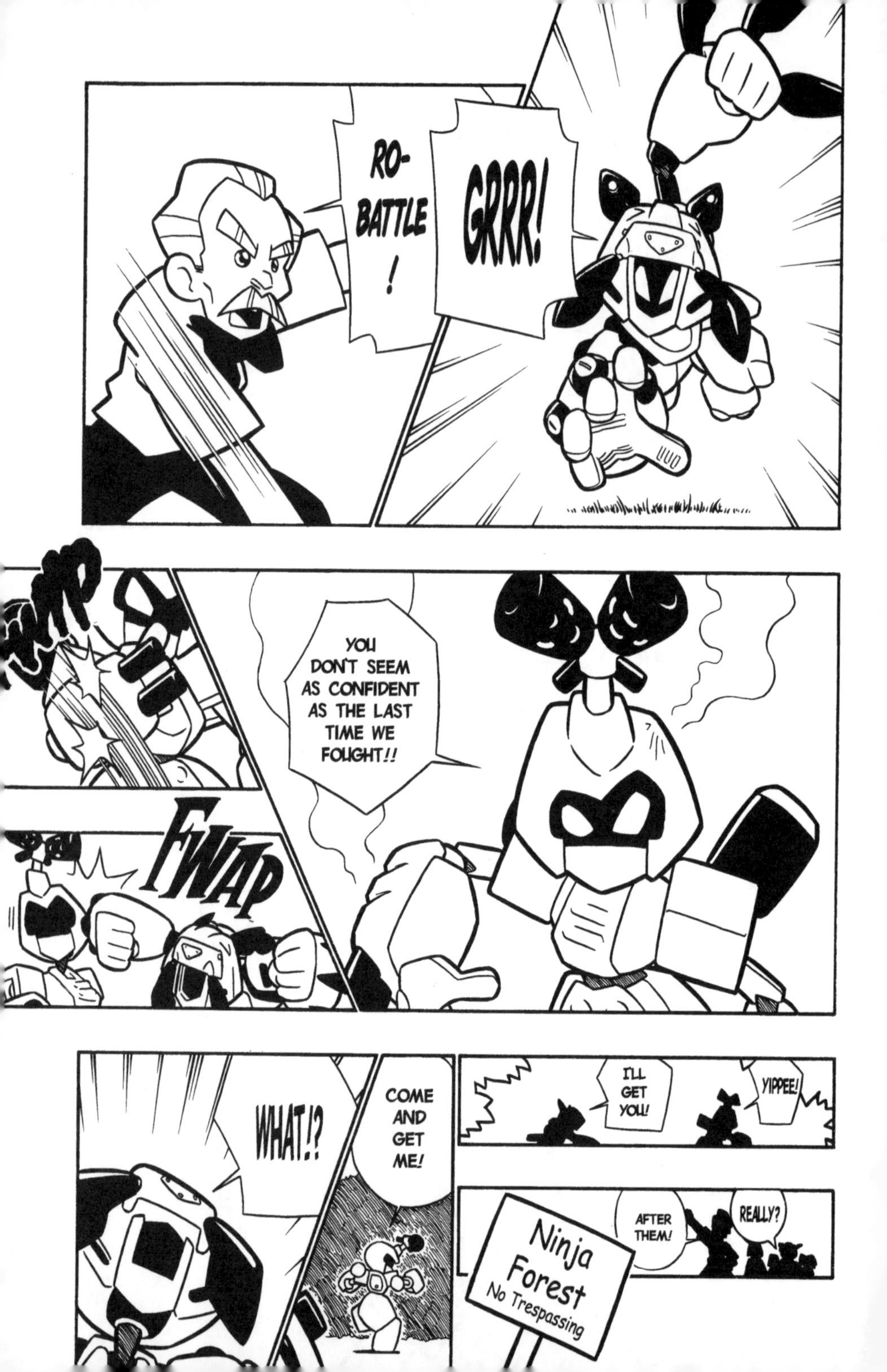
RO-BATTLE!
GRRR!
FWAP
YOU DON'T SEEM AS CONFIDENT AS THE LAST TIME WE FOUGHT!!
WHAT!?
COME AND GET ME!
I'LL GET YOU!
YIPPEE!
Ninja Forest
No Trespassing
AFTER THEM!
REALLY?

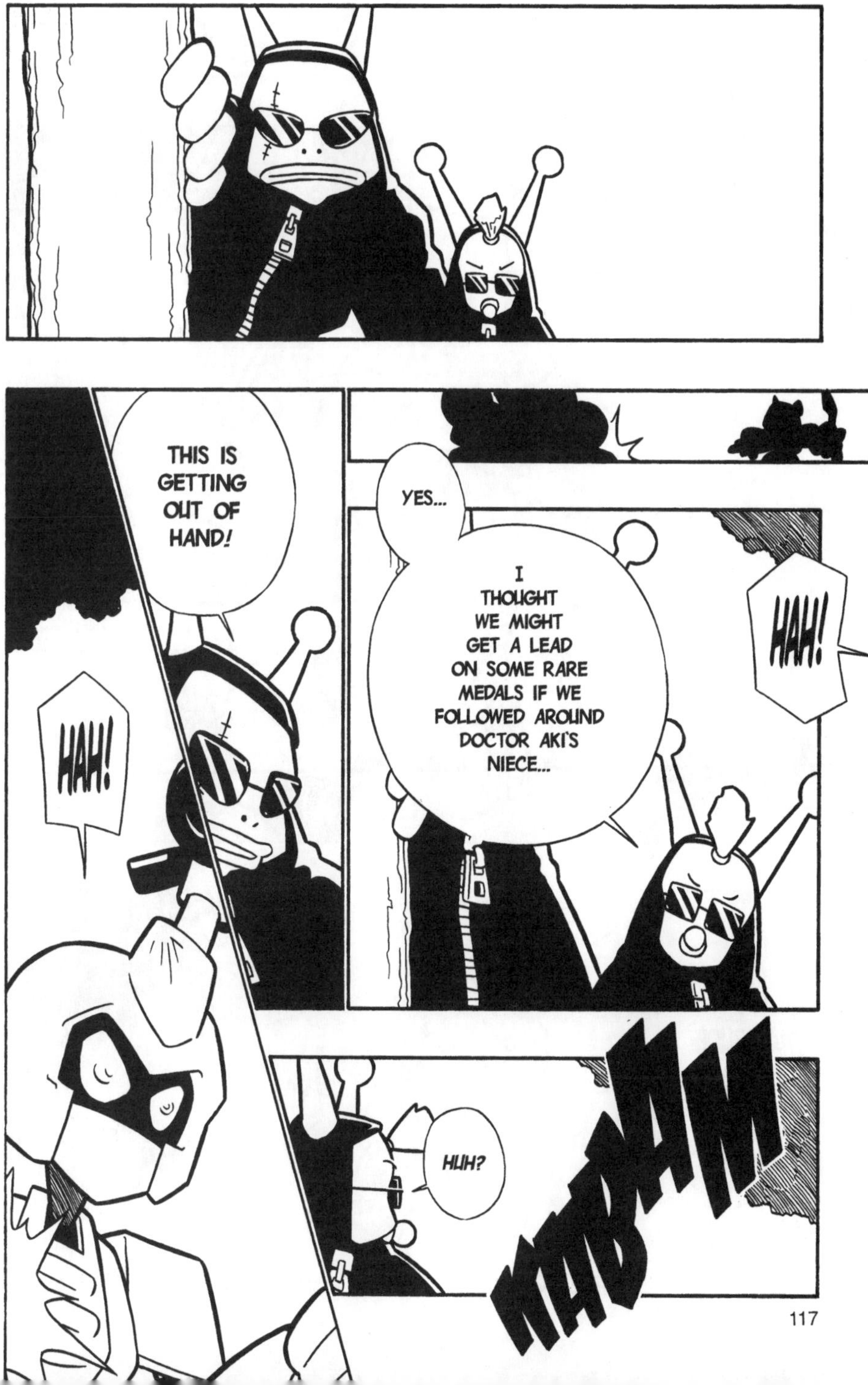
THIS IS GETTING OUT OF HAND!
HAH!
YES...
I THOUGHT WE MIGHT GET A LEAD ON SOME RARE MEDALS IF WE FOLLOWED AROUND DOCTOR AKI'S NIECE...
HAH!
HUH?
KABAM!

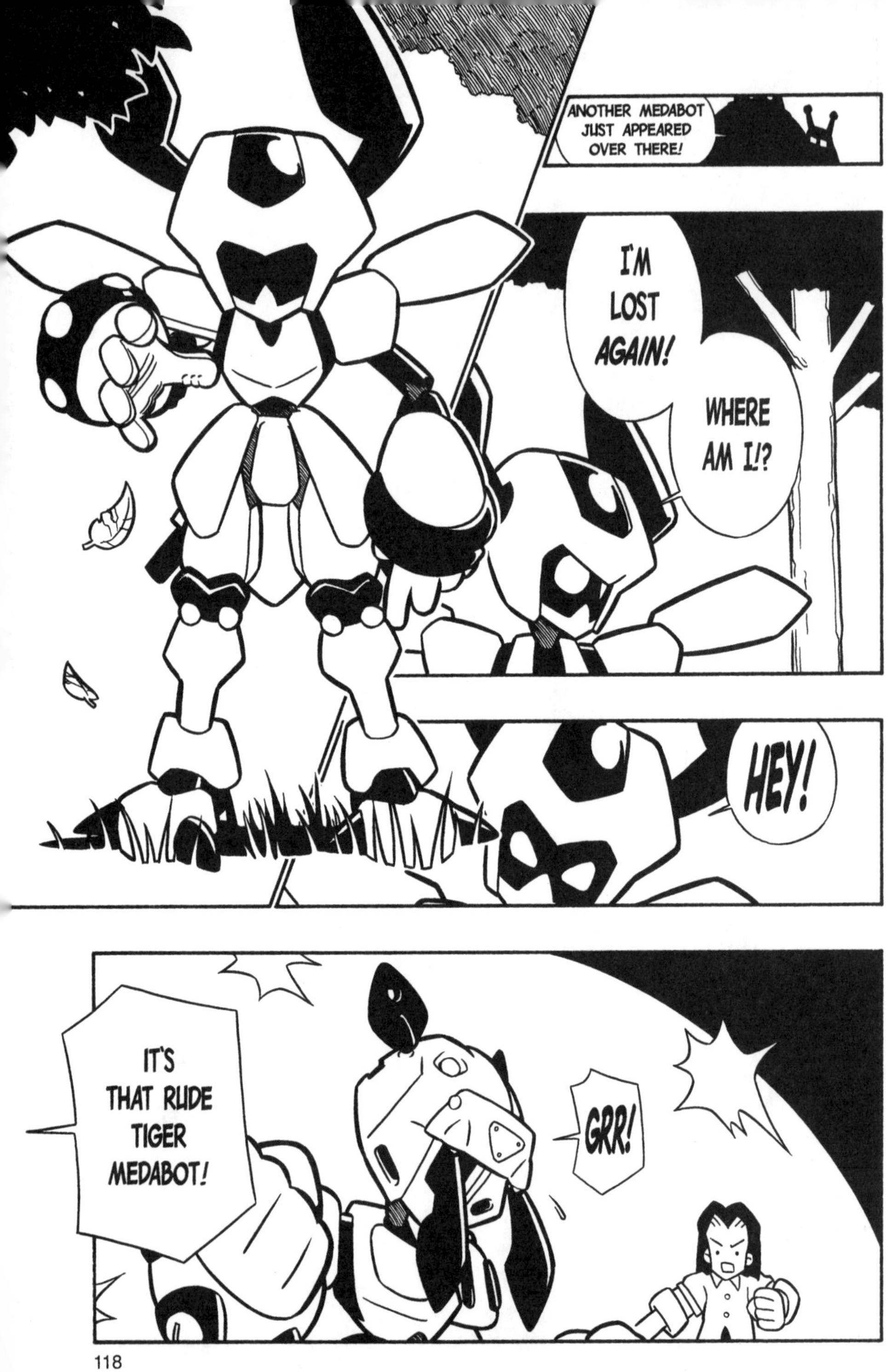
ANOTHER MEDABOT JUST APPEARED OVER THERE!
I'M LOST AGAIN!
WHERE AM I!?
HEY!
IT'S THAT RUDE TIGER MEDABOT!
GRR!

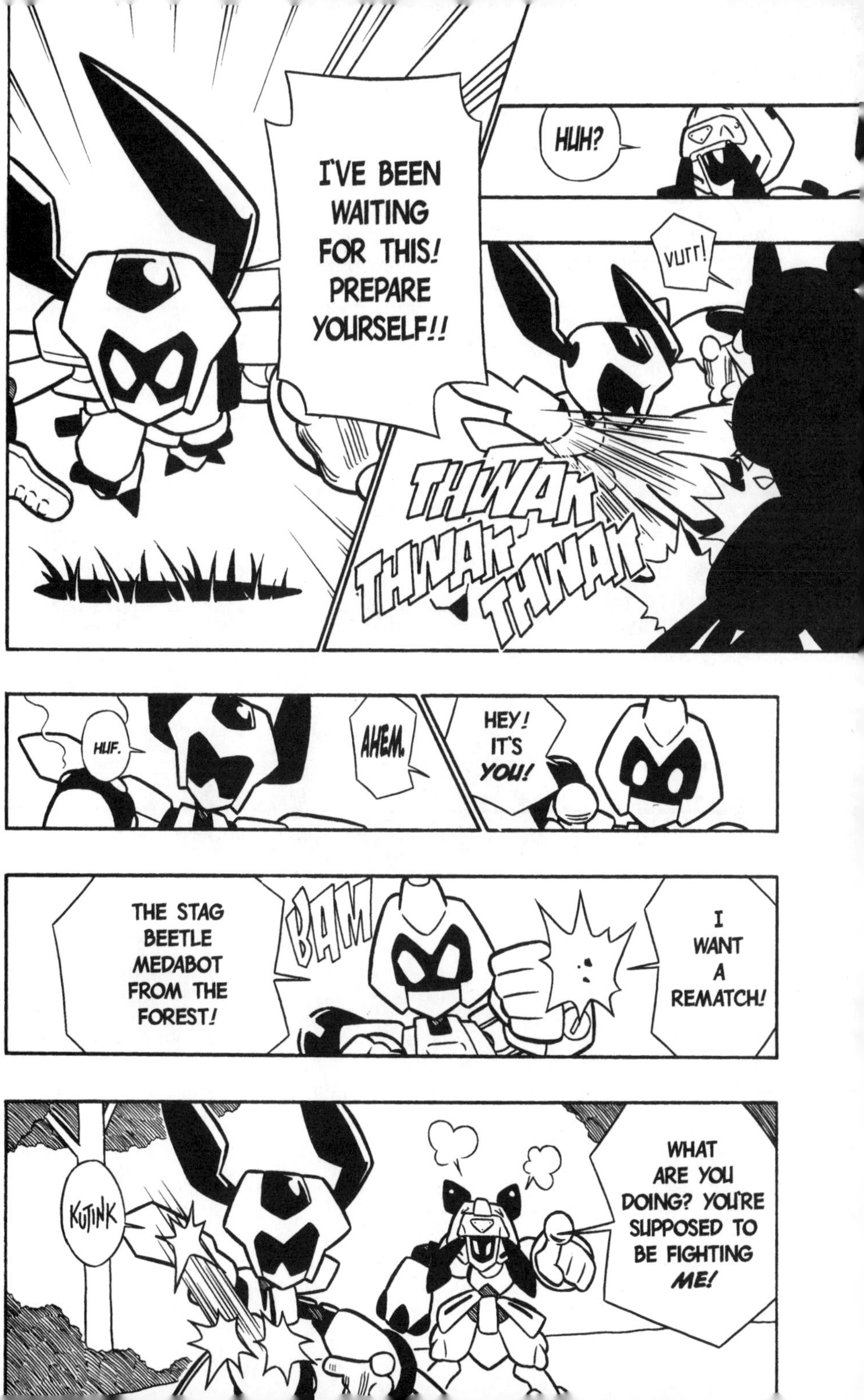
I'VE BEEN WAITING FOR THIS! PREPARE YOURSELF!!
HUH?
VUTT!
THWAK THWAK THWAK
HUF.
AHEM.
HEY! IT'S YOU!
THE STAG BEETLE MEDABOT FROM THE FOREST!
BAM
I WANT A REMATCH!
KUTINK
WHAT ARE YOU DOING? YOU'RE SUPPOSED TO BE FIGHTING ME!

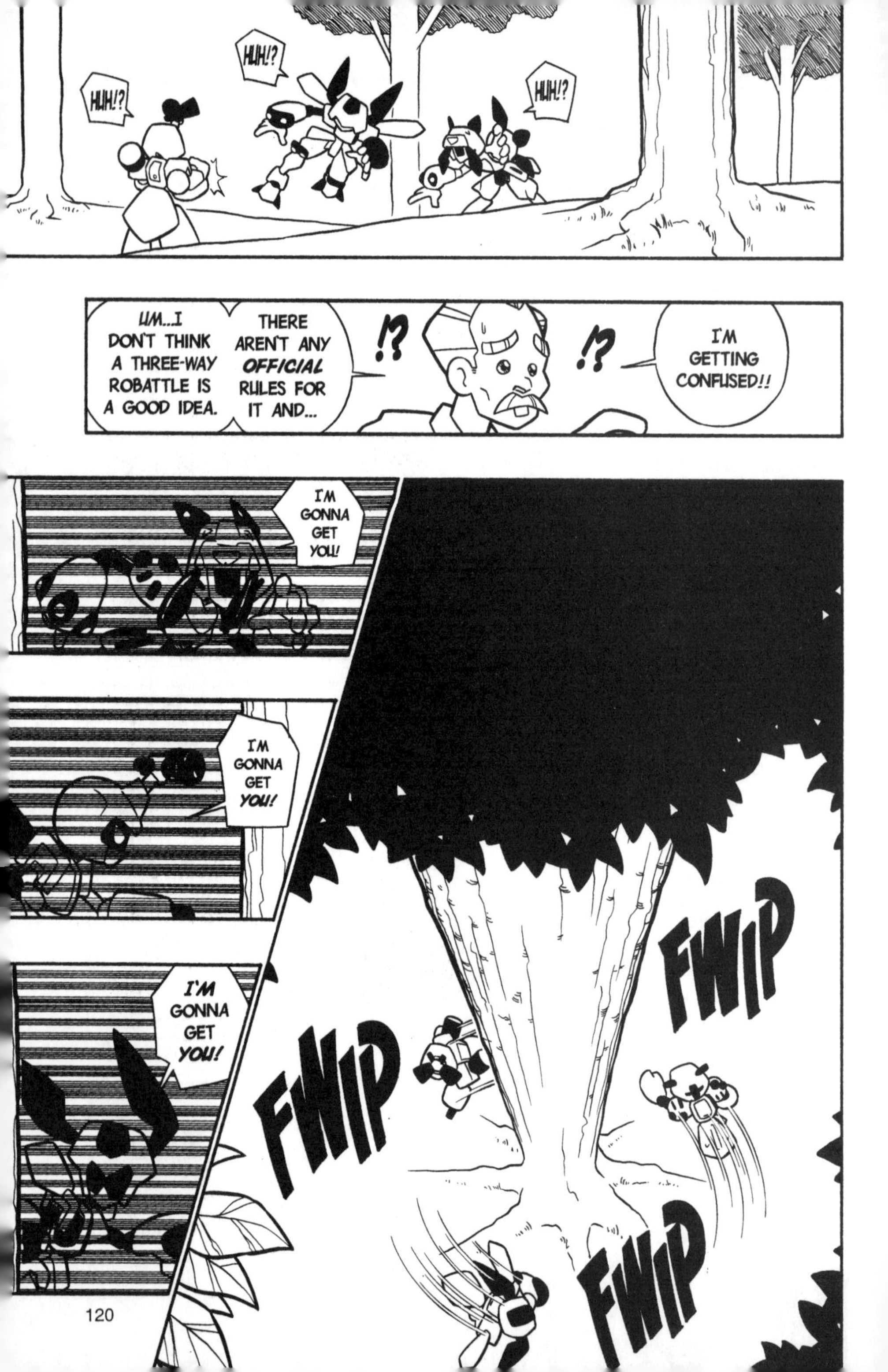
HUH!?
HUH!?
HUH!?
UM...I DON'T THINK A THREE-WAY ROBATTLE IS A GOOD IDEA.
THERE AREN'T ANY OFFICIAL RULES FOR IT AND...
!?
!?
I'M GETTING CONFUSED!!
I'M GONNA GET YOU!
I'M GONNA GET YOU!
I'M GONNA GET YOU!
FWIP
FWIP
FWIP

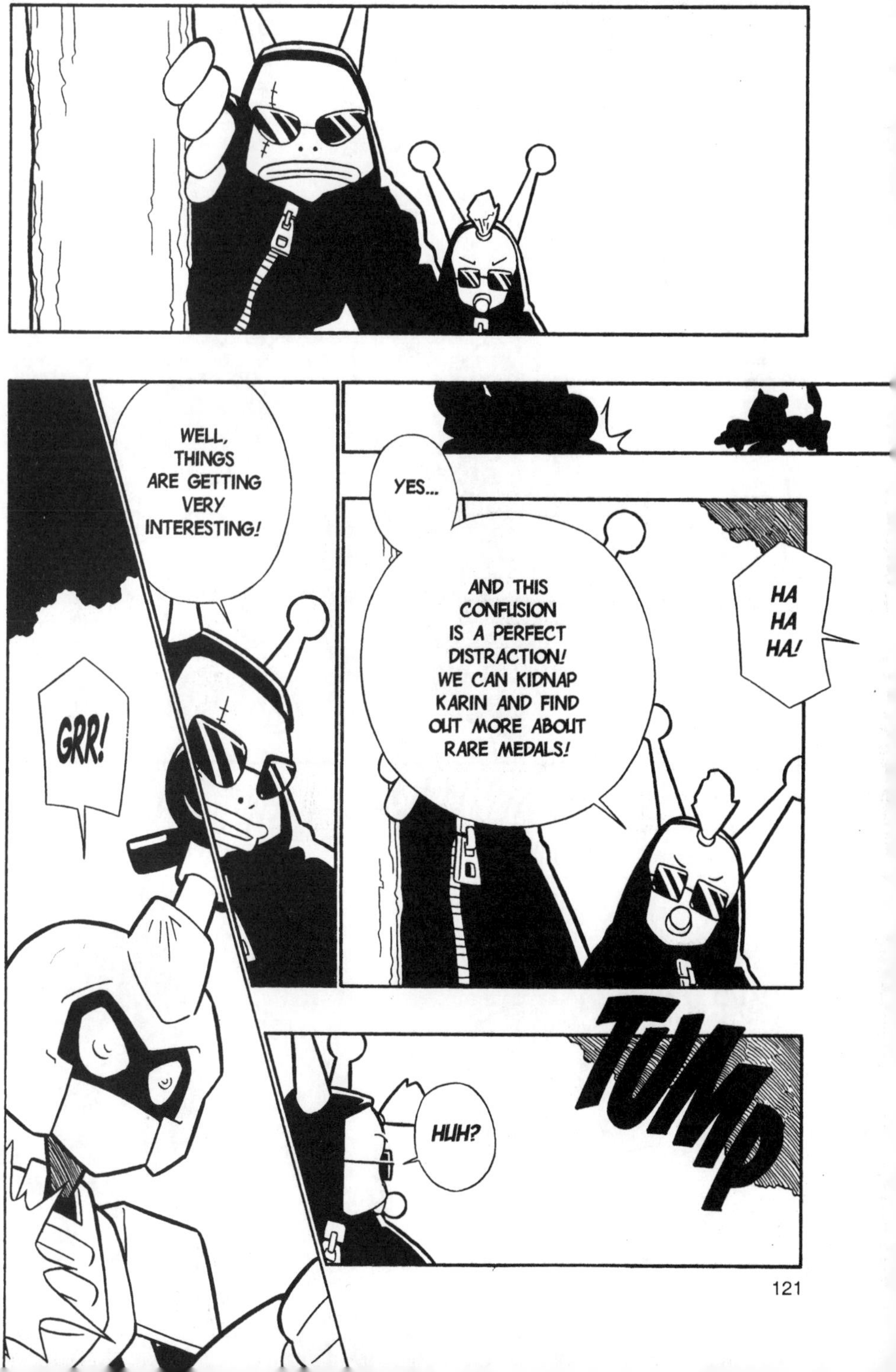
WELL, THINGS ARE GETTING VERY INTERESTING!
GRR!
YES...
AND THIS CONFUSION IS A PERFECT DISTRACTION! WE CAN KIDNAP KARIN AND FIND OUT MORE ABOUT RARE MEDALS!
HA HA HA!
TUMP
HUH?

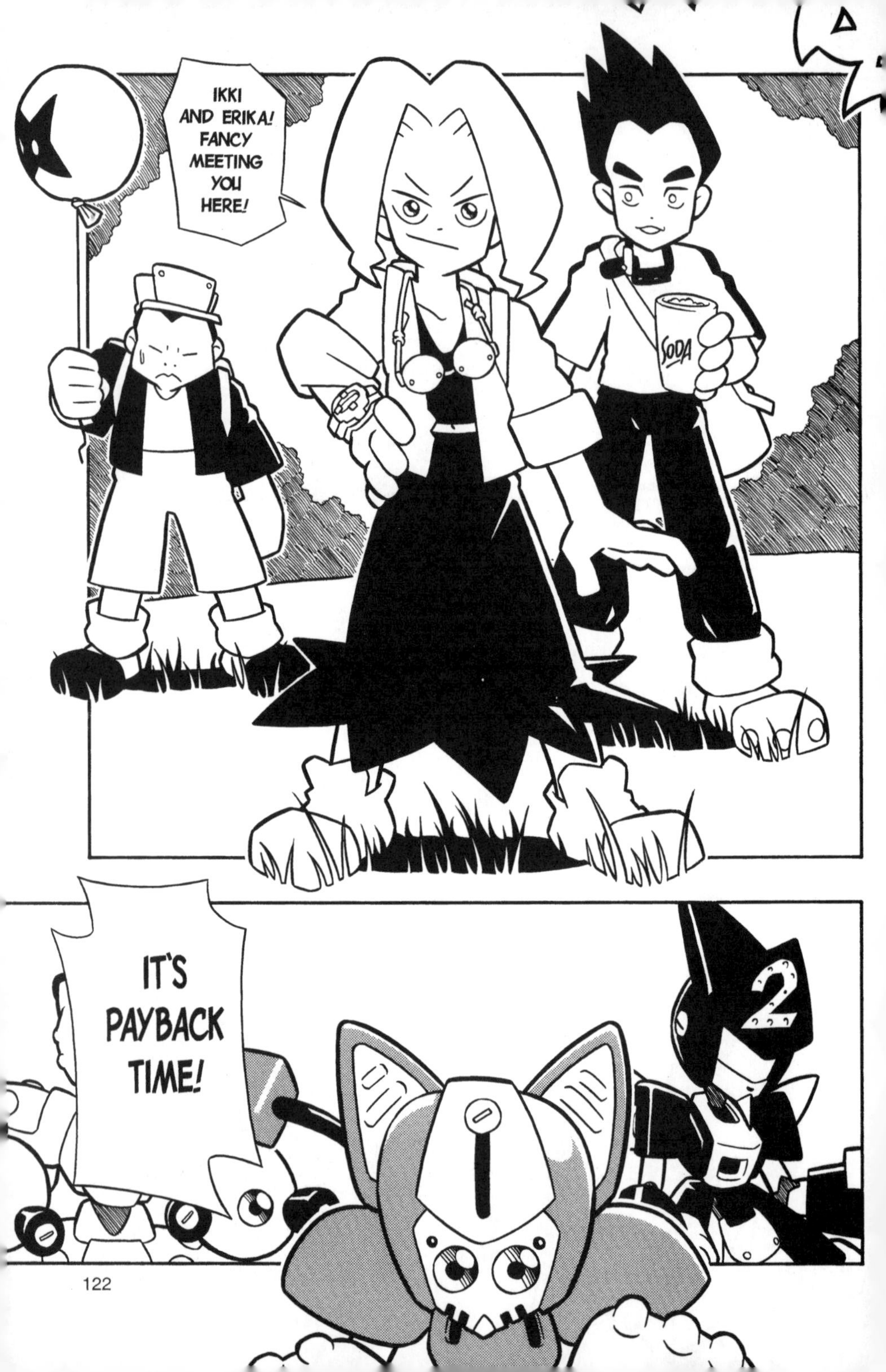
IKKI AND ERIKA! FANCY MEETING YOU HERE!
IT'S PAYBACK TIME!

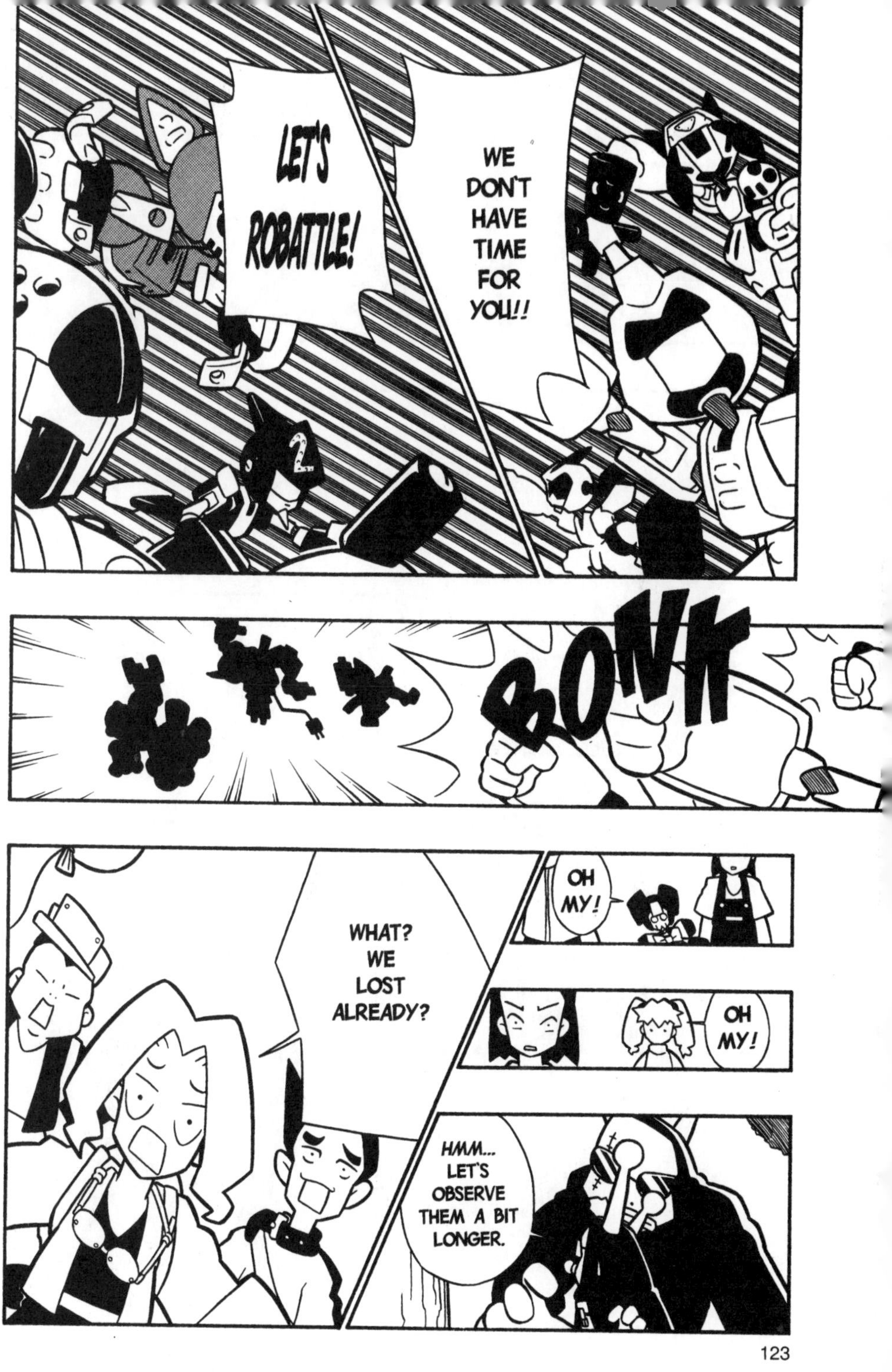
LET'S ROBATTLE!
WE DON'T HAVE TIME FOR YOU!!
BONK
WHAT? WE LOST ALREADY?
OH MY!
OH MY!
HMM... LET'S OBSERVE THEM A BIT LONGER.

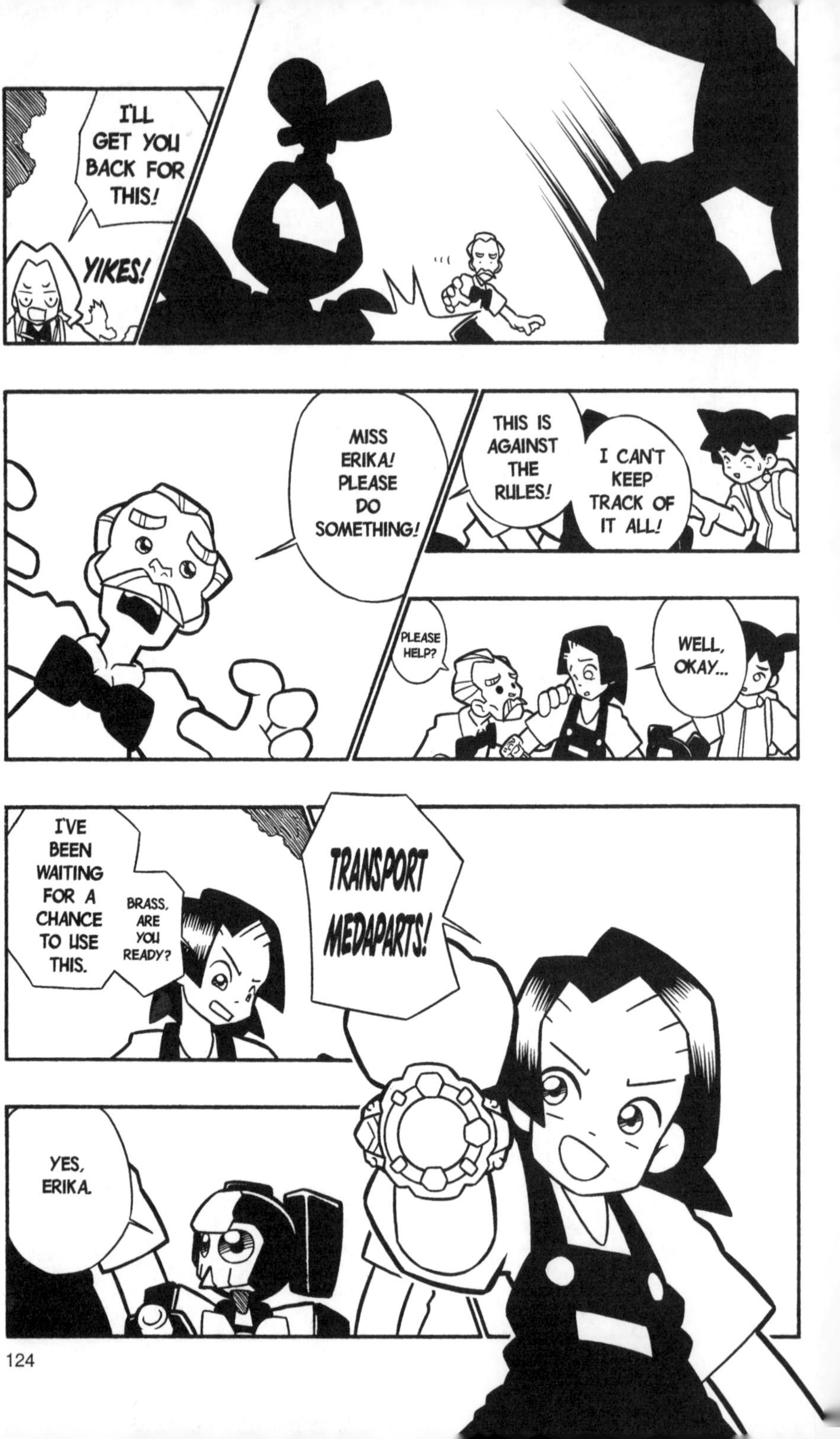
I'LL GET YOU BACK FOR THIS!
YIKES!
MISS ERIKA! PLEASE DO SOMETHING!
THIS IS AGAINST THE RULES!
I CAN'T KEEP TRACK OF IT ALL!
PLEASE HELP?
WELL, OKAY...
I'VE BEEN WAITING FOR A CHANCE TO USE THIS.
BRASS, ARE YOU READY?
TRANSPORT MEDAPARTS!
YES, ERIKA.

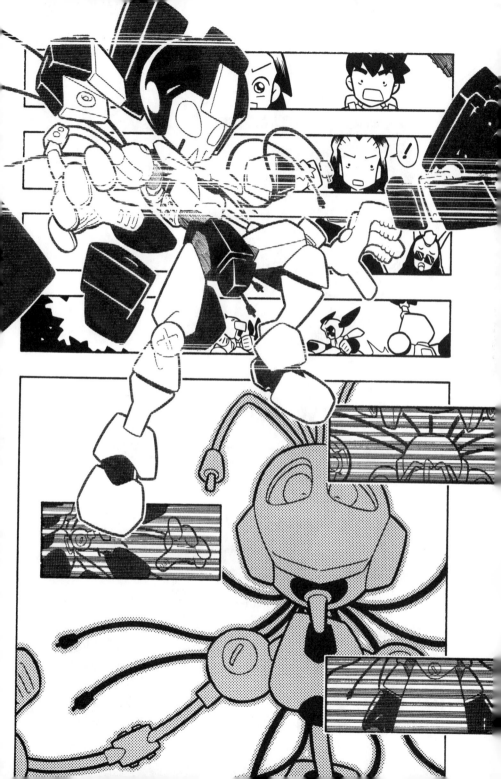

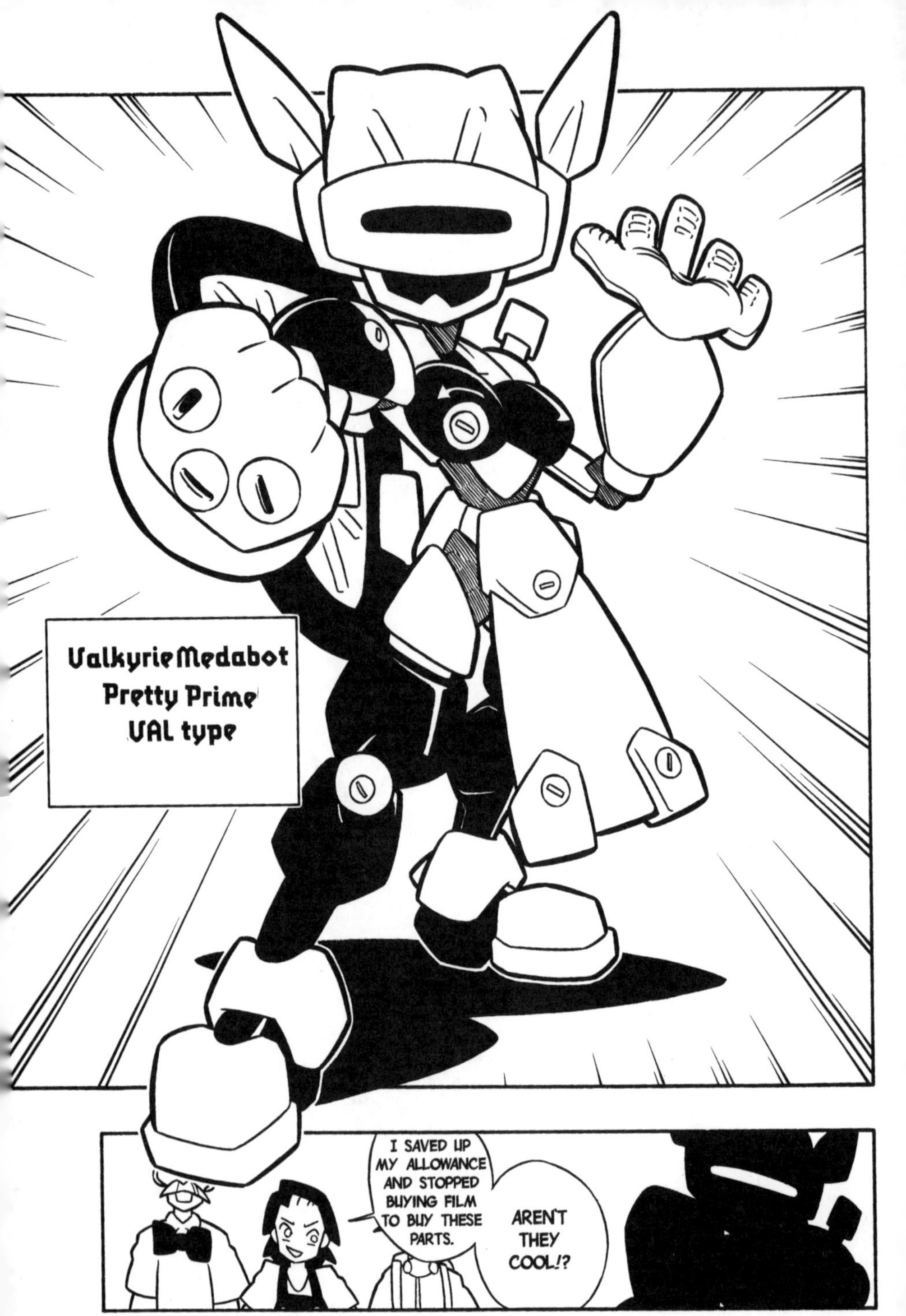
Valkyrie Medabot
Pretty Prime
VAL type
I SAVED UP MY ALLOWANCE AND STOPPED BUYING FILM TO BUY THESE PARTS.
AREN'T THEY COOL!?

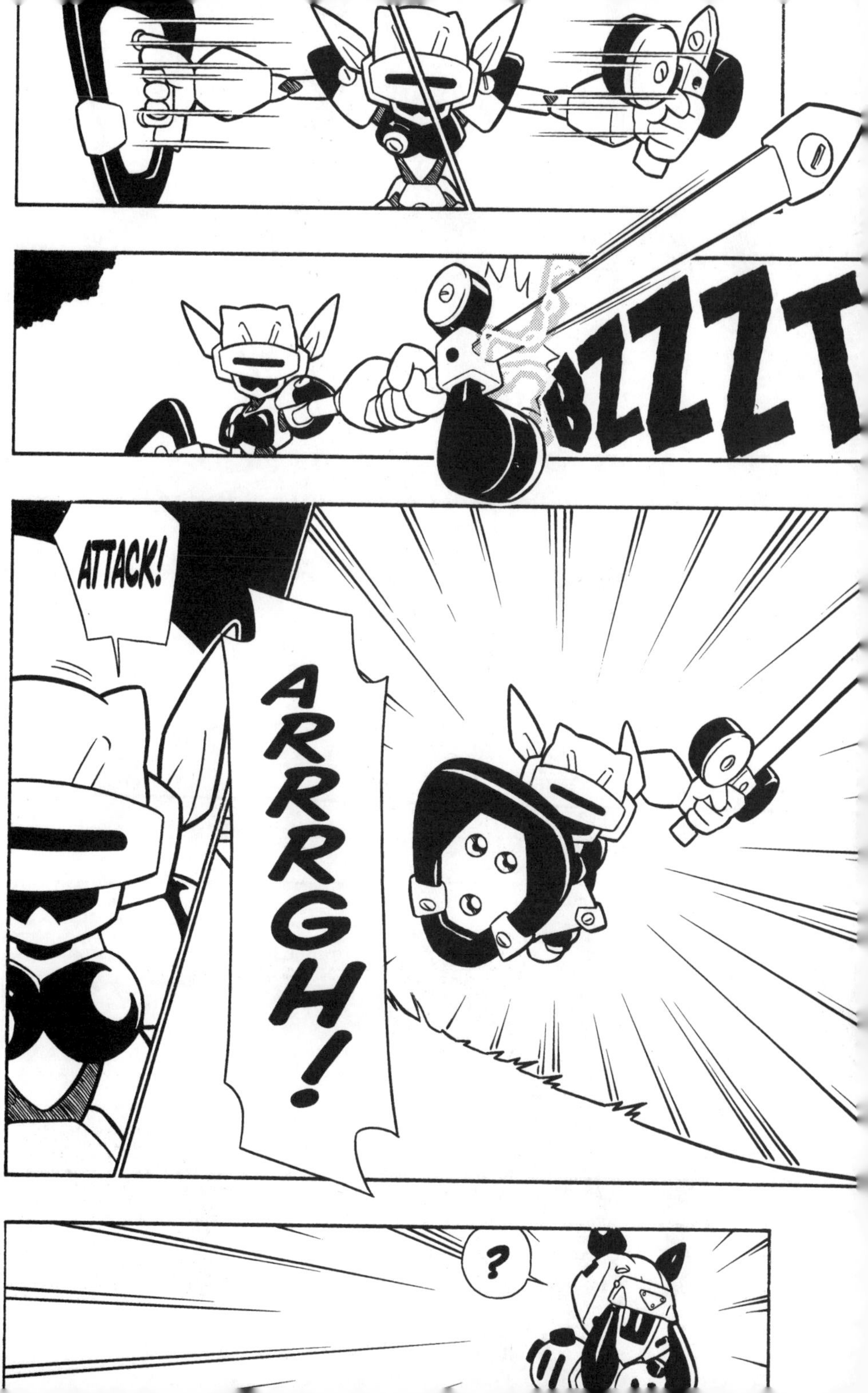
BZZZT
ATTACK!
ARRRGH!
?

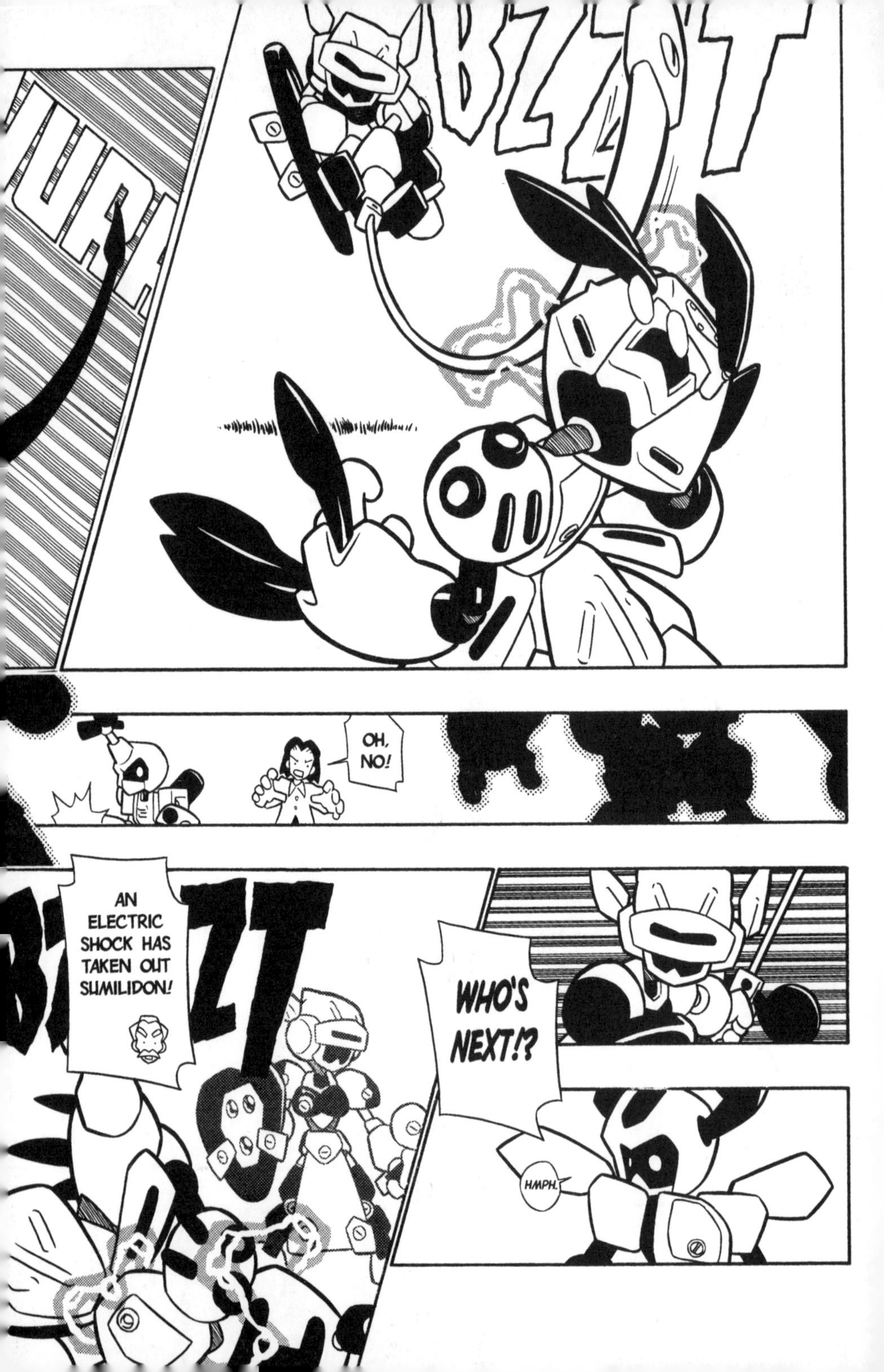
OH, NO!
AN ELECTRIC SHOCK HAS TAKEN OUT SUMILIDON!
WHO'S NEXT!?
HMPH.

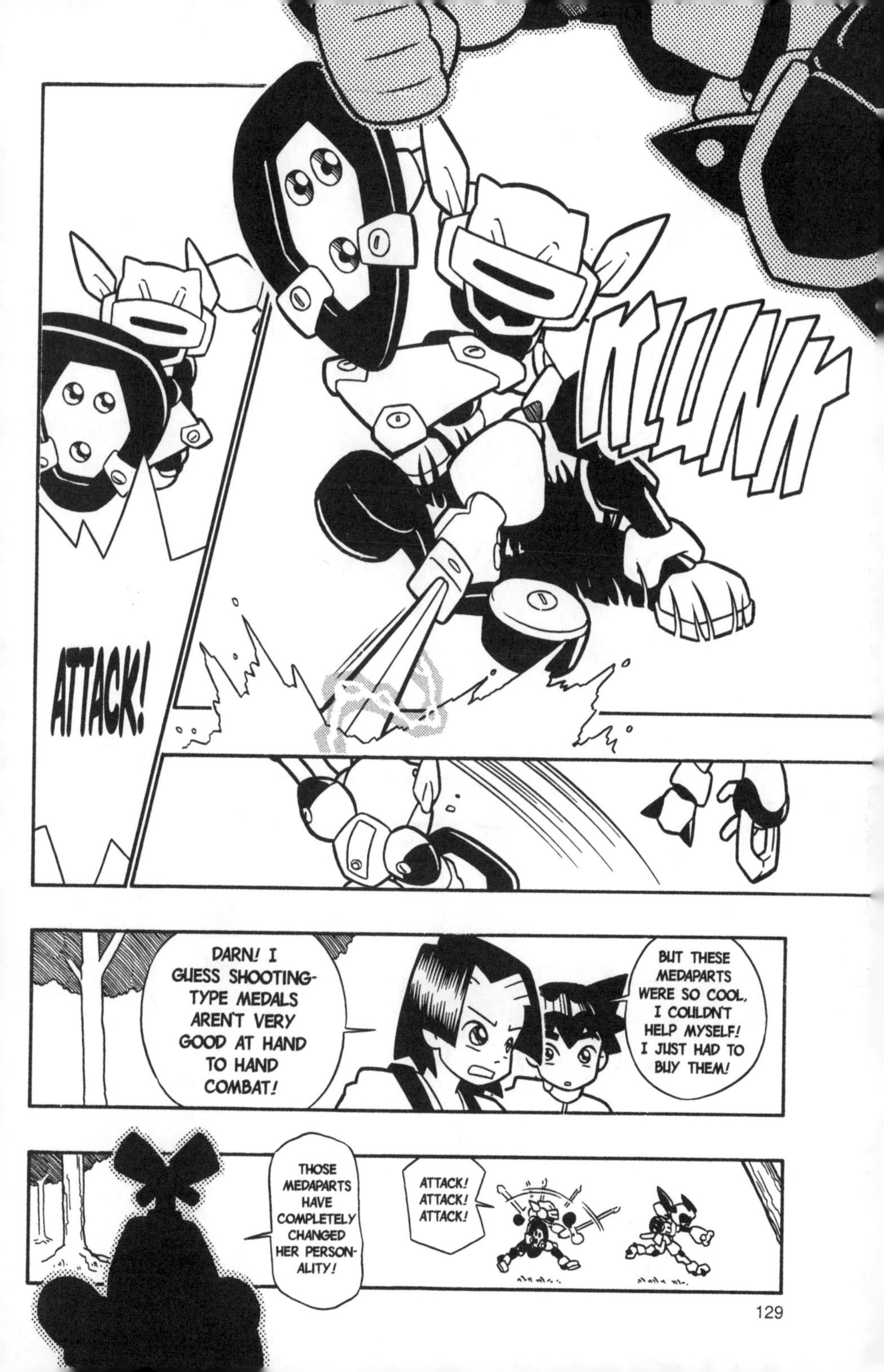
KLUNK
ATTACK!
DARN! I GUESS SHOOTING-TYPE MEDALS AREN'T VERY GOOD AT HAND TO HAND COMBAT!
BUT THESE MEDAPARTS WERE SO COOL, I COULDN'T HELP MYSELF! I JUST HAD TO BUY THEM!
THOSE MEDAPARTS HAVE COMPLETELY CHANGED HER PERSON-ALITY!
ATTACK! ATTACK! ATTACK!

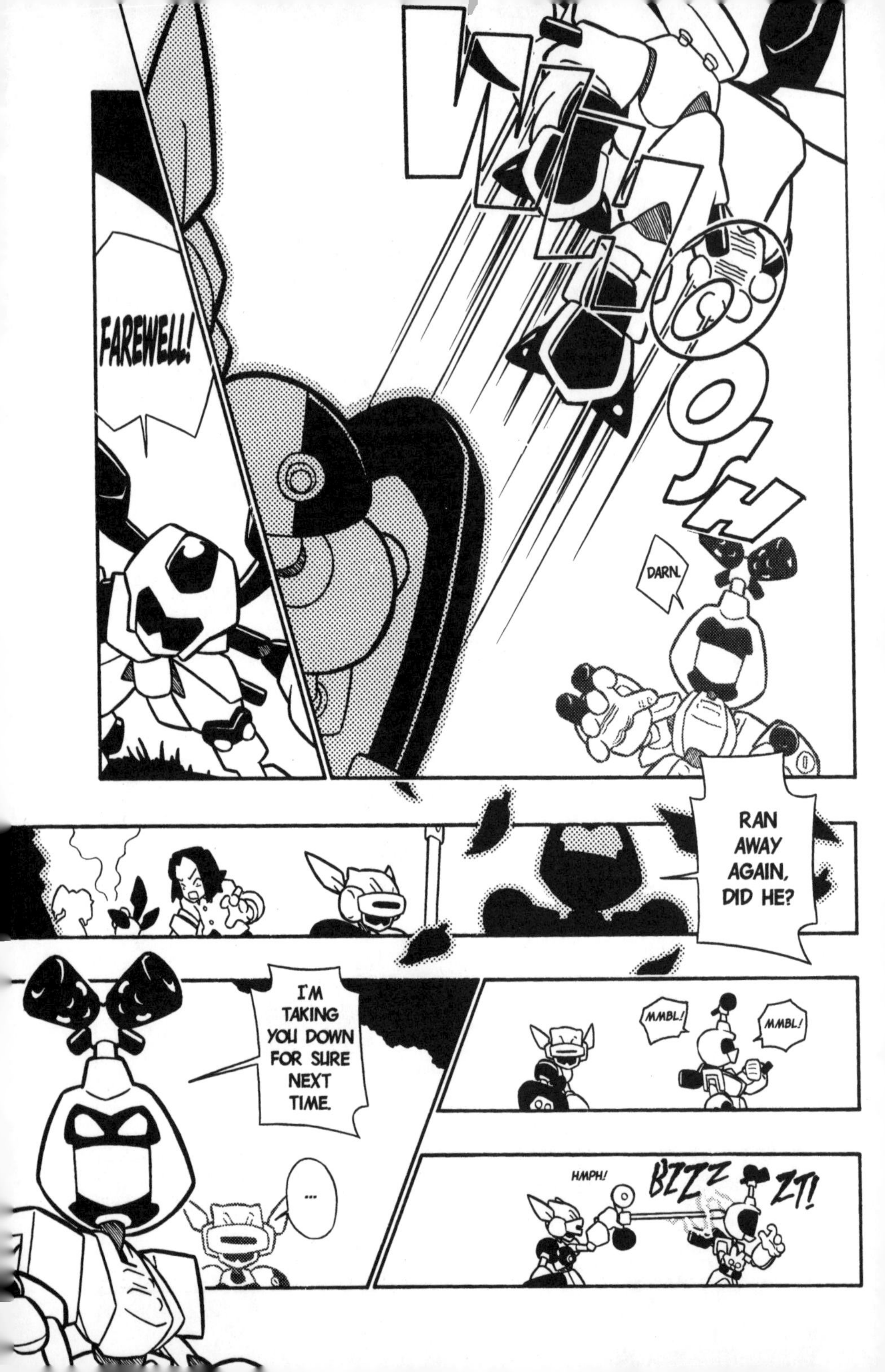
FAREWELL!
WHOOOSH
DARN.
RAN AWAY AGAIN, DID HE?
I'M TAKING YOU DOWN FOR SURE NEXT TIME.
...
MMBL!
MMBL!
HMPH!
BIZZZ ZT!

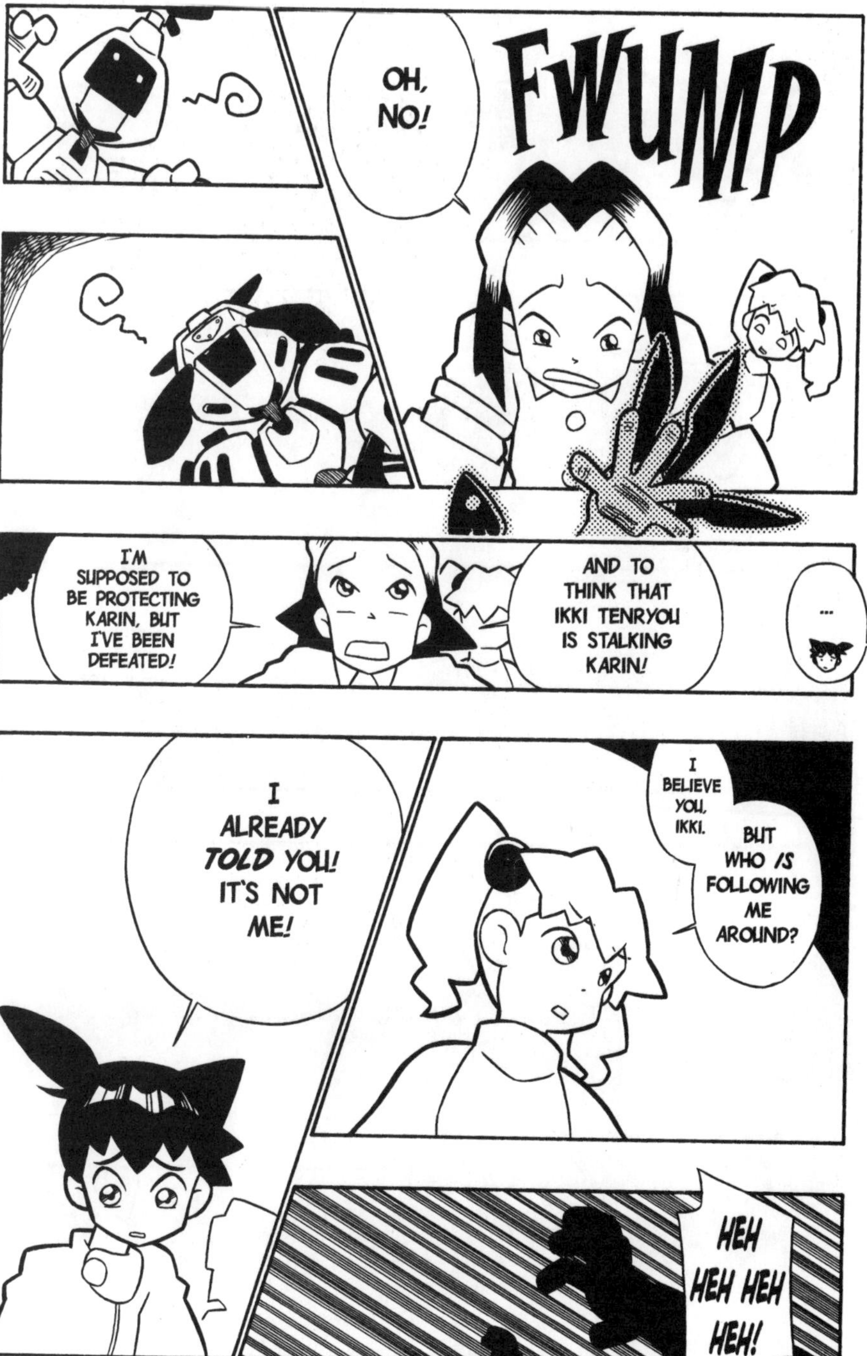

OH, NO!
FWUMP
I'M SUPPOSED TO BE PROTECTING KARIN, BUT I'VE BEEN DEFEATED!
AND TO THINK THAT IKKI TENRYOU IS STALKING KARIN!
...
I ALREADY *TOLD* YOU! IT'S NOT ME!
I BELIEVE YOU, IKKI.
BUT WHO *IS* FOLLOWING ME AROUND?
HEH HEH HEH HEH!

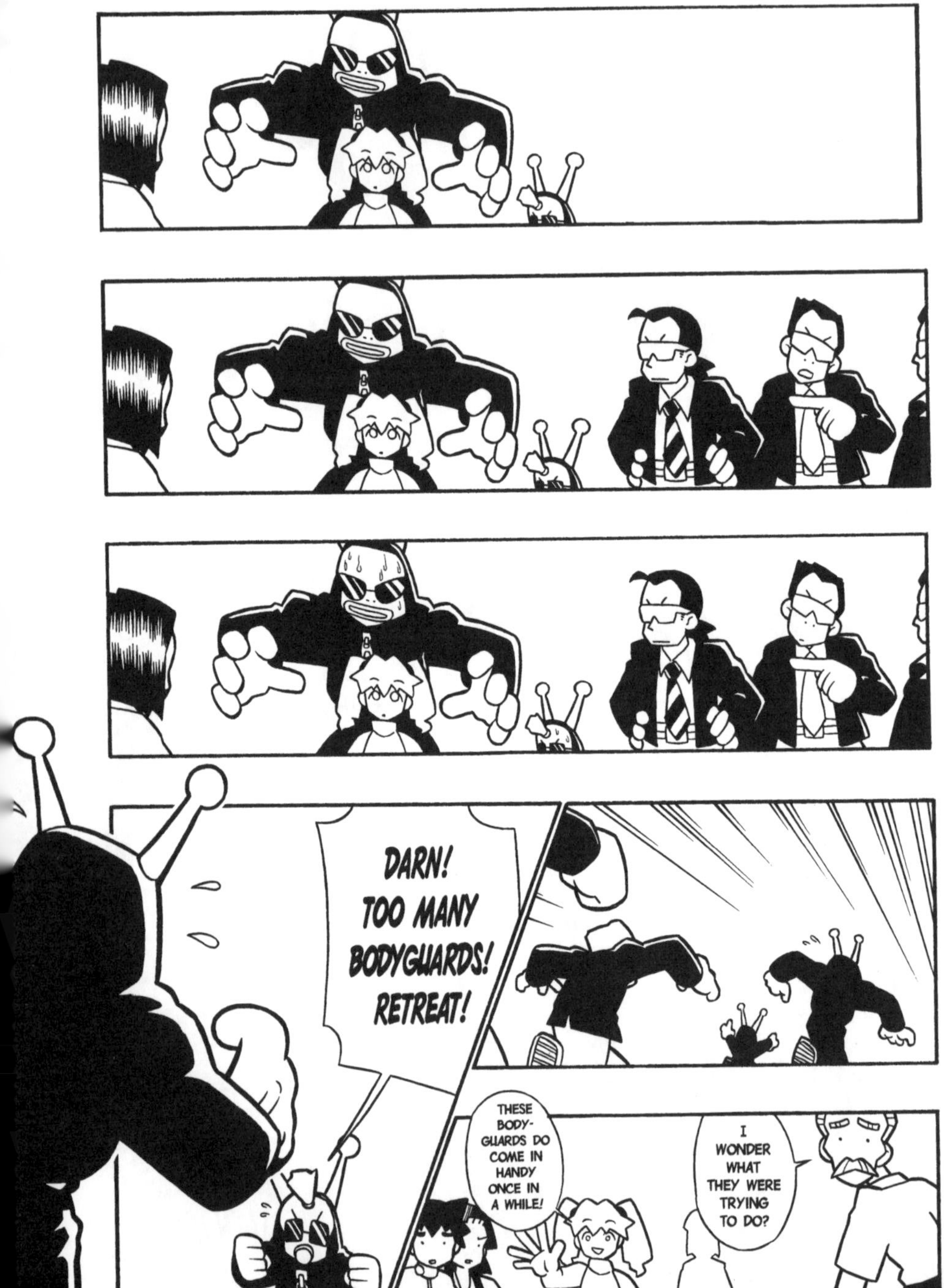
DARN! TOO MANY BODYGUARDS! RETREAT!
THESE BODY-GUARDS DO COME IN HANDY ONCE IN A WHILE!
I WONDER WHAT THEY WERE TRYING TO DO?

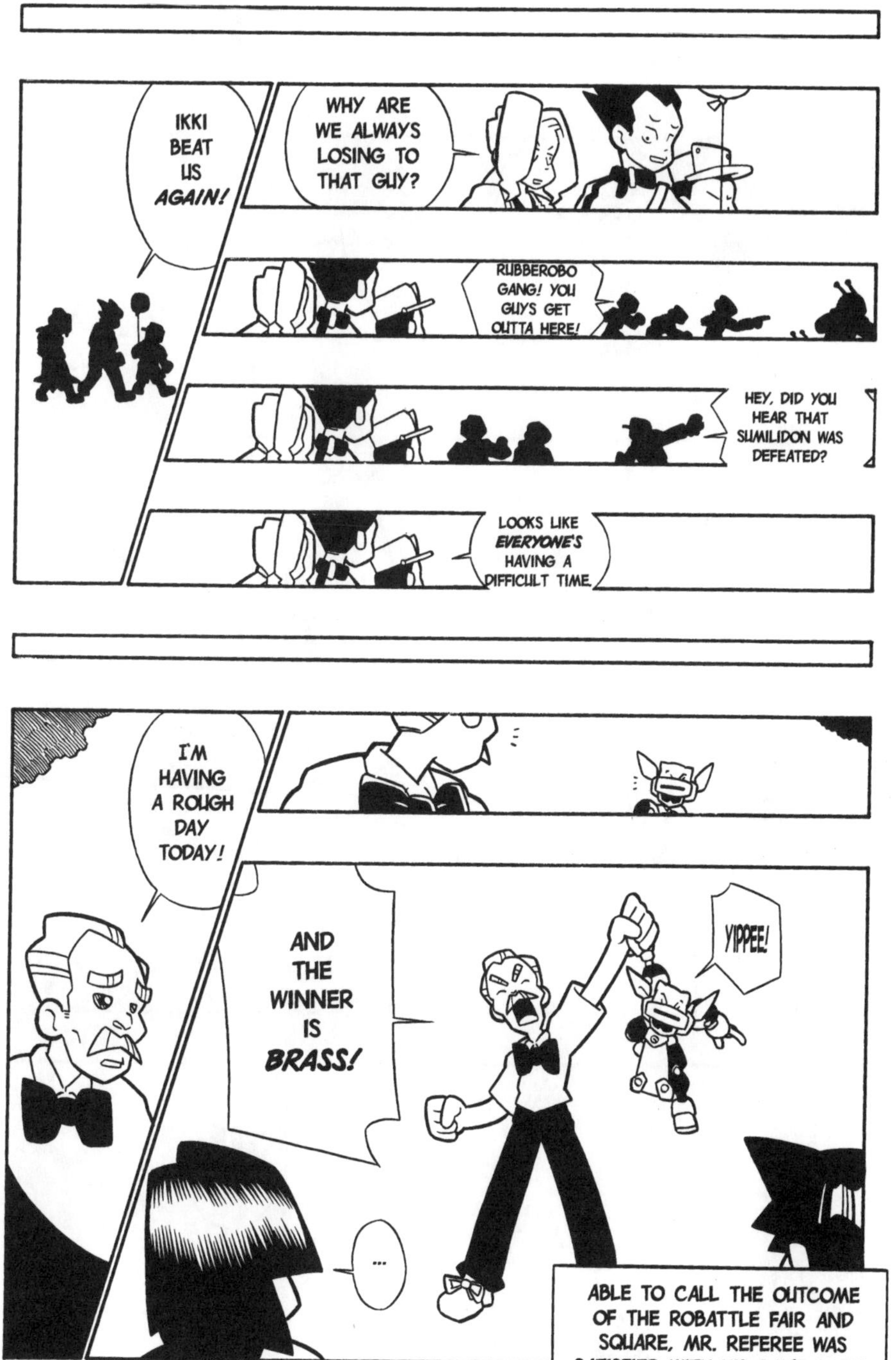

IKKI BEAT US *AGAIN!*
WHY ARE WE ALWAYS LOSING TO THAT GUY?
RUBBEROBO GANG! YOU GUYS GET OUTTA HERE!
HEY, DID YOU HEAR THAT SUMILIDON WAS DEFEATED?
LOOKS LIKE *EVERYONE'S* HAVING A DIFFICULT TIME.
I'M HAVING A ROUGH DAY TODAY!
AND THE WINNER IS *BRASS!*
YIPPEE!
...
ABLE TO CALL THE OUTCOME OF THE ROBATTLE FAIR AND SQUARE, MR. REFEREE WAS SATISFIED WITH HIS DAY'S WORK.

WHAT'S BEEN ON OUR MINDS

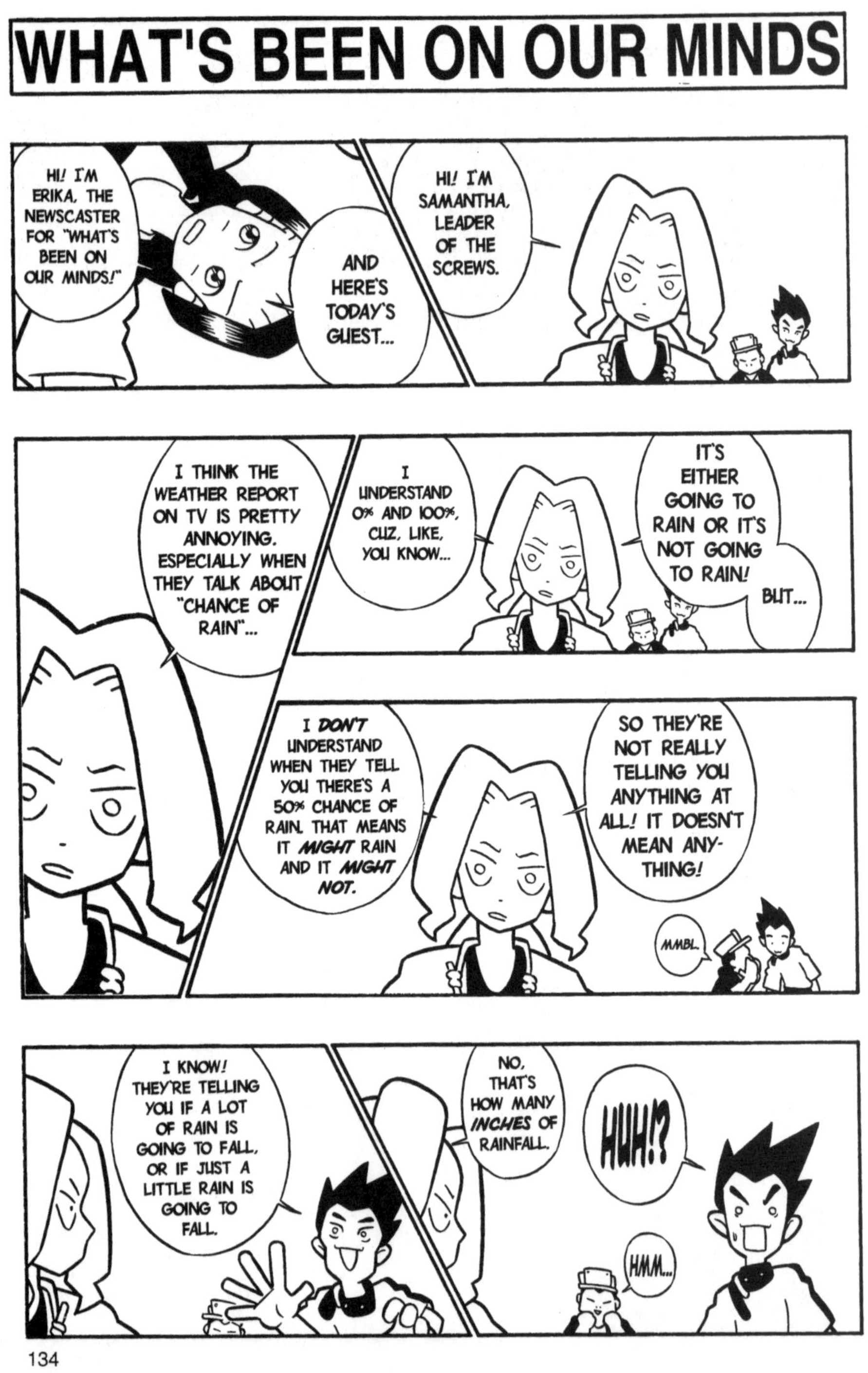
HI! I'M ERIKA, THE NEWSCASTER FOR "WHAT'S BEEN ON OUR MINDS!"
AND HERE'S TODAY'S GUEST...
HI! I'M SAMANTHA, LEADER OF THE SCREWS.
I THINK THE WEATHER REPORT ON TV IS PRETTY ANNOYING. ESPECIALLY WHEN THEY TALK ABOUT "CHANCE OF RAIN"...
I UNDERSTAND 0% AND 100%, CUZ, LIKE, YOU KNOW...
IT'S EITHER GOING TO RAIN OR IT'S NOT GOING TO RAIN!
BUT...
I *DON'T* UNDERSTAND WHEN THEY TELL YOU THERE'S A 50% CHANCE OF RAIN. THAT MEANS IT *MIGHT* RAIN AND IT *MIGHT NOT*.
SO THEY'RE NOT REALLY TELLING YOU ANYTHING AT ALL! IT DOESN'T MEAN ANY-THING!
MMBL.
I KNOW! THEY'RE TELLING YOU IF A LOT OF RAIN IS GOING TO FALL, OR IF JUST A LITTLE RAIN IS GOING TO FALL.
NO, THAT'S HOW MANY *INCHES* OF RAINFALL.
HUH!?
HMM...

Fact or Fiction!?
Is this the Latest in Medabot Technology!?

Composite sketch of the Riceball Head

Dr. Aki recently unveiled the newest Medabot model, but there have been unsubstantiated reports that another Medabot has been newly developed. The existence of this new model, called a Riceball Head Medabot, has not been confirmed at this time.

Today's Stories

World News
A1
Local
B1
Business
B6
Weather
B10

Dr. Aki, the Father of the Medabots.

Dr. Aki denies the existence of the Riceball Head.

"I like a good joke as much as the next guy, but even I wouldn't create something that silly!" comments Dr. Aki.

Medabot Data Files

Sumilidon
Type: Saber-Tooth Tiger
Special Attack: Shadow Sword
Medabot Number: STG-19207

Banisher
Type: Gang Leader
Special Attack: Strong
Appearance
Medabot Number:
BAN-2114

Medabot Data Files

Blackram
Type: Devil
Special Attack: Bombarder
Medabot Number: DVL-42212

Totalizer
Type: Tortoise
Special Attack: Laser
Beam
Medabot Number: TOT-
201520

Medabot Data Files

Churlybear
Type: Bear
Special Attack: Gravity
Beam
Medabot Number: BER-
2581

Agadama
Type: Racoon
Special Attack: Hand-to-Hand Combat
Medabot Number: TAN-20114

Medabot Data Files

Neutranurse
Type: Nurse
Special Attack: Healing
Medabot Number: NAS-14119

Nin-Ninja
Type: Ninja
Special Attack: Ninja-Sword
Medabot Number: NIN-14914

Medabot Data Files

Pretty Prime
Type: Valkyrie
Special Attack: Long Sword
Medabot Number: VAL-22112

New characters... New adventures...

Four New Pokémon
Gold & Silver Tales...

MUDDY PICHU™

WOBBUFFET **WATCHES CLOUDS**

Swinub's Nose

Wake Up, Lugia!

In April, look for the latest in the series of collectible children's storybooks written and drawn by Japan's greatest artists.

Full color...18 pages...$5.50 USA/$8.95 CAN

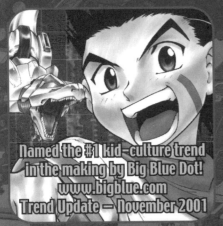

AVAILABLE FROM 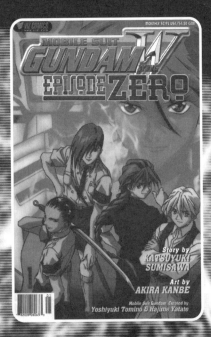 VIZ COMICS™

Gundam Wing: Blind Target takes place after the TV series and before Endless Waltz. Heero, Wufei, Duo, Trowa, Quatre and Relena are determined to keep peace in the midst of a terrifying plot by a group who wishes to obtain the Gundams for their own dubious ends.

By Akemi Omode
Art by Sakura Asagi
Graphic Novel
b&w, 152 pages
$12.95 USA/$20.95 CAN

Gundam Wing: Episode Zero takes a look at the G Boys' and Relena's origins before Operation Meteor. In Gundam Wing: Episode #8, the latest installment, gain some insight into what events helped shape and influence the personalities and drive for each member of the Gundam team.

By Katsuyuki Sumisawa
Art by Akira Kanbe
monthly comic
b&w, 32 pages
$2.95 USA/$4.95 CAN